DUTCH COURAGE

Special Forces in the Netherlands
1944–1945

JELLE HOOIVELD

AMBERLEY

Een volk ... dat niet bereid is tegen de verdrukker op te staan en voor zijn vrijheid te vechten, verdient slechts roemloos ten onder te gaan in de oceaan der vergetelheid.

(A nation ... that is not willing to rise against its suppressor and to fight for its freedom, merely deserves to perish ingloriously in the ocean of oblivion.)

Johannes van Bijnen
National Sabotage Commander, LKP

First published 2016
This edition published 2016

Amberley Publishing
The Hill, Stroud,
Gloucestershire, GL5 4EP

www.amberley-books.com

ISBN 978 1 4456 5741 7 (print)
ISBN 978 1 4456 5742 4 (ebook)

British Library Cataloguing in Publication Data.
A catalogue record for this book is available from the British Library.

Typesetting and Origination by Amberley Publishing.
Map illustrations by Thomas Bohm, User Design, Illustration and Typesetting.
Printed in Great Britain.

CONTENTS

ACKNOWLEDGEMENTS

The original Dutch edition of this book was published in April 2014, under the auspices of the Netherlands Institute for Military History (NIMH) of the Dutch Ministry of Defence, by Boom Uitgevers Amsterdam. Both books would not have been published without the assistance and cooperation of many people. Naturally, I would like to thank the people who were involved in realising the Dutch version, titled *Operatie Jedburgh: Geheime Geallieerde Missies in Nederland 1944–1945*. Firstly, I am extremely grateful for the cooperation of the Jedburgh veterans and their families, former secret agents, and former Dutch resistance members. They gave so much of their time for interviews, telephone conversations, and correspondence. Besides an amazing amount of information, I received many photos which were included in both books. In this respect, I would especially like to thank American Jedburgh veteran Willard 'Bud' Beynon † and his grandson Brian Donahue.

Secondly, I would like to thank Dr Arthur ten Cate, Senior Researcher at the Netherlands Institute of Military History (NIMH), and Ben Schoenmaker, Professor of Military History at Leiden University and head of the *Operationele Dienstverlening* department of the NIMH, for their confidence and enduring assistance throughout the realisation of *Operatie Jedburgh*.

My debt of gratitude is also due to the valuable comments and/or linguistic advice about the original Dutch manuscript of the following people: Wybo Boersma, Serge Blom, Brigade General and Professor (retired) Hans Bosch, Maarten Cieremans †, Marlies Enklaar, Dr Coen Hilbrink, Henk Hooiveld, Annette Niessen-Brinkgreve, Hermien Boekema-Roothaan, Joke Scheepstra, Joke Scheffer, Captain (retired) Jelle Schepers, Lieutenant Colonel (retired) Dr Jan Schulten, and Dr Jo Wolters.

I am also grateful to Dianne Lodder for her assistance with the translation of the Dutch manuscript, significantly speeding up the publication process. Tessa Neerings, too, provided useful aid. I would also like to thank the next of kin of former Dutch resistance members, countless volunteers of Dutch local historical societies, researchers, and authors, who were very eager to share information and images. Dr Steven Kippax's and John Howes's assistance, providing me plentiful copies of files of the British National Archives, saved a lot of time throughout the years, enabling me to spend much more time on researching and writing. Johan van Doorn provided much background information about the liberation of the Netherlands, which was added to the English manuscript. Gerryt Hooning, Dr Steven Kippax, Dianne Lodder, and Hans van Tour very kindly proofread the English manuscript.

For the restoration and preparation of the photographic material, I thank Mariska Boekema. A special thanks goes out to my agent, Shaun Barrington, and to my editor at Amberley Publishing, Aaron Meek. I am also grateful to my family and friends for their steadfast encouragement.

All support of the aforementioned persons in no way detracts from the fact that all responsibility for the content of this book lies entirely with me. The opinions expressed in this book are, thus, completely my own.

Jelle Hooiveld, Deventer,
The Netherlands

FOREWORD

This book started with another. Sometime in 2005, I bought a hand-to-hand fighting manual in an American bookshop on eBay. It was an original 1942 edition of W. E. Fairbairn's legendary book *Get Tough*, which presented combat techniques as taught to the British commandos and U.S. armed forces in the Second World War. This made for interesting 'learning material' to an Economics student – which I was at that time. My fascination for major conflicts, though, especially the Second World War, and my lifelong interest in special forces and intelligence operations, motivated me to buy plentiful numbers of books about military topics as well. The techniques presented in *Get Tough* could even be useful in real life! And $15 plus shipping costs to the Netherlands for this original copy seemed worth the money.

After about two weeks, the package finally arrived. When I opened the book, I immediately noticed a slightly faded but still clearly readable name, written down by its first owner. The ink revealed the following name: 'Lucien E. Conein, U.S. Army'. Always curious, I entered his name in Google's search engine. To my surprise, thousands of results appeared! A *New York Times* headline immediately caught my attention: 'Lucien Conein, 79, Legendary Cold War Spy'. The book that I held in my hands apparently once belonged to 'one of the last great cold war spies, whose swashbuckling tales of war and death and sex … form an enduring legend at the Central Intelligence Agency …' Conein turned out to be a renowned U.S. intelligence officer whose career spanned over fifty years. Among other things, Conein ran agents behind the Iron Curtain in the 1950s and was instrumental in the November 1963 coup against Ngô Đình Diệm, President of the Republic of Vietnam. Impressively, Lucien Conein was one of President John F. Kennedy's key CIA officers in the early stages of the conflict in Vietnam.

Interestingly enough, Conein had also seen action in France in the Second World War. Initially, he enlisted in the French Army, as he was born in Paris. After the fall of France in June 1940, Conein made his way to the United States, eventually joining the newly created U.S. Office of Strategic Services (OSS). In the summer of 1944, Conein was parachuted by OSS behind enemy lines in the south of France. As a so-called 'Jedburgh' officer, Conein liaised with the armed resistance and organised guerrilla warfare against the German occupier.

After conducting more research about this mysterious Allied unit, I found out that the Jedburghs were highly elite, specially trained forces, formed from a small pool of approximately three hundred men, mainly American, British, and French volunteers. Much to my surprise, a handful of Dutch officers had also been part of Operation Jedburgh. Intrigued by these special forces, I started spending considerable time collecting information, especially about the Dutch officers. I soon found out that most of the Dutch Jedburghs had been endowed with the *Militaire Willems-Orde 4e Klasse*, the Knight's Cross of the Military Order of William 4th Class – the Netherlands' highest military award. Talking about Dutch Courage!

After these revelations, I felt urged to find every bit of information about the Dutch Jedburghs. It turned out that there was not a single book published that told the complete story of the Dutch Jedburgh teams in the occupied Netherlands during 1944–45. Unfortunately, it also became clear that few Dutch Jedburghs had survived the war. The Dutchmen who had survived had already passed away of natural causes. However, in early 2007, I came into contact with the family of Lykele 'Lee' Faber. He was a former Dutch secret agent from the Bureau Bijzondere Opdrachten (BBO), the Dutch equivalent of OSS. Through BBO, he was attached to a Jedburgh team that was parachuted over the Netherlands during the infamous Operation Market Garden. Faber was still alive and well, but lived in Canada. To my delight, he came back to the Netherlands every May, to celebrate Liberation Day. Shortly before his yearly trip to the Netherlands, I contacted him by telephone. I was thrilled when he agreed to an interview.

We met in early May 2007 in the village of Geldermalsen, in the centre of a beautiful Dutch region called the Betuwe. I came to know Faber as a very impressive and inspiring person, but not a 'typical' military man. Faber was a quiet, extremely humble, and mysterious person. He did bring his maroon beret, which he had worn during two hazardous missions behind enemy lines in the Netherlands. He would not let me photograph him wearing his beret, though; that was 'too much'. It was an excellent lesson in Dutch modesty to a (cocky) young student.

Already during our meeting, I decided that I had to write a book about this man and his courageous Dutch and foreign Jedburgh colleagues. However, I was still studying Economics and Business Administration at two Dutch colleges. In my few spare hours I contacted other Jedburgh and BBO veterans, their families, and former Dutch resistance members. I also acquired files from archives in the Netherlands, Germany, United States, Great Britain, and Canada. I got a kick every time I opened a historical file that had not been disclosed yet. Slowly but steadily I uncloaked the secrecy around the Dutch Jedburgh officers and their operations in my – or our – home country.

Indeed, partly due to prolonged secrecy, the operations of the Dutch Jedburgh teams were only described fragmentarily and summarily throughout the years. Only recently, a small number of books were published that partly covered the Dutch teams. These books were focused on the groups that were deployed during Operation Market Garden. The other half of the teams that operated in the Netherlands – deployed either before or after Market Garden – were not included in these publications. Moreover, these books were based almost solely on British and American sources. The Dutch team leaders, their cooperation with the Dutch resistance, their awards and post-war lives, largely remained shrouded in mystery.

Up until April 2014, when my Dutch book *Operatie Jedburgh: Geheime Geallieerde Missies in Nederland 1944–1945* was published by the Dutch Ministry of Defence via Boom Publishers Amsterdam, the integral Dutch contribution to Operation Jedburgh remained unknown. *Operatie Jedburgh* told the public, for the first time, what *really* went on behind the lines in the occupied Netherlands. In addition to British and American documents, a vast amount of Dutch sources – including archival files that are still semi-classified – were included in the book. Following the publication of *Operatie Jedburgh*, an English-written news item appeared on the website of the Dutch government. I received many reactions from abroad asking whether the book was also published in English. After having disappointed many, I finally decided to translate the manuscript and tell the story of the Dutch Jedburgh teams to the rest of the world. However, scarce free hours were available besides my work as a lecturer, coordinator, and Ph.D. candidate. With the assistance – and understanding – of others, I was able to complete a revised English edition of *Operatie Jedburgh*.

Dutch Courage is divided into six chapters. The opening chapter tells the history of the Jedburghs, their recruitment and selection, and the special training they received in England and Scotland. Chapter two deals with the situation in the occupied Netherlands around 1944, and it describes the infiltration of the first Dutch Jedburgh team. This group was parachuted close to the German border approximately one week before the start of Operation Market Garden. In chapters three and four, the progress of this major Allied offensive in the Netherlands is described, but this section mainly highlights the contribution of the four Jedburgh teams attached to the involved Allied airborne divisions.

Chapter five focuses on the actions and experiences of two Jedburgh teams that continued to operate in the Netherlands after the failure of Market Garden. One team transformed former resistance fighters into regular military units. The hazardous activities of another Jedburgh team that kept operating behind enemy lines until March 1945 are also described in this chapter.

The next chapter describes the efforts of the last two Jedburgh groups that were deployed in the occupied Netherlands. These teams were parachuted with members of the British Special Air Service (SAS) to support the liberation of the central and northern Netherlands. The final part of this book reviews all Dutch Jedburgh operations and mentions the awards of the (fallen) Dutch Jedburghs. Finally, the post-war careers and lives of the Dutch Jedburgh members are described. The book also includes many not yet internationally published photos of the Dutch Jedburgh teams and the key resistance fighters with whom they cooperated during their missions.

I chose not to cover the infamous '*Englandspiel*', which took place in the early stages of the war in the Netherlands, in detail. I presumed that most readers of this book are already familiar with this disastrous German counter-intelligence operation. The same goes for the major Allied (airborne) operations that took place in the Netherlands during the 1944–45 liberation campaign. These offensives merely function as the 'military context' of the Jedburgh operations. Only general background information about the Allied offensives in the Netherlands, that which I deemed absolutely necessary to understand the deployment and the exploits of the Jedburgh teams, is provided.

The Netherlands

0   25   50km

NOORDZEE

Leeuwarden   ●Groningen

●Assen

IJSSELMEER

Zwolle

Haarlem●   ●Amsterdam

IJssel

Apeldoorn

●Enschede

Leiden●

●'s-Gravenhage   ●Amersfoort

●Delft   ●Utrecht

Rhine

Schiedam● ●Rotterdam   ●Arnhem

Waal

●Dordrecht   ●Nijmegen

GERMANY

Maas

Maas   ●'s-Hertogenbosch

Rhine

Breda●   ●Tilburg

●Essen

Duisberg●

●Eindhoven   Krefeld●   Wuppertal●

Maas   Düsseldorf●   ●Solingen

●Antwerpen   Mönchen-Gladbach

●Gent   ●Keulen

●Brussel   Maastricht●

●Aken

BELGIUM

Luik●

Main rivers
National borders
Provincial borders

Deployment of Jedburgh teams in the Netherlands, 1944–1945

Legend:

— National borders
— Provincial borders
— Main rivers
— Smaller rivers
Lakes
Inundation

🪂 By parachute
✈ By glider
🚙 On the ground

① Team Dudley, 12 September 1944.
② Team Clarence, 17 September 1944.
③ Team Claude, 17 September 1944.
④ Team Daniel II, 17 September 1944.
⑤ Team Edward, 17 September 1944.
⑥ Team Stanley II, in early October 1944.
⑦ Team Gambling, 4 April 1945.
⑧ Team Dicing, 7 April 1945.

0   10   25km

Operation Market Garden – 17 September 1944

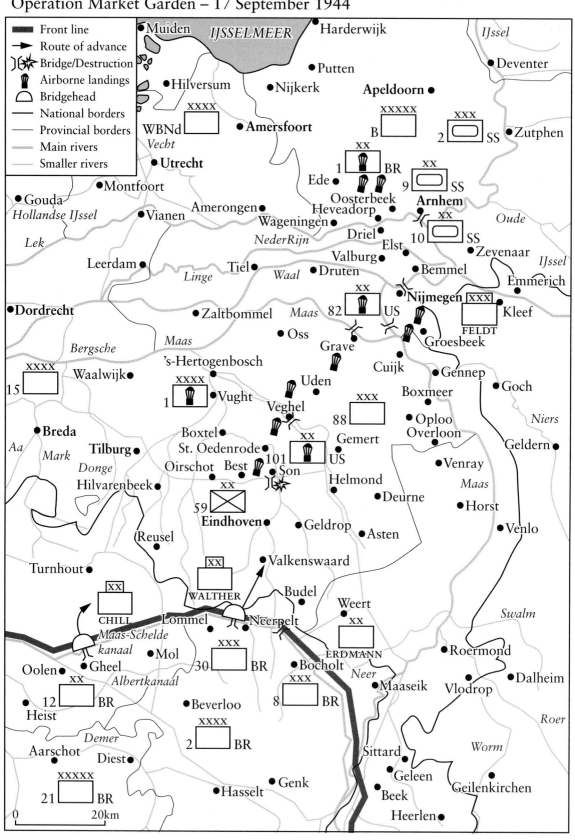

Legend:
- Front line
- Route of advance
- Bridge/Destruction
- Airborne landings
- Bridgehead
- National borders
- Provincial borders
- Main rivers
- Smaller rivers

0   20km

Operation Market Garden – 26 September 1944

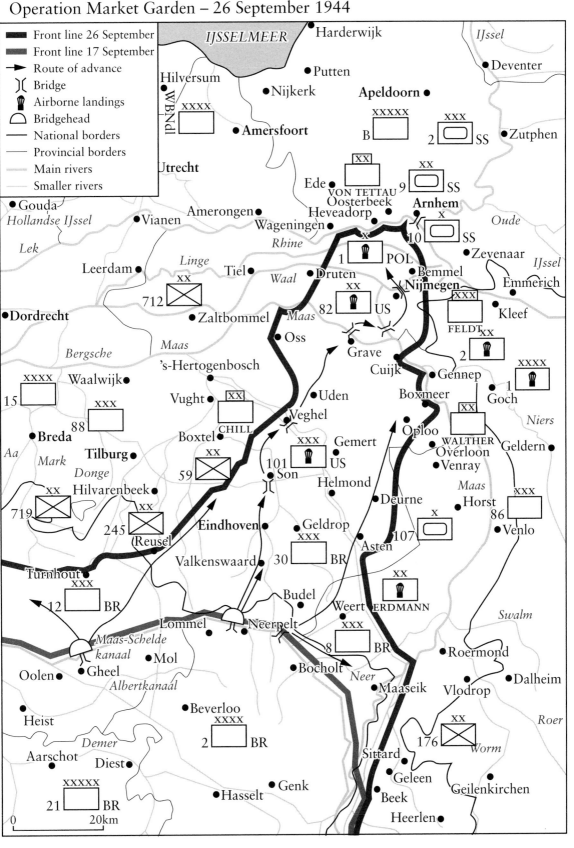

Activities of team Dudley – September–November 1944

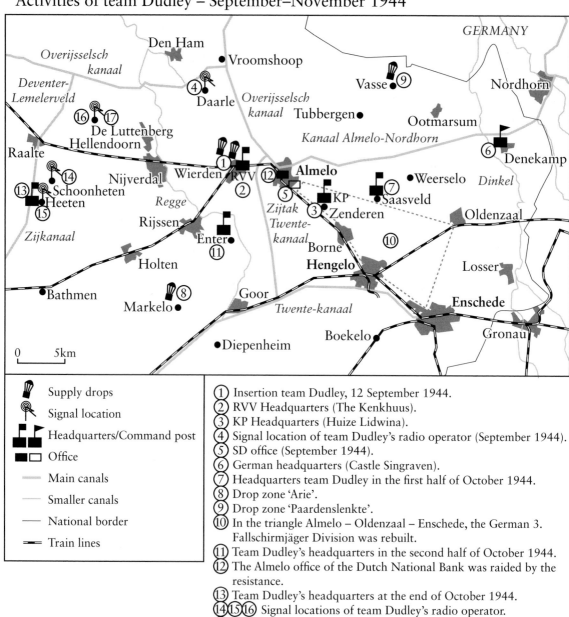

Supply drops

Signal location

Headquarters/Command post

Office

Main canals

Smaller canals

National border

Train lines

1. Insertion team Dudley, 12 September 1944.
2. RVV Headquarters (The Kenkhuus).
3. KP Headquarters (Huize Lidwina).
4. Signal location of team Dudley's radio operator (September 1944).
5. SD office (September 1944).
6. German headquarters (Castle Singraven).
7. Headquarters team Dudley in the first half of October 1944.
8. Drop zone 'Arie'.
9. Drop zone 'Paardenslenkte'.
10. In the triangle Almelo – Oldenzaal – Enschede, the German 3. Fallschirmjäger Division was rebuilt.
11. Team Dudley's headquarters in the second half of October 1944.
12. The Almelo office of the Dutch National Bank was raided by the resistance.
13. Team Dudley's headquarters at the end of October 1944.
14,15,16. Signal locations of team Dudley's radio operator.
17. Apprehension of team Dudley's radio operator.

The Betuwe – December 1944

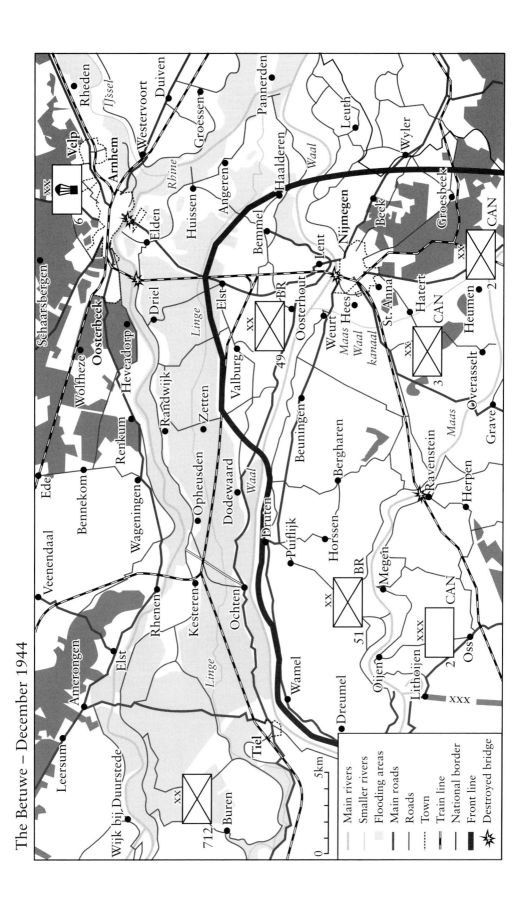

Legend:
Main rivers
Smaller rivers
Flooding areas
Main roads
Roads
Town
Train line
National border
Front line
Destroyed bridge

0   5km

Activities of team Gambling, April 1945

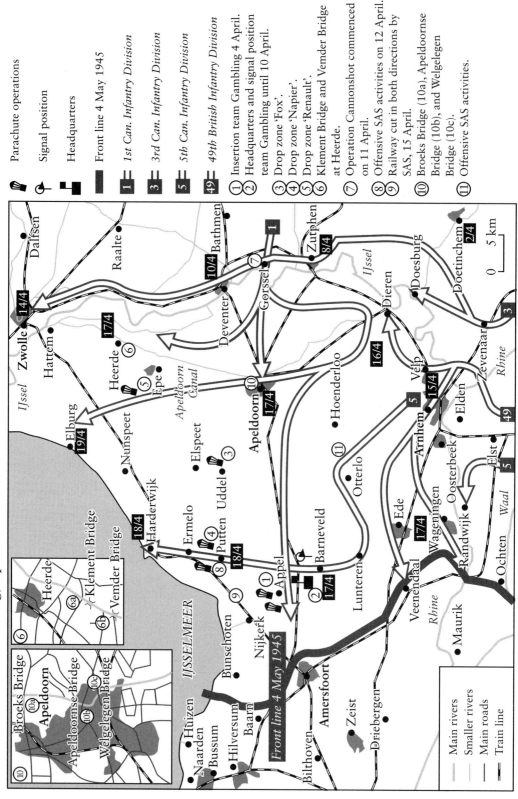

Legend

- 🪂 Parachute operations
- ⚲ Signal position
- ▪️ Headquarters
- ▬ Front line 4 May 1945
- **1** 1st Can. Infantry Division
- **3** 3rd Can. Infantry Division
- **5** 5th Can. Infantry Division
- **49** 49th British Infantry Division

1. Insertion team Gambling 4 April.
2. Headquarters and signal position team Gambling until 10 April.
3. Drop zone 'Fox'.
4. Drop zone 'Napier'.
5. Drop zone 'Renault'.
6. Klement Bridge and Vemder Bridge at Heerde.
7. Operation Cannonshot commenced on 11 April.
8. Offensive SAS activities on 12 April.
9. Railway cut in both directions by SAS, 15 April.
10. Broeks Bridge (10a), Apeldoornse Bridge (10b), and Welgelegen Bridge (10c).
11. Offensive SAS activities.

Activities of team Dicing, April 1945

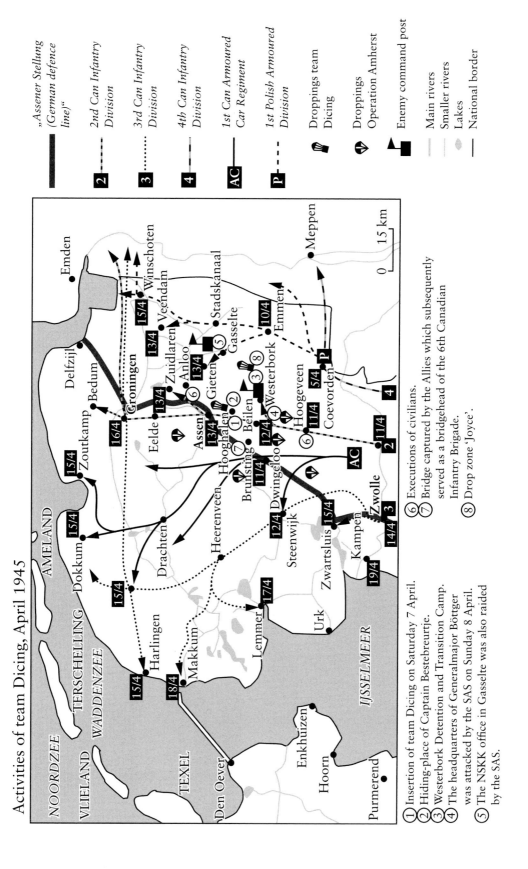

Legend:

- "Assener Stellung (German defence line)"
- 2nd Can Infantry Division [2]
- 3rd Can Infantry Division [3]
- 4th Can Infantry Division [4]
- 1st Can Armoured Car Regiment [AC]
- 1st Polish Armoured Division [P]
- Droppings team Dicing
- Droppings Operation Amherst
- Enemy command post
- Main rivers
- Smaller rivers
- Lakes
- National border

0   15 km

① Insertion of team Dicing on Saturday 7 April.
② Hiding-place of Captain Bestebreurtje.
③ Westerbork Detention and Transition Camp.
④ The headquarters of Generalmajor Böttger was attacked by the SAS on Sunday 8 April.
⑤ The NSKK office in Gasselte was also raided by the SAS.
⑥ Executions of civilians.
⑦ Bridge captured by the Allies which subsequently served as a bridgehead of the 6th Canadian Infantry Brigade.
⑧ Drop zone 'Joyce'.

THE JEDBURGH CONCEPT

The origin of the Jedburgh teams

In July 1940, a clandestine British organisation was established that was to undermine the Nazi regime by organising sabotage and subversive activities on the European continent.[1] It was named Special Operations Executive (SOE). If SOE could succeed in transforming the numerous resistance groups in mainland Europe into 'underground armies', the enemy would (also) be disrupted from within.[2] In order to achieve this objective, SOE secretly sent agents, weapons, and supplies to the European resistance.

During the spring of 1942, SOE consulted with senior British Army officers about the role it could play in the Allied invasion of Western Europe. A plan, primarily developed by SOE staff officer Lieutenant Colonel P. A. (Peter) Wilkinson, was extensively discussed. He envisaged the deployment of special military units in occupied territory who, unlike regular secret agents, would operate in military uniform.[3] These forces were to be deployed as small teams in occupied France to work with the resistance:

> SOE will drop additional small teams of French speaking personnel carrying arms for some forty men each. The role of these teams will be to make contact with local authorities or existing SOE organizations, to distribute the arms, to start off the action of the patriots, and, most particularly, to arrange by W/T [wireless telegraphy] communication the dropping points and reception committees for further arms and equipment … Each team will consist of one British officer, one W/T operator with set and possibly one guide.[4]

The British military command saw potential in Wilkinson's proposal and allowed SOE to further develop this plan. It was given the randomly assigned code name 'Jedburgh', after the Scottish border town.[5]

In March 1943, SOE participated in Operation Spartan – a major Allied military exercise in central and southern England – and simulated the deployment of Jedburgh teams in support of resistance forces.[6] After several other exercises it

Lieutenant Colonel Wilkinson played an
important role in the development of the
Jedburgh concept. (CART)

was concluded that the Jedburgh groups had to operate at least sixty kilometres
behind enemy lines. From deep inside occupied territory, they would operate
against the enemy's lines of communication, and, in cooperation with the armed
resistance, carry out guerrilla warfare.

Later that year, SOE involved the American intelligence service, the Office
of Strategic Services (OSS), in the Jedburgh project.[7] In December 1943, the
so called 'Jedburgh Basic Directive' was issued by SOE and OSS. This directive
indicated that the area of operations had been widened; the emphasis was still
on France, but Belgium and the Netherlands were included as well. SOE and OSS
foresaw that the presence of Jedburgh teams behind enemy lines would boost
the morale of the resistance. The Jedburghs were also to act as representatives of
the supreme Allied command and train, support, and assist the resistance groups.
The Jedburgh forces would not act as intelligence agents, although they were to
provide Allied headquarters with important information, such as enemy troop
movements and the locations of German headquarters.

It was decided to form one hundred multinational Jedburgh teams of three
men, consisting of a team leader, a second officer, and a sergeant/radio operator.[8]
In addition to mainly British, American, and French soldiers, the plan involved
the recruitment of about nine Dutch officers for special operations in occupied
Netherlands.[9]

Jedburgh recruitment

In the second half of 1943 SOE and OSS started recruiting American, British, French, Belgian, and Dutch personnel for Operation Jedburgh. A special committee, known as the Jedburgh Student Assessment Board, would be testing the candidates on their physical and psychological features and abilities. SOE and OSS were primarily looking for officers who possessed self-confidence, were self-reliant, and, regardless of the situation, could think quickly and properly. Due to the expected (long-term) stressful conditions behind enemy lines, mental endurance and emotional stability were also important requirements for the Jedburgh candidates. In the role of resistance adviser, the aspirant also had to be an ample diplomat.[10]

The search for British officers and radio operators commenced in October 1943. They were recruited by displaying posters in barracks and military camps with the announcement: 'Volunteers who are interested in parachuting and guerrilla warfare and with a knowledge of French, step forward.'[11] SOE eventually recruited fifty-five British Jedburgh officers and about forty-five radio operators.[12]

OSS recruiters initially looked for volunteers in military encampments in the United States. The focus here was on bases with soldiers who had already gone through parachute training. The American service was especially interested in personnel with knowledge of foreign languages and a desire to perform hazardous duties. Later Jedburgh officer Major J. M. (John) Olmsted commented: 'He [the recruitment officer] told us that he could say little about the proposed job, he was looking for volunteers to work behind enemy lines and figured that chances for survival were roughly fifty-fifty.'[13]

OSS initially recruited approximately a hundred Jedburgh candidates. However, after the first selection round in the United States, only around fifty officers were left.[14] After the Jedburgh Assessment in England, this group shrunk even further to only thirty-five men.[15] The Americans were therefore compelled to search for Jedburgh candidates in units who were already stationed in the United Kingdom. Eventually, OSS recruited about fifty-five officers and sixty-two radio operators.

The recruitment of the French took place in the United Kingdom and in the French colonies in North Africa. As early as July 1943, officers of SOE and OSS had been sent to Algeria. Moreover, the French intelligence service, the Bureau Central de Renseignements et d'Action (Central Bureau of Intelligence and Operations, BCRA), was already looking in Casablanca (Morocco) to replace agents who had been killed or imprisoned in occupied France.

The French candidates were sent to the United Kingdom in November 1943 for tests. Eventually, the BCRA enlisted around one hundred French officers and fourteen radio operators. In addition to the mainly French, American, and British candidates, a small group of Belgian and Dutch personnel was included in the Jedburgh programme.[16]

In September 1943, SOE's Dutch counterpart, the Bureau Militaire Voorbereiding Terugkeer (MVT, Preparation Bureau for Military Return) of the Dutch government-in-exile, had received a request to recruit a number of Dutch officers for 'special operations in occupied Dutch territory'.[17] Due to the dangers involved in these missions, MVT's commandant, Colonel M. R. (Mattheus) de Bruyne, decided to only recruit volunteers.

Colonel De Bruyne recruited the Dutch Jedburgh candidates. (NIMH)

4

The Dutch Jedburgh candidates were found in the Prinses Irene Brigade, which had been established in January 1941 and was made up of Dutchmen who had escaped to England.

De Bruyne selected a small group of officers, who reported to him later that month. They all expressed their willingness to carry out special operations in the occupied Netherlands and returned to their unit pending further orders. Early in December 1943, the Dutch officers were subjected to the arduous tests of the Jedburgh Student Assessment Board. Just four of about nine Dutchmen qualified for the Jedburgh programme: First Lieutenant H. (Henk) Brinkgreve and Second Lieutenants A.D. (Arie) Bestebreurtje, J. (Jaap) Groenewoud and J. (Jaap) Staal.[18] Who were these Dutchmen and what was their story?

Henk Brinkgreve was born in Utrecht on 6 June 1915 and graduated from grammar school in the city of Leiden. In the summer of 1933, he enlisted as a volunteer in the Royal Dutch Army and was assigned to the 4e Regiment Veld Artillerie. In September 1934, Brinkgreve began studying law in Leiden. After obtaining his bachelor's degree, Brinkgreve studied briefly at the Paris-Sorbonne University. Just before his final exams, Brinkgreve was mobilised.

During the German invasion of the Netherlands in May 1940, Brinkgreve acted as a fire-control officer with the 20e Regiment Artillerie in the Peel-Raamstelling, a Dutch defence line behind the Maas River in the south-east of the Netherlands. After the Dutch capitulation he moved south and managed to join retreating Belgian forces; Brinkgreve was evacuated to England via the French port of

Henk Brinkgreve. (The National Archives)

Cherbourg. In March 1942 he joined SOE and served for some time with a secret British commando unit, the Small Scale Raiding Force (SSRF, also known as No. 62 Commando). In September 1942, Brinkgreve participated in a successful raid on the lighthouse of the Casquets in the Channel Islands.[19] After his time with SSRF, Brinkgreve worked in the intelligence department of the previously mentioned Bureau MVT.

Second Lieutenant Arie Bestebreurtje was born on 12 April 1916 in Rotterdam. He moved with his family to Berlin in 1923 when his father, a senior corporate officer for Lever Brothers, was transferred to Germany. Bestebreurtje completed secondary school in Zurich, Switzerland and moved on to study international law at the universities of Zurich and Geneva, eventually earning a Ph.D. As a talented athlete and speed skater, Bestebreurtje became the Swiss All-round national speed skating champion in 1941.[20]

In order to contribute to the battle against Nazi Germany, Bestebreurtje left neutral Switzerland later that year.[21] His aversion to the Nazis grew along the

Arie Bestebreurtje.
(The Bestebreurtje family)

way to England. After witnessing a bullfight in Madrid, Bestebreurtje noticed a German staff car outside the arena with a fluttering swastika flag. Bestebreurtje remarked about what happened next:

> I walked back and forth past the car, getting angrier by the minute. Finally, I reached over and tore the flag off the fender and ran ... I had half the German army, or so it seemed, chasing me through the streets of Madrid. They chased me for more than an hour before I lost them.[22]

From Portugal, Bestebreurtje travelled on to New York, where his parents lived at that time. In the United States Bestebreurtje briefly attended Yale University. He went to England in December 1941 and was appointed second lieutenant in the Dutch infantry in August 1942. Before joining the Jedburghs, Bestebreurtje was attached to several Allied military units, including the South Wales Borderers.[23]

Jacobus 'Jaap' Groenewoud was born in Amsterdam on 8 November 1916. In 1935 he was declared unfit for military service due to poor eyesight. Shortly before the outbreak of the Second World War, he migrated to South Africa and became a student at the University of Cape Town. In December 1940, Groenewoud took

Jaap Groenewoud. (Airborne Museum Hartenstein)

employment with Sesco Works in Johannesburg as an accountant. After several further attempts to enlist, Groenewoud was summoned in September 1941 by the Dutch Military Mission in Pretoria. To his luck he was finally considered fit for service and assigned to the so-called '1e Contingent', which consisted of about eighty Dutch-South African volunteers.

In January 1942, Groenewoud embarked for England. The following summer, Groenewoud was awarded a temporary commission of reserve second lieutenant. Subsequently, he served several weeks with a battalion of the Canadian Black Watch Regiment.[24] Soon thereafter, Groenewoud was sent to Officer Training School in Aldershot. After completing officer training, he was transferred to the British Home Guard. When he was recruited for Operation Jedburgh, Groenewoud was serving with the 18th Battalion of the Welch Regiment. About his performance in this unit, the following was reported to the Dutch military attaché in London:

> The assessed ... was the best platoon commander of the battalion. He was an outstanding instructor and did excellent with people and knew how to inspire them. He has made himself known during his detachment as a first class officer ... [25]

Jaap Staal. (M. Staal)

The fourth Dutch officer who qualified for Jedburgh training was Jacob 'Jaap' Staal, born on 8 July 1913 in the city of Assen in the north-east of the Netherlands. As of August 1933, he was assigned as a conscript in the 4e Regiment Veld Artillerie, where Brinkgreve also served. Staal went on long furlough in August 1936 and emigrated to South Africa two years later. He got married in December 1940. In January 1942, Staal was also assigned to the first contingent of Dutch-South African volunteers. He was commissioned in August 1942 in England as a second lieutenant. From August 1943, Staal was on detachment to the British Army, including an artillery unit named the Queen's Own Dorset Yeomanry.[26]

In order to be seconded to SOE, the Dutch Jedburgh candidates were required to have (at least) the rank of first lieutenant. By Dutch Royal Decree, Bestebreurtje, Groenewoud and Staal were temporarily promoted to this rank. Henk Brinkgreve, already a first lieutenant, was temporarily appointed captain. Due to the dangers involved in Operation Jedburgh, Colonel De Bruyne served a request to the Dutch Minister of War to award these officers with a 'commando' allowance on their pay. This request was approved soon after.[27]

Jedburgh training

In late 1943, SOE and OSS began their search for a suitable location to establish a Jedburgh training school. One of the estates inspected in October 1943 was the sixteenth-century Milton Hall, an English country house in the county of Cambridgeshire. This complex, located about six kilometres outside the town of Peterborough, was isolated, and its surroundings were very suitable for field exercises. After its requisition by SOE, Milton Hall's numerous rooms were converted into classrooms, demonstration areas and bedrooms. Interestingly, the plentiful paintings, armour, swords, and shields in the main building were left untouched. The training centre was, according to a later Jedburgh officer, therefore 'truly a warrior's domain'.[28]

The estate of Milton Hall was the Jedburghs' home. (J. Dowse)

According to the original plan, the training programme of the Jedburgh students was to commence on 1 January, 1944. Training was expected to be completed on 1 April that year. The training curriculum was largely based on SOE's regular agent course.[29] However, the training of the Jedburghs was longer and put more focus on organising guerrilla warfare.

Due to a shortage of equipment and personnel, the Jedburgh school did not become available before early February 1944. In the meantime, the Jedburgh trainees were sent to regular SOE training schools. At these training centres, the recruited men met each other for the first time.[30] American Jedburgh officer John Olmsted commented about their first gathering, 'There were many colorful characters in this group of mixed nationalities. Ari[e] [Bestebreurtje] was probably as interesting as any. He had been an up and coming [sic] young speed skater ... and was not at all abashed by the boisterous Americans.'[31]

During the first month, the training programme involved mainly basic military subjects such as unarmed combat, demolition, tactics, fieldcraft, radio signalling, and physical training.[32] The trainees were given French language classes. The Jedburgh students also immersed themselves in all aspects of unconventional warfare, including organising resistance groups and applying guerrilla tactics, but also covering counter-espionage, security, and escape and evasion. Furthermore, the recruits were trained in the use of foreign weapons – including German and French arms. Their parachute training took place at an SOE school near Manchester. At this location each Jedburgh candidate made at least three jumps during a three-day course. This included one day jump and two night jumps, qualifying them officially as parachutists;[33] throughout their training, more (night) jumps followed repeatedly.

On 5 February 1944, the Jedburgh recruits reported for the first time to Milton Hall. Since the mansion was a secret training centre, the Jedburgh students were ordered to declare that they were part of a regular commando school. This sometimes led to awkward situations, though, when the trainees ran into 'real' commandos. At Milton Hall, everything went differently compared to their former military lives. According to American Major Olmsted, an unusually informal atmosphere quickly developed at the Jedburgh school:

> We were in the enviable position of having volunteered for a mission that was considered by the big boys as somewhat out of the ordinary, as well as being somewhat dangerous, so were given a freedom of action that was something entirely new in the service.[34]

The Jedburgh trainees soon developed their own battle cry: 'forty-eight ... forty-nine ... fifty ... some shit!' It would be heard regularly in and around the

Aerial photograph of Milton Hall, 1944. (NARA)

mansion. This battle cry could be traced back to an incident in a U.S. barrack: one of the paratroop officers, who had arrived too late, was ordered to execute fifty push-ups for punishment. The officer, who counted every push-up aloud, eventually rose with a red face and added 'some shit!', with venom in his voice. During the first weeks at Milton Hall the recruits completed the basic training. There was also a lot of a heavy physical training, including long marches and unarmed combat. In the 'silent killing' course, the Jedburghs were taught how to take out an opponent by using a commando knife, a garrote (a sort of strangle cord), or even bare hands.[35] They were also taught how to shoot 'intuitively' with firearms – a new and faster way of shooting. As the main focus of Operation Jedburgh would be on France, the programme did initially not include separate Dutch language classes. The Dutch Jedburgh trainees therefore also participated in the French classes.[36]

The second phase of Jedburgh training commenced in the second half of February 1944. The emphasis was now on field exercises, which would continue until their deployment to occupied Europe. Part of this training were the 'schemes' which were designed to mimic the conditions behind enemy lines. These manoeuvres took at least twenty-four hours and could last up to ten days.

Above: Exercise area in Milton Hall's rear courtyard. (NARA)

Below: Jedburgh students scale a wall during training at Milton Hall. (NARA)

Jedburghs following lessons at Milton Hall. (NARA)

Jedburgh students in demolition class. (NARA)

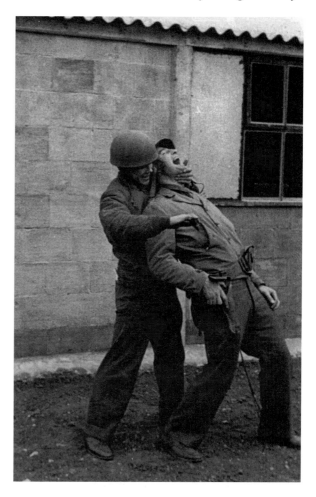

Two Jedburghs practicing silent killing. (The Todd family)

One scheme, for instance, involved ambushing the staff of a German general with 'resistance fighters' who were led by a Jedburgh team.

During such exercises the role of the enemy was played by the guards of Milton Hall, the local police, or the British Home Guard. According to Dutch Jedburgh officer Arie Bestebreurtje they were also parachuted into Scotland, at which time the British authorities were alerted that disguised German paratroopers had landed.[37] It was very hard for the Jedburgh trainees to evade capture – and imprisonment – during these exercises. The training therefore felt very realistic to the men.[38] Between numerous hours in the field, guest speakers held lectures on various topics at Milton Hall. There were also talks by agents and commandos who had already gained experience in enemy occupied territory.[39]

At the end of February 1944, Brigadier E. E. (Eric) Mockler-Ferryman, SOE's director for operations in north-west Europe, personally visited Milton Hall. During this visit, the brigadier gave the Jedburgh candidates a

Jedburghs on exercise in the British countryside. Seen here are Olmsted, Brinkgreve, and Scott. (W. Irwin)

A Jedburgh team is parachuted during an exercise. (NARA)

concrete picture of the tasks they could be called upon to perform in occupied Europe.[40] Until then, the trainees had only been briefed very generally about their future missions. The brigadier informed the Jedburgh students that they were going to perform a strategic role, and would primarily act as liaison officers on behalf of Allied headquarters to resistance groups in occupied France, Belgium, and the Netherlands; in addition, the Jedburghs were to arm the resistance and act as military instructors and advisers. Because the Jedburghs would operate far behind enemy lines, their missions could be of long duration.

As regards the leadership of the resistance groups, Mockler-Ferryman apprised the men that if an underground organisation did not function satisfactorily, the Jedburghs could be ordered to (re)organise it, possibly taking over command. This required extremely cautious and sensitive methods, though, as the Jedburghs had to avoid creating the impression that they were sent to take over resistance leadership.

According to Brigadier Mockler-Ferryman, there was also another possible method of employing Jedburgh groups: to act as a reception committee for a (large) body of airborne troops. Subsequently, the Jedburghs would operate as liaison between these forces and the resistance groups in the area. At Milton Hall, the brigadier stressed that the Jedburgh forces would not carry out so-called '*coup-de-main*' operations, small offensive actions wherein a particular target was raided – they were considered 'too precious' for that. The brigadier finally noted that the definitive orders for the Jedburgh teams would depend on the needs of Allied commanders in the field and the condition of the resistance groups in occupied territory.

From mid-March 1944, the first teams were formed at Milton Hall. The men were allowed to choose their own team members. The only requirement specified by Milton Hall was that each team, in addition to a radio operator, would consist of at least one American or British officer and one French, Belgian, or Dutch officer.[41]

Since February 1944, Dutch Captain Brinkgreve had shared a room with three American officers and a French soldier. One of his roommates was American W. E. (William) Colby, who later became director of the CIA (1973–76). Another American roommate was Major J. M. (John) Olmsted. Brinkgreve and Olmsted felt connected and built a friendship before long. When the Dutch officer asked Major Olmsted to team up, he agreed immediately.[42] The other Dutchmen at Milton Hall also joined with American officers. Arie Bestebreurtje teamed up with Lieutenant G. M. (George) Verhaeghe, and Jaap Groenewoud with Lieutenant H. A. (Harvey) Todd. Lieutenant Staal, finally, formed a partnership with Captain M. (McCord) Sollenberger.

Above: Teammates Brinkgreve and Olmsted. (The Beynon family)

Left: The American Lieutenant Verhaeghe, teammate of Lieutenant Bestebreurtje. (The Beynon family)

Left: The American Lieutenant Todd, teammate of Lieutenant Groenewoud. (The Beynon family)

Right: The American Captain Sollenberger, teammate of Lieutenant Staal. (The Sollenberger family)

After the officers formed a duo, they jointly selected a radio operator. Brinkgreve and Olmsted had their eyes on the twenty-one-year-old Irish Sergeant J. P. S. (John) Austin. Brinkgreve and Austin had already served together in the Small Scale Raiding Force. Lieutenants Bestebreurtje and Verhaeghe asked the twenty-year-old American Sergeant W. W. (Willard) Beynon to join them. Staal and Sollenberger would unite with the American Sergeant J. R. (James) Billingsley. Lieutenants Groenewoud and Todd picked Sergeant C. A. (Carl) Scott, also from the United States, as their radio operator.

Apart from the Dutch Jedburgh officers and Lieutenant Verhaeghe, who had Flemish roots, the men of the Dutch Jedburgh Section barely spoke Dutch. After the Dutch teams were formed, their members stopped participating in the French language and geography classes. From then on the focus was

The wireless operators from the Dutch Jedburgh section at Milton Hall: Scott, Austin, Beynon and Billingsley. (The Beynon family)

entirely on the Netherlands.[43] The small and independent Dutch Jedburgh element would swiftly become the most tightly knit group within the entire school.[44]

Establishing a new SOE-counterpart for the Netherlands

Back in December 1940, SOE had formed an independent section for operations in the occupied Netherlands. The following year, the first Dutch SOE agent was sent into occupied territory. SOE's initial activities in the Netherlands, however, resulted in disaster. A Dutch agent, who was arrested in 1942, had been forced by the Germans to continue to send telegrams to England. Subsequently, dozens of Dutch organisers, radio operators, and instructors were parachuted, nearly all of whom were arrested. Only in the second half of 1943 was SOE's 'Plan for

Holland' halted. More than fifty Dutch agents with tons of supplies had fallen into Germans hands.[45] Hundreds of Dutch resistance members fell victim to this so-called '*Englandspiel*' as well.

Allied confidence in the Dutch resistance was severely damaged by this fiasco.[46] Moreover, the building and expansion of the Dutch armed resistance was delayed significantly. Assuming that the resistance groups who were in touch with SOE and the Dutch MVT (SOE's initial Dutch equivalent) were heavily infiltrated by the Germans, the Dutch Minister of War, O. C. A. (Otto) Van Lidth de Jeude, set up a new 'sabotage department' in March 1944. This organisation became the Bureau Bijzondere Opdrachten (BBO, Bureau of Special Assignments).[47] Dutch Major General J. W. (Johan) van Oorschot was proposed by the Dutch government-in-exile as head of this new secret service.

Before the outbreak of the Second World War, Van Oorschot had been commandant of the third department of the Dutch General Staff (GS III) and was responsible for military intelligence. He had been forced into early retirement because of his connection to the so-called 'Venlo Incident' in November 1939. This was a secret German operation in the Dutch border town of Venlo, which involved the abduction of two British Secret Intelligence Services (SIS) agents. These British officers had tried to organise an assassination attempt on Adolf

Major General Van Oorschot was head of the Dutch BBO. (NIMH)

Hitler, believing that they were in contact with German opposition elements. Van Oorschot had secretly pledged assistance to the British, thereby violating his nation's neutrality.

Although punished by the Dutch authorities, Van Oorschot still had a good reputation in England: '[Van Oorschot was] a man who never feared to shoulder responsibility nor hesitated to take prompt action where such was necessary.'[48] With no objections from the British side, the Dutch general was quickly installed as head of BBO.

BBO established its headquarters in London. General Van Oorschot, who was not fully informed about the actual status and working methods of the Dutch resistance, recruited two Dutch resistance members who had recently arrived in England, K. (Kas) de Graaf and F. J. (Karel) Klijzing. These men were temporarily appointed officers and were to lead the everyday activities of the bureau.[49]

Around this time, SOE and the Special Operations branch of OSS were integrated into a joint headquarters. In March 1944, Supreme Allied Command

A letter stamp of BBO. Striking is the use of the term 'Special Forces'. (C. Hijszeler)

made this London-based command centre responsible for all matters relating to the resistance in north-west Europe.[50] Later, it was officially named 'Special Force Headquarters' (SFHQ), internally also referred to as 'Special Forces Headquarters'.

SFHQ soon created a Low Countries section for operations within Belgium and the Netherlands. Within this department a separate Dutch section was established, lead by the British Major R. I. (Richard) Dobson – in close collaboration with BBO.[51] To ensure proper coordination between the resistance and the Allied armies in occupied Europe, SFHQ also founded special liaison elements, named 'Special Force Detachments', and attached them to the Allied headquarters in the field.

Major Dobson was head of the Dutch Section of SFHQ. (The National Archives)

Jedburgh officers at the bar, Milton Hall. (NARA)

Swiftly after its creation, BBO contacted the Dutch Section at Milton Hall to discuss the deployment plans of the teams for Operation Jedburgh. Parallel to this, BBO also coordinated its activities with the other Dutch secret service that sent agents to occupied territory: the Bureau Inlichtingen (BI, Bureau of Intelligence). This organisation had been founded in England in 1942 by the Dutch government-in-exile.[52] BBO and BI would soon work closely together, both in England and in the occupied Netherlands.

The last preparations

The first conference with SFHQ and BBO about the deployment of Dutch Jedburgh teams took place at Milton Hall in early April 1944.[53] After several other meetings, it was concluded that the Dutch Jedburghs teams had to operate in a different manner to the French groups. In France, the resistance could use the cover of extensive forests and inaccessible mountainous terrain, far from inhabited areas and out of direct reach of the Germans. This allowed the French resistance to gather, train, and carry out their operations in relative ease and safety, enabling many opportunities for (fierce) guerrilla warfare.

In contrast, the Dutch rural area consisted mainly of open fields and small, cultivated forests that were all easily accessible. In addition, due to the excellent infrastructure the German security forces were able to exercise strict control over Dutch territory – just 33,000 square kilometres – and its population. This task was carried out by numerous German police and counter-intelligence services, such as the Geheime Staatspolizei (Gestapo, Secret State Police), the Sicherheitsdiens*t* (SD, Security Service) and the Abwehr (Military Intelligence Service). Moreover, the Germans were supported by the Dutch national police, members of the Nationaal-Socialische Beweging (NSB, National Socialist Movement), and related organisations such as the Landwacht (national-socialist police auxiliaries).

The activities of the Dutch underground were further hampered by the high density of the population.[54] After Belgium, the Netherlands was the most densely populated country in Europe. Sustained guerrilla warfare, as conducted in several parts of France, was therefore impossible. From this perspective, the Veluwe area, in the central-eastern Netherlands, with its continuous forests, and the less populated northern provinces, such as Overijssel, Drenthe, Groningen, and Friesland, were most suitable for guerrilla-type resistance activities.

Despite the difficult and dangerous conditions in occupied Netherlands, BBO commander Van Oorschot saw opportunities for the Dutch Jedburgh teams that partially coincided with the French Jedburgh groups: like the French teams, the Dutch groups had to make contact with the resistance and provide them with weapons and military advice. The Dutch Jedburghs groups also had to restrain the resistance from 'wild', irresponsible actions and prevent premature action. However, unlike the Jedburghs who were sent to France, the teams operating in the Netherlands could be ordered to carry out *coup-de-main* operations.[55] Finally, the Dutch teams could, unlike the French groups, be sent on intelligence-gathering missions.[56]

At a later stage, as the front lines approached their area of operations, the Dutch Jedburgh groups and the resistance would act more openly and offensively, eliminating German pockets of resistance, sabotaging enemy lines of communication, and preventing enemy demolitions of critical infrastructure. After they were overrun by Allied forces, the Jedburgh would assist in maintaining (public) order in cooperation with the resistance groups.[57] According to Major Olmsted, everyone from the Dutch Jedburgh Section was fully aware of the fact that assignments in occupied Netherlands were going to be 'extremely difficult'.[58] Nevertheless, the morale within the group was excellent and the Jedburghs could not wait 'to be done with training and get going'.[59]

On 1 May 1944 the entire Jedburgh group gathered for the last time. That day a final sporting event was organised. The Dutch athlete Lieutenant Bestebreurtje earned himself a creditable second place, only after an American Jedburgh officer of the French section.[60] Soon after, fifteen Jedburgh teams left Milton Hall for Algeria; when the time came, these groups would be parachuted into southern France.[61]

Around May, the Dutch Jedburgh officers started preparing their teams for deployment in occupied territory. Several teams were alerted for a ten-day hike in Scotland. Each team took its own route, covering 160 to 360 kilometres, partly through extremely remote areas. The Dutch Jedburgh Section also went on Small Boat Training in Scotland. This is where they learned how to handle kayaks, canoes, skiffs, and sailing boats.[62] In late May, many Jedburgh teams were ordered to follow an Air Landing Course, in which they were taught how to select and prepare (improvised) runways for small transport aircraft. This way the Jedburghs could, if deemed necessary, quickly evacuate important people and material from behind enemy lines.

By the end of May 1944 the equipment of the Jedburghs was also nearly complete.[63] It was decided that each Jedburgh would carry his own national insignia. All nationalities wore American jump boots and a British airborne helmet. The Dutch Jedburghs wore the standard British Battledress. Over this they wore a British camouflage parachutist jacket, called the Denison smock. All Jedburghs also had mounted a Special Force Wing on their uniforms, showing the letters 'SF', which was especially designed for (and by) the Jedburgh unit.[64]

Jedburghs on small boat training in Scotland, spring of 1944. From left to right: Bestebreurtje, Verhaeghe, Scott, Beynon, and Groenewoud. (The Beynon family)

The Jedburghs receiving sailing lessons in Scotland, spring of 1944. From left to right: Billingsley, Sollenberger, Staal, Brinkgreve, a sail instructor, Austin, and Olmsted. (The Beynon family)

SOE put together a special radio transmitter for the Jedburgh teams, the so-called 'Jed-Set'. This device was packed in a backpack and weighed about twenty kilos. In an emergency situation, the operator could generate electricity by using a hand generator. In terms of armament, the troops were equipped with an American M1A1 Carbine (with folding butt) and the U.S. M1911 Pistol. They were also issued with a British Fairbairn–Sykes Fighting Knife. Another typical piece of equipment carried by the Jedburghs was an escape kit, which contained a double-sided fabric map of the area of operations, a miniature compass, and a small saw.

Meanwhile SFHQ had finalised the operational procedure for the deployment of teams. The head of SFHQ would, along with the commander of the Jedburghs, decide when and where a team was to be parachuted. Depending on the type of mission, it was decided whether a team should be reinforced with commandos and/or regular agents. Thereupon the team would be alerted to prepare the mission. In the final briefing, which would normally last three to four hours, the

Above and below: Insignia of the Dutch Jedburghs. (Private collection)

Right: British type parachute helmet
worn by all Jedburghs. (J. Siemensma)

Below: All Jedburghs wore a British
camouflage parachutist jacket, called
the Denison smock. (J. Siemensma)

Jedburgh 'SF' wing. (C. Bassett)

U.S. M1A1 Carbine.

U.S. M1911 Pistol.

Right: Fairbairn–Sykes Fighting Knife.

Below: The Escape Kit contained a double-sided fabric map, a small compass, and a miniature saw.

team was given the latest details of the mission, including the exact location of the drop zone, the agents which were already active in the concerned area, and code phrases that were needed to lay contact with the resistance. Afterwards the team would be transported to the airport and parachuted over occupied territory that very night.

On the evening of 5 June 1944 – the day before the invasion of Western Europe started – the first Jedburgh team was sent to France. Team Hugh was parachuted over Brittany to support the resistance and interrupt German lines of communication. By August 1944 almost all Jedburgh teams were deployed. In general, they worked successfully with the resistance in many French regions and were able to support the Allied ground offensive.[65] The Jedburgh groups rendered valuable assistance to resistance groups in sabotage and other offensive operations, but also played an important intelligence-collecting role.[66]

The teams who remained in England were very disappointed – even resentful – that their training efforts failed to be rewarded. The Jedburgh teams who were destined for the Netherlands were tossed between hope of being deployed and the frustration of missions cancelled at the last minute. Due to the rapid advance

Leisure time on the balcony at Milton Hall. From left to right: Sollenberger, Olmsted, and Groenewoud. (The Groenewoud family)

of the Allied forces through Europe, some members of the Dutch Jedburgh Section even began to immerse themselves into Oriental languages, hoping that they might go into action against the Japanese.

A Jedburgh officer in battle dress uniform. (NARA)

2

THE SITUATION IN THE OCCUPIED
NETHERLANDS

The armed resistance in the Netherlands

On 10 May 1940 the German army invaded the Netherlands. After a brief but fierce battle the Dutch armed forces capitulated. Gradually, small resistance groups emerged. These carried out simple acts of sabotage, such as cutting telephone wires and slashing the tires of German vehicles. As the German occupation endured, some of these groups began to concentrate on robberies, sabotage, assassinations, and other forms of armed resistance. The most important Dutch armed resistance groups were the Raad van Verzet (RVV, Council of Resistance), the Landelijke Knokploegen (LKP or KP, National Riot Squads), and the Ordedienst (OD, Order Service).

In August 1940 a resistance cell developed in The Hague around nobleman J. (Johan) Schimmelpenninck, the director of the Dutch office of a French wine trading company. In order to structure the activities of several independent small resistance groups, Schimmelpenninck created the OD. This national network of resisters consisted mostly of former army officers. The initial goal of the OD was to prevent a power vacuum after the German occupier was defeated; it did not take long before the Germans infiltrated the OD. A large number of arrests followed, including Schimmelpenninck himself. He was succeeded by Reserve Captain P. J. (Pieter) Six, who intended to transform the OD in a sort of 'military authority administration'.[1] However, as the occupation continued, the OD increasingly focused on armed resistance.

The driving force behind the RVV was Reserve First Lieutenant J. (Jan) Thijssen. He initially built a nationwide radio network that could support both the Dutch resistance and the Allies. In cooperation with the OD, Thijssen had his network ready for use by 1942. When he discovered that the OD only wanted to use his radio network for its own purposes and postpone activities until the liberation phase, the more aggressive Thijssen began developing new plans. He then focused on uniting the resistance groups that were involved in espionage and sabotage.[2] Thijssen was able to expand his organisation but did not succeed in turning the RVV into an 'umbrella' organisation for the Dutch armed resistance.

As a result of the increase in the number of persons in hiding during the occupation, the Landelijke Organisatie voor Hulp aan Onderduikers (LO, National Organisation for Assistance to People in Hiding) was confronted with a growing need of ration coupons. The LO therefore decided to form special groups, so called 'Knokploegen' (KP, Riot Squads) to raid coupon distribution offices. The KP squads eventually grew into an independent subsidiary of the LO, known as the LKP. Around the end of 1943, the LKP had so many affiliates that, from then on, it was truly a nationwide organisation.[3]

The KP groups conducted many successful raids and other acts of armed resistance. In May and June 1944, for instance, the Koepel Prison and the House of Detention in the city of Arnhem were attacked. The raiders were able to free LO commander F. (Frits) Slomp and more than fifty other political prisoners. At the end of August 1944, just before the advancing Allied ground forces reached the Netherlands, Reserve First Lieutenant J. A. (Johannes) van Bijnen was appointed Landelijk Sabotage Commandant, or National Sabotage Commander of the LKP.[4] Van Bijnen had developed sophisticated sabotage plans to support the liberation of the Netherlands.

Left: Jan Thijssen was the driving force of the RVV. (Private collection)

Right: Johannes van Bijnen from the LKP. (Private collection)

Due to the lack of communication between the occupied Netherlands and England, the Dutch government-in-exile in London was for a long time under the impression that the resistance groups in the Netherlands were much less active than they actually were. This changed in the course of 1944. With increasing radio traffic from the occupied nation, it gradually became clear that the resistance in the Netherlands was much more extensive than expected, but unfortunately also very fragmented and inharmonious.[5]

Within several weeks after its establishment, the Dutch BBO sent its first agents to the Dutch resistance. Between April and August 1944, the bureau parachuted a total of twenty-two men into the occupied Netherlands;[6] the Dutch underground also received several BI agents in this timeframe. Conditions in and above the Netherlands proved – as expected – to be very difficult: seven BBO agents were killed in plane crashes, while another was injured upon landing. During these operations, three transport planes of the Special Duties squadrons of the RAF were lost.[7] To make matters worse, three agents were arrested shortly after their arrival. Unfortunately, BI also suffered several casualties.[8]

Despite these heavy losses, important progress had been made in the occupied Netherlands. During the spring and summer of 1944, the still active agents made or restored contacts between the resistance groups and London. Moreover, for

General Eisenhower was the Supreme Allied Commander of the Allied forces. (NARA)

the first time since the end of the *Englandspiel*, supplies had been delivered again to the Dutch resistance.[9] The prospect of the arrival of the Allies, and the fresh inflow of weapons and explosives from England, resulted in a surge in sabotage acts. The various resistance movements hardly collaborated in their actions, however, which lessened the effect on the German war machine in the Netherlands.

Eventually, some degree of coordination between the various resistance organisations developed. In early September 1944, the OD, RVV, and KP were, through a broadcast on Radio Oranje (the radio station of the Dutch Government-in-exile), officially declared a military organisation. From then on, the groups were conjointly referred to as the Nederlandse Binnenlandse Strijdkrachten (NBS or BS, Netherlands Forces of the Interior). Within the BS, the resistance parties were to work together on an equal footing.[10] Prince Bernhard of the Netherlands was appointed its commandant. The prince, in turn, was to act under orders of the Supreme Allied Commander, General D. D. (Dwight) Eisenhower.

The Allies approaching the Netherlands

On 6 June 1944 the invasion of north-western Europe began in Normandy. In the weeks that followed the Allies were able to establish and expand their beachhead. By August the Allies were rapidly advancing through France. Meanwhile, all Allied airborne divisions in Europe were put under command of the newly formed First Allied Airborne Army. The commander of this airborne army was the American Lieutenant General L. S. (Lewis) Brereton. The American part of his army was formed by XVIII US Airborne Corps, commanded by Major General M. B. (Matthew) Ridgway. The British section was made up of the I British Airborne Corps led by British Lieutenant General F. A. M. (Frederick) Browning.

One of the first operations of the First Allied Airborne Army should have been Operation Transfigure, a massive airborne landing between Orléans and Paris aimed to disrupt the German retreat from north-western France. However, due to the rapid advance of Lieutenant General G. S. (George) Patton's Third U.S. Army, this offensive was cancelled.[11]

At the end of August 1944 the Allies liberated Paris, whereupon ground forces rapidly advanced towards Belgium and Germany. Meanwhile, the First Allied Airborne Army developed a new plan to support the Allied advance. This operation, code-named Linnet, to be executed in the Lille–Tournai area, was aimed at hampering the retreat of German troops through Belgium.

Lieutenant General Patton advanced rapidly through France with his Third U.S. Army. (NARA)

Lieutenant General Brereton was the commandant of the First Allied Airborne Army, seen here in the rank of Major General.

When SFHQ learnt of this operation, it proposed to add Belgian Jedburgh teams to the Allied Airborne Army. The Jedburghs were to be assigned to the headquarters of the airborne divisions that had been selected for this operation: the US 17th and 101st Airborne Divisions and the British 53nd (Lowland) Division. A single Jedburgh team would be placed with each divisional headquarters.[12]

The Jedburghs teams would thus – for the first time – be deployed together and simultaneously with conventional forces. Apparently SFHQ was, in view of a rapid liberation of Belgium, looking for a way to provide the Belgian groups a chance to become operational. In this new setup, the Jedburghs were to establish contact with the Belgian resistance in the bridgehead and, among other things, recruit guides and labourers in the local population and gather intelligence. Due to the continuing rapid Allied advance Operation Linnet was cancelled too, depriving the Belgian Jedburghs of seeing action.

On 3 September 1944, the Allies liberated Brussels. Antwerp, with its important port, welcomed its liberators the next day.[13] Operation Linnet II, another planned airborne operation – this time between the cities of Liege in Belgium and Maastricht in the Netherlands – was, like so many other plans for the deployment of the airborne divisions, cancelled too. The Allied ground forces were simply advancing too fast.

With the Allies approaching the Netherlands fast, the Dutch people were whipped into a liberation frenzy. On 5 September 1944, German units from France and Belgium withdrew through the Netherlands, clogging the Dutch roads; collaborators fled in large numbers as well. That day, which would be remembered as *Dolle Dinsdag* or Mad Tuesday, Dutch and Allied flags were hoisted everywhere and the streets flooded with cheering and exuberant people. What the Dutch did not know, however, was that the Allies could not enter the Netherlands yet; the long logistical supply lines originating in France – the port of Antwerp could not be put into operation yet – caused major supply problems. This would severely delay the Allied steamroller advance. Due to this Allied hold-up, the Germans were, unfortunately, able to recover and regroup.

During August 1944, SFHQ and BBO had held several conferences about the deployment of the Dutch Jedburgh teams. As the Dutch Jedburghs now had their teams ready for action, BBO commander Van Oorschot suggested to the Dutch Minister of War to promote the Jedburgh officers. This proposal was supported by SOE as 'the named officers belong to the best that were in training for the Jedburgh task'.[14] By Royal Decree the Dutch Jedburgh officers were promoted to the next higher rank.

At the end of August 1944, the Dutch Jedburgh teams were instructed to abort their manoeuvres in Scotland and return to their headquarters in Peterborough immediately. The men realised, to their great delight, that something important was imminent. On 2 September 1944, the Dutch Jedburgh officers were ordered to report the next day at SFHQ in London for further instructions.[15] After nine months of training, deployment had finally arrived. Captain Bestebreurtje recollects, 'I had a feeling of exhilaration. That is the only way I can describe the way I felt about finally getting into the fracas.'[16]

After the cancellation of the Linnet operations, Field Marshal B. L. (Bernard) Montgomery, Commander of the 21st Army Group, had given the First Allied Airborne Army orders to develop a plan for a massive offensive that was aimed at conquering the Dutch river crossings at Grave, Nijmegen and Arnhem.[17] This operation was code-named Comet and involved the British 1st Airborne Division, the British 52nd Division, and the 1st Polish Independent Parachute Brigade.[18] These forces would be under tactical command of the I British Airborne Corps. Three Dutch Jedburgh teams were incorporated in this Allied plan.

Captain Staal's Jedburgh team, code-named Edward, was added to the headquarters of the I British Airborne Corps. Team Claude, under command of Captain Groenewoud, was assigned to the British 1st Airborne Division. Finally,

Field Marshal Montgomery was the commander of the 21st Army Group. (Library and Archives Canada)

team Clarence, led by Captain Bestebreurtje, was attached to the British 52nd Division. These Dutch teams were denominated as the 'Dutch Liaison Mission' (DLM). Team Edward would be in command of the DLM. The tasks of the teams were similar to those in Operation Linnet. In addition, the Jedburgh groups had to advise the corps and the division commanders on the way the Dutch resistance was to support Operation Comet.

The deployment of team Dudley

On 5 September 1944, Major Brinkgreve's team, code-named Dudley, was informed that it would be parachuted into the occupied Netherlands that night. Besides Brikgreve, this group consisted of the American Major Olmsted and Irish Sergeant Austin. Team Dudley was to unite and mobilise the resistance in the border province of Overijssel. One of their primary objectives was securing bridges that were important for the Allied advance through Overijssel, thereby enabling a quick entry into Germany's industrial heartland.[19] For Brinkgreve, it would be the first time since May 1940 that he was to be deployed on Dutch soil.

Jedburgh team Dudley on exercise in Scotland, Brinkgreve, Austin, and Olmsted. (The Beynon family)

Brinkgreve's colleague John Olmsted was born on 23 September 1914 in Lake Crystal in Minnesota. After graduating from college, he taught at a high school in Nebraska. Olmsted enlisted in 1939 with the 35th Infantry Division. In August 1942, he volunteered for parachute training and became part of the 541st Parachute Infantry Regiment.[20] About a year later, Olmsted was recruited by OSS. Team Dudley's wireless operator, John Austin, was born on 27 August 1922 in Castleconnell, Ireland. He volunteered for military service immediately after his eighteenth birthday in 1940. Austin initially joined the Royal Berkshire Regiment.[21] Before long, he joined SOE and wound up in its Small Scale Raiding Force, where he met Brinkgreve.

During the briefings it became clear that they would be dropped on an RVV drop zone in the Twente region of Overijssel – less than fifteen kilometres from the German border. The Allied ground forces were expected to reach them within several weeks. Each team member was issued *f* 10,000 in cash and would be parachuted in military uniform.

That day, Prince Bernhard paid a visit to the team – he wished the men good luck in accomplishing their difficult and dangerous mission.[22] After dinner, team Dudley left for the airfield. Just as the Jedburghs were ready to take off, the news came that the mission was cancelled for that evening due to bad weather conditions in the Netherlands. At the airfield the Jedburghs met two BBO agents who were also destined for the Netherlands: T. (Tobias) Biallosterski and his wireless operator P. (Pieter) de Vos. They should have been dropped that same night in the province of Noord-Holland.

Three days later, team Dudley was again alerted by SFHQ. At 2200 hours their aircraft took off.[23] Unfortunately, the bomber crew could not find the drop zone in Overijssel. The aircraft, with the Jedburghs still aboard, returned to England. BBO agents Biallosterski and de Vos had more luck; they were parachuted successfully that night.[24] On Monday, 11 September, the day the First U.S. Army reached the border city of Aachen in Germany, the Jedburghs took off again. John Olmsted stated:

> Our air crew was a different one and the pilot was excellent. The old RAF Stirling came over the drop zone like a homing pigeon and twenty minutes after midnight of September 11th-12th we were swinging in our harness over a reception committee that we fervently hoped was our own.[25]

Jedburgh team Dudley landed in the hamlet of Hoge Hexel in the municipality of Wierden, just west of the city of Almelo. After landing, the Jedburghs were brought to the local RVV headquarters where they met the local commander, Captain A. F. (Albert) Lancker. BBO agents J.(Jaap) Hinderink and J.(Jaap) Beekman, who had been dropped earlier into the Netherlands, were also present.[26]

Team Dudley's drop zone in the hamlet of Hoge Hexel, recent photograph. (Stichting Historische Kring Wederden)

The resistance in Overijssel

Although team Dudley had the task to unite the different resistance organisations in Overijssel, the relationship between the RVV and the KP would actually deteriorate further. Uniting the various underground groups in Overijssel would prove to be a challenging and time-consuming task for the Jedburghs. What was the history of the resistance in this Dutch border province?

On behalf of the RVV, the forty-nine-year-old Captain Lancker was sent to Overijssel in the summer of 1943. Before the war, Lancker had been an officer of the Royal Netherlands East Indies Army (KNIL). During the German invasion in May 1940, he fought in the Peel-Raamstelling, a defence line in the south of the Netherlands. After arriving in Overijssel, Captain Lancker succeeded in gaining authority over resistance men in a dozen places in the north-west of the Twente and Salland, two neighbouring, non-administrative regions in the province. The local '*Kenkhuus*' was the headquarters of the RVV, close to the hamlet of the Piksen. By the summer of 1944 this section of the RVV consisted of about ninety men who could be called upon to undertake action when required.[27] Until September 1944, though, the activities of the RVV were mostly of a preparatory nature.

From the spring of 1943, KP squads were also active in Overijssel. The first KP group in Twente was formed in Wierden, near the Piksen. Before long, KP groups were also established in the nearby cities of Almelo and Enschede. As of March 1944 these KP squads cooperated very closely, their members becoming more and more offensive as 1944 progressed.[28] In September 1944, the 'KP Twente' was formed. This group was commanded by the thirty-one-year-old J. (Johannes) ter Horst, a baker from Enschede. He had already earned his spurs in the resistance and had been involved in the previously mentioned impressive raid on the Arnhem House of Detention in June 1944 (see p. 34).[29] The headquarters of the Twente KP was the villa Huize Lidwina at Zenderen, strategically located between Almelo and the city of Hengelo. From this resistance nerve centre, many successful sabotage actions were orchestrated by Ter Horst in early September 1944.

Next to the RVV and KP, the OD was active in Overijssel. In the spring of 1944, former KNIL officer Colonel G. D. E. J. (George) Hotz was appointed OD Commander of the province. Hotz's headquarters was at that time located in Zwolle, in the north-western part of the province. The Overijssel OD had largely refrained from offensive activities against the Germans. The organisation was also still recovering from waves of arrests during the first years of the occupation.

Captain Lancker was the commander of Salland brigade of the RVV.
(C. B. Cornelissen)

Johannes ter Horst was commandant of the KP in Twente. (The Ter Horst family)

The remote Huize Lidwina, headquarters of the KP in Twente. (C. Hilbrink)

Besides the Jedburghs, several teams of the British Special Air Service (SAS) were deployed in the Netherlands in the final stage of the war. The SAS was founded in 1942 and worked, like the Jedburghs, behind enemy lines. Its forces specialised in penetrating the enemy front and conducting small-scale raids, targeting the enemy's rear elements and supply lines.[30] During the Second World War the SAS grew to the size of a brigade, which also included French and Belgian elements. A small group of Dutch personnel was detached to the SAS Brigade as well.

The first SAS team parachuted into the occupied Netherlands was a Belgian team code-named Fabian. This group entered the country a few days after Jedburgh team Dudley. They were parachuted near the town of Nijkerk in the province of Gelderland, approximately forty-five kilometres from Arnhem. Team Fabian, under command of Lieutenant G. S. J. A. (Gilbert) Kirschen, was ordered to collect intelligence about German troop movements and the locations of launch sites of the much feared V-2 rockets, which were fired at London and Antwerp.[31] Despite the usually offensive character of SAS operations, team Fabian was explicitly ordered not to carry out any offensive actions.

A V-2 rocket on a mobile launch platform. (NIMH)

Meanwhile, Prince Bernhard, commander of the Dutch Interior Forces (BS), had crossed from England to Belgium. From his headquarters in castle Rubens near Brussels, he was to coordinate the actions of the Dutch resistance during Operation Comet. However, Comet would be cancelled too, due to bad weather and the growing Allied concern about the build-up of German forces in the Netherlands.[32] Subsequently, Field Marshal Montgomery proposed an even more extensive offensive. This operation, which was to be the largest after the Normandy landings, was given the code name Market Garden.[33]

3

The Start of Operation Market Garden

The plan

After the cancellation of Comet, Montgomery's staff hastily prepared plans for Operation Market Garden. The airborne element of this operation, Market, employed the American 82nd and 101st Airborne Division, as well as the British 1st Airborne Division and the 1st Polish Independent Parachute Brigade. These airborne forces would be placed under tactical command of the British I Airborne Corps and were ordered to seize the bridges at Grave, Nijmegen, and Arnhem – just as in Operation Comet.

The XXX British Corps, under command of Lieutenant General B. G. H. (Brian) Horrocks, whose vanguard was at that time located near the Belgian-Dutch border, was to move north and cross the Rhine at the city of Arnhem as part of Operation Garden. If this bold plan succeeded, the Allies would be able to advance from the Arnhem bridgehead to the IJssel River – an offshoot of the Rhine – and subsequently head straight for the Ruhr region, Germany's industrial heart. An additional advantage of this Allied advance to the north was that it would cut German supply lines to the west of the Netherlands, also eliminating the threat of V-2 rockets fired against Britain from that region.[1]

In more detail, the American 101st Airborne Division, led by Major General M. D. (Maxwell) Taylor, was tasked to capture the rail and road bridges over the Aa River and the Zuid-Willemsvaart Canal near Veghel, the bridges over the Dommel Stream near Sint-Oedenrode as well as the bridge over the Wilhelmina Canal at Son.[2] The American 82nd Airborne Division, commanded by Major General J. M. (James) Gavin, was to occupy the bridges over the Waal River at Nijmegen, over the Maas River at Grave, and the Maas–Waal Canal. The division also had to capture the high grounds at the village of Groesbeek, to the south-east of Nijmegen.[3]

The main objectives of Operation Market Garden were the bridges over the Rhine at Arnhem. This task was given to the British 1st Airborne Division under command of Major General R. E. (Robert) Urquhart. The 1st Polish Independent Parachute Brigade of Major General S. F. (Stanislaw) Sosabowski was added to

Major General Taylor, commanding officer of the U.S. 101st Airborne Division. (National Liberation Museum Groesbeek)

Major General Gavin, commander of the U.S. 82nd Airborne Division. (National Liberation Museum Groesbeek)

Major General Urquhart commanded the British 1st Airborne Division. (Airborne Museum Hartenstein)

this division as reinforcement. The British and Polish forces would land farthest behind enemy lines and, consequently, were responsible for the toughest part of the operation.

With the transition from Comet to Market Garden, the number of deployed troops increased significantly. In total, approximately 35,000 men would be parachuted or sent in by glider. The Allies had insufficient transport capacity to deploy all these forces in just one day. It was decided to transport the three airborne divisions to the Netherlands over three days in several waves.[4] Contrary to the landings on D-Day in Normandy, the parachutists would be deployed by day. This was due to the negative Allied experience with night drops in June 1944, which had resulted in airborne units being scattered over a very large area.

On the ground, the XXX British Corps would have to advance approximately 100 kilometres from Neerpelt in Belgium to Arnhem. The corps had to cover this distance within just several days. Advance speed was essential since the lightly armed paratroopers in Arnhem would not be able to hold the bridges much longer. Yet the plan of XXX British corps was perilous: the advance from Belgium to Arnhem depended on just a single major road.[5] Still, the Allies took this for granted, as the defensive capability of the German forces in the Netherlands was thought to be very weak.[6] In order to hinder the Germans from sending reinforcements to the Netherlands, the Dutch government-in-exile was to call for a nationwide railway strike at Allied headquarters' request.

In the days leading up to Operation Market Garden, however, the Allies received increasingly more intelligence reports stating that the Germans were regrouping in the Netherlands. Allied headquarters also acquired messages indicating that the (re-established) German I. Fallschirmarmee was building a defence line along the Belgian-Dutch border. On 7 September, the Allies were apprised that the remnants of the German II. SS-Panzerkorps, led by SS-Obergruppenführer W. (Wilhelm) Bittrich, had arrived in the Netherlands after retreating from France.

In addition, Allied headquarters learned that the highly experienced German Generalfeldmarschall O. M. W. (Walter) Model, commandant of Heeresgruppe B, had established his headquarters in Oosterbeek, just a few kilometres outside Arnhem.[7] Moreover, on 14 September 1944, the Dutch espionage group 'Albrecht' relayed to England that the 9th SS-Panzer-Division 'Hohenstaufen' – one of Bittrich's two divisions – had arrived near Arnhem.[8] Though battered, the division still posed considerable danger. The Allies decided to ignore this information as they were convinced that the Germans had barely any fighting strength left. Operation Market Garden was to continue – by hook or by crook.

The Dutch Liaison Mission

As in the setup for Operation Comet, SFHQ attached Jedburgh teams to the British airborne corps and all participating airborne divisions. However, the transformation of Comet to Market Garden entailed that airborne corps were sent into battle with three airborne divisions instead of two. This also meant that an extra Jedburgh team had to be formed at the last minute; after the deployment of team Dudley in Overijssel, only three Dutch teams remained available for operations.

Two British Jedburghs and two Dutch BBO agents were selected to form the additional Jedburgh team, which was code-named Daniel II. The two British servicemen – originally not part of the Dutch Jedburgh Section – were Major R. K. (Robert) Wilson and Sergeant G. W. (George) Mason. The Dutch half of the team was made up by First Lieutenant A. (Bram) du Bois and Sergeant L. (Lee) Faber.

Lieutenant Du Bois was born in the village of Sloten on 12 April 1916, and enlisted in September 1936 as a conscript in the Dutch army. Du Bois, who studied law in Amsterdam, was mobilised in August 1939. When the Germans invaded the Netherlands, he saw action in the Peel-Raamstelling as a second lieutenant. After the capitulation, he reached the French port of Brest and was evacuated to England. He was sent to Canada by the Dutch government-in-exile as part of the Netherlands Military (recruitment) Mission. After returning to England, Du Bois, by now a first lieutenant, served briefly with No. 12 Commando. Thereafter he was trained by SOE and eventually seconded to BBO.[9]

Sergeant Faber was born on 14 September 1919 in Koudekerke in the south-western province of Zeeland. After finishing high school in Middelburg in 1939, he had various jobs in different parts of the Netherlands. In 1941, Faber was sent to forced labour in the city of Chemnitz, an industrial centre in eastern Germany. Two years later, whilst working in Amsterdam as a desk officer of the PTT (the Dutch Post and Telegraph organisation), he came into contact with the organised resistance. Faber was engaged in March 1943 to the sister of the well-known resistance member J. (Jean) Weidner, who was involved in the so-called 'Dutch-Paris' escape line. Later that year, Faber decided to leave his home country. He had a perilous journey through France, Andorra, and Spain before eventually reaching England in March 1944. After being trained as a radio operator by SOE, Faber was seconded as a sergeant to BBO.[10]

In the setup of Market Garden, Jedburgh team Edward, in overall command of the DLM, remained attached to the I British Airborne Corps. Captain Groenewoud and his team Claude also remained with their original formation, the 1st Airborne Division. Team Clarence, led by Captain Bestebreurtje, was tasked to the American 82nd Airborne Division. Their assignments were on par with those detailed for Operation Comet. Team Claude was additionally tasked by the staff of the 1st Airborne Division to assist British supply troops in collecting all means of transport in the area. Finally, Team Daniel II was attached to the American 101st Airborne Division.

On the morning of 11 September 1944, team Clarence reported at the headquarters of the 82nd Airborne Division. Captain Bestebreurtje, who spent several summers in and around Nijmegen, started to assist the American division in their preparations immediately. He was soon called 'Captain Harry' because his name was found too difficult to pronounce. The Dutch Jedburgh officer had great knowledge of the operational area, which impressed Major General Gavin. Bestebreurtje would continue to impress his American colleagues during Operation Market Garden – Gavin would later describe the Dutchman as an 'extraordinary officer'.[11]

On 14 September, the other Dutch Jedburgh teams reported at headquarters of the I British Airborne Corps in Moor Park, north of London. That day, Captain Staal briefed the staff on the Jedburgh teams' role during the operation. The Jedburghs also assisted the corps in carrying out field studies and gathered information about the expected military situation in the area of operations.[12] The Jedburgh teams were able to collect 'much valuable information' via the Dutch intelligence services for British corps headquarters.[13]

Sergeant Mason was team Daniel II's first radio operator. (The National Archives)

Lieutenant Du Bois was attached to team Daniel II. (A. Donk-Du Bois)

Sergeant Faber was attached to team Daniel II. (Archive De Roever)

Meanwhile, SFHQ had decided to reinforce several Dutch Jedburgh teams. Additional members were required because the Jedburghs were to be deployed – simultaneously – with the Allied forces and had only limited time to organise and utilise the Dutch resistance. Two British SOE members were added to Jedburgh team Edward; Captain R. M. (Richard) Mills would act as an additional liaison officer and Second Lieutenant L. R. D. (Leonard) Willmott as the team's second wireless operator. Captain Mills, born on 17 January, 1916, came from the Royal Welch Fusiliers; thereafter, he was a staff officer at a Special Force Detachment.[14] Willmott, born on 23 June 1921, originated from the Royal Corps of Signals. He had already been active for SOE as a radio operator in occupied Greece. Mills and Willmott were not specially trained as Jedburgh forces.

Captain Groenewoud's team was reinforced with First Lieutenant M. J. (Martin) Knottenbelt of No.2 (Dutch) Troop, a commando unit within No. 10 (Inter-Allied) Commando. Knottenbelt was born on 12 March 1920, in Jakarta in the Dutch East Indies. He emigrated to England and studied at Oxford University. In August 1941, Knottenbelt was promoted to Reserve Second Lieutenant. Early 1942, he successfully completed British Commando training. The following year, Knottenbelt was promoted to first lieutenant. In 1944 he was attached to No. 44 (Royal Marine) Commando and saw action against the Japanese in Burma. Early September 1944, Knottenbelt was voluntarily transferred to BBO, where his secondment to the Jedburghs came about.

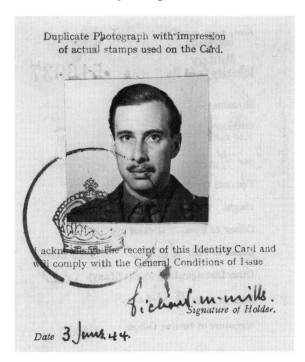

Duplicate Photograph with impression of actual stamps used on the Card.

I acknowledge the receipt of this Identity Card and will comply with the General Conditions of Issue

Signature of Holder.

Date 3 June 44.

Major Mills reinforced Jedburgh team Edward. (The National Archives)

Second Lieutenant Willmott was the second wireless operator of team Edward. (The National Archives)

Lieutenant Knottenbelt was attached to Jedburgh team Claude, post-war photograph. (NIMH)

Apart from Knottenbelt, a large contingent of Dutch commandos would also participate in Operation Market Garden. Like the Jedburghs, they were divided over the various airborne divisions. In addition to their regular infantry duties, they were to liaise with the Dutch resistance in the area. Another Dutchman who would be deployed during the Airborne offensive was Lieutenant Commander A. (Arnold) Wolters. He had been a reserve officer in the Royal Netherlands Navy until 1940. During 1941–42, Wolters had worked for the Dutch Centrale Inlichtingendienst (CID, Central Intelligence Service) of the Netherlands War Department in London.

Shortly before Market Garden, Wolters was appointed by the Dutch government-in-exile as the future military commissioner for the city of Arnhem and was assigned to the 1st Airborne Division. He was to work under command of the British Colonel H. N. (Hilaro) Barlow, deputy commander of the British 1st Airlanding Brigade. The latter was expected to form resistance groups for sabotage and intelligence tasks in the Arnhem area. Once the city was liberated, Barlow was to become the Town Mayor of Arnhem.[15] From then on, Jedburgh team Claude would act under his orders.[16]

Dutch Lieutenant Commander Wolters was appointed as future military commissioner for the city of Arnhem. (NIMH)

The resistance in the operational zone

While preparing for their missions, the Jedburgh teams gathered as much information about the underground as they could. However, they soon found out that there was little information about the Dutch resistance groups in the operational zone. Although radio traffic with the occupied Netherlands had increased during 1944, a lot of Dutch resistance elements were still not in direct contact with England. So which underground groups were actually active in and around the operational zone of Market Garden?

One of the most active groups in Eindhoven, in the sector of the 101st Airborne Division, was Partisanen Actie Nederland (PAN, Partisans Action Netherlands). This resistance movement was founded by student A. (Ad) Hoynck van Papendrecht in late August 1943. His organisation consisted of several small, armed groups that conducted sabotage and other offensive actions. Early in 1944, he came into contact with the KP squad of T. (Theo) Dirks that was mainly active in the villages west of Eindhoven. Before long the resistance leaders coordinated their activities with each other.

The headquarters of the PAN was based in Eindhoven. During 1944, Hoynck van Papendrecht also liaised with national KP headquarters (LKP). It was agreed that the PAN would go into action when the LKP commenced their nationwide sabotage of the railways, in support of the arrival of the Allied forces in the Netherlands. In return, the LKP would provide the PAN with much needed weapons and explosives.[17]

Besides the PAN, there were several other (independent) resistance organisations in the vicinity of Eindhoven, including a very active group in the village of Eerde, led by a pastor. This resistance cell was able to steal explosives from German forces, which were subsequently used in attacks on railways shortly before Operation Market Garden commenced.[18]

In the vicinity of Nijmegen, the sector of the 82nd Airborne Division, there were also several active resistance movements. One of these groups was led by T. (Theo) Dobbe, who was involved in clandestine work as early as 1940. Dobbe settled in Nijmegen in the spring of 1943 and founded a KP squad, amalgamating several independent groups. Later, various members of the KP from the neighbouring province of Noord-Brabant also joined his organisation.

In the autumn of 1943, Dobbe met LKP chief executive L. (Liepke) Scheepstra, who was actively coordinating and integrating KP activities throughout the nation. Dobbe's group was soon absorbed in the LKP. Unfortunately, Dobbe was arrested on Mad Tuesday – two weeks before Market Garden – while trying to assassinate a notorious collaborator. He was executed that same day. Besides Dobbe's group, there were various other resistance organisations active in and near Nijmegen, including 'De Pandoeren'.[19] In the nearby Groesbeek area, several OD units operated. The local OD grew considerably during Market Garden, as many people who had been in hiding found their way to this group.

The main resistance group in the Arnhem area, the sector of the British 1st Airborne Division, was former Reserve First Lieutenant P. C. (Pieter) Kruyff's KP squad. He had first come into contact with the organised resistance in October 1940. Kruyff initially focused on collecting residual Dutch arms and ammunition. The former Dutch officer moved to Arnhem at the end of 1940 and became the commander of a well-organised KP group, and established his headquarters at Velper Square in the town centre.

Kruyff's organisation was composed of different branches, including a sabotage section.[20] The centre of gravity of the movement was its intelligence operation. The collected information was passed on by Kruyff to several other underground organisations, including the aforementioned group Albrecht, which was in contact with Dutch authorities in England. Former Dutch Navy officer C. L. J. F. (Charles) Douw van der Krap was also part of the Arnhem KP. After the Dutch capitulation, he had refused to sign the so-called 'Erewoordverklaring' – a declaration that one

Theo Dobbe was the founder of the KP Nijmegen. (Private collection)

Liepke Scheepstra was one of
the key figures within the LKP.
(The Scheepstra family)

Pieter Kruyff was the head of the
KP Arnhem. (The Kruyff family)

would not resist German authority – and was subsequently imprisoned. After an escape attempt, Douw van der Krap was sent to Colditz Castle in eastern Germany, a notorious high-security POW camp. He later escaped from another prison, eventually joining the Dutch underground.[21]

Already at the beginning of September 1944, Allied headquarters instructed the Dutch resistance to start widespread sabotage. Attacks on railways in the south, centre, and east of the Netherlands were especially encouraged. Much to the delight of the Allies, an intensive sabotage campaign followed. The KP and PAN in the southern provinces of Noord-Brabant and Limburg sabotaged many railway lines.[22] The resistance in the province of Gelderland also carried out approximately thirty attacks on railway targets in and around Arnhem.[23] In the more northern province of Overijssel, particularly in the Twente region, plenty of sabotage acts took place. Night after night, the Twente KP cut important railways to Germany. Roads were also blocked and the destruction of canal sluice gates severely hampered canal traffic in the province.[24]

On the night prior to Market Garden, the Dutch government-in-exile would also call for a nationwide railway strike via Radio Oranje. The Dutch response

Navy officer Douw van der Krap, left in the picture, here in German captivity. After escaping he joined the KP Arnhem. (NIMH)

A derailed locomotive in Almelo. The Twente KP organised a successful sabotage campaign in early September 1944. (C.B. Cornelissen)

was highly productive: almost all railway personnel ceased working and went into hiding. Due to this massive walkout, German reinforcements and equipment could not be transported by rail during the first days of Market Garden.[25]

Meanwhile in Overijssel

While Operation Market Garden was being prepared in England, Jedburgh team Dudley had become operational in Overijssel. Major Brinkgreve organised a meeting on 12 September 1944 with local RVV commandant Lancker and several other regional resistance leaders. The purpose of this gathering was to obtain a general idea of the situation in the area. Major Olmsted and Sergeant Austin were engaged with burying the containers and parachutes that were dropped with them the night before. They also formed an improvised depot to facilitate the distribution of weapons and explosives to the Overijssel resistance.

Though the Jedburghs were dropped in military uniform, arrangements were made for the men to obtain forged identity cards; it had already become clear that it was impossible to move around without civilian clothing. Lancker's radio operator, BBO agent Jaap Beekman, whose radio set had become unusable, received one of the transmitters that were brought by team Dudley. SFHQ in London, which was waiting anxiously for a sign of life from the Jedburghs, received the first telegram the next day:

> Arrived safely with all containers and equipment. Contact made leader RVV district Overijssel. Available approx. 500 men in 18 groups varying strength. Arms and equipment none. Send supplies 8 containers … Love Pappy [Major Olmsted], Henk [and] Sergeant Austin.

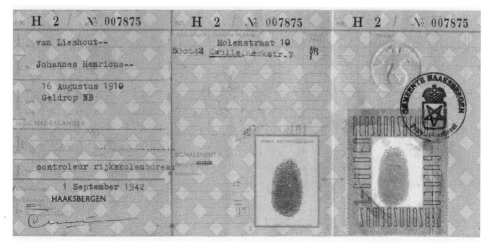

Forged identity papers of Major Henk Brinkgreve. (The Brinkgreve family)

Team Dudley made immediate arrangements with SFHQ for supply drops, since the resistance in Overijssel was in desperate need of weapons and equipment. Major Brinkgreve had already exchanged his uniform for civilian clothes, which he had brought from England. Major Olmsted and Sergeant Austin now wore overalls over their uniforms.

Above: The American Major Olmsted, Jedburgh team Dudley's second officer. (The Beynon family)

Right: Forged identity papers of BBO wireless operator Jaap Beekman. (Archive De Roever)

On Wednesday, the Jedburgh team commenced their weapon instructions.[26] Before long, the local KP leader, the aforementioned Johannes ter Horst, visited Captain Lancker's headquarters. He had just heard that Allied paratroopers had landed in the area. During the conversation, Ter Horst insisted that the Jedburghs should join his organisation. Unlike the RVV, the KP had conducted many instances of sabotage in the area. To Lancker's great displeasure, the Jedburghs would soon decide to head for the nearby KP Twente headquarters.[27]

On Friday 15 September, radio operator Sergeant Austin went out to find a new location from whence he could signal. In the meantime, increasingly more people visited the local RVV headquarters where the two Jedburgh officers were still present. The news that parachutists had landed quickly spread in the region of Twente. In the evening, German trucks suddenly drove into the woods where the men were hiding. Fortunately, the Jedburghs and the resistance fighters were not discovered. As a precaution, the RVV headquarters would move the following night, while Sergeant Austin moved his radio set to a safe house several kilometres north.

From then on, Austin would mostly operate independently, away from his officers. Contact between them would mainly take place via couriers. This was done in order to reduce the risk of the entire team being discovered by the enemy, who was intensely tracking radio signals. These precautions were very wise as

The Irish Sergeant Austin was Jedburgh team Dudley's wireless operator. (The Beynon family)

the German SD had now set up a station in the nearby city of Almelo.[28] Until then, only SD men from Enschede and Arnhem had been deployed in the hunt for the resistance in Twente and its surroundings.[29] The situation thus became (even) more precarious for the local resistance and the Jedburghs. It would not take long before the SD would deliver a massive blow to the local underground.

On Saturday, 16 September, the day before Operation Market Garden commenced, team Dudley reported to headquarters in England that the situation in the east of the Netherlands was deteriorating fast. All Dutchmen aged 17 to 45 were forced by the Germans to help build fortifications along the IJssel River. The Germans were also rapidly sending in reinforcements from Germany. In Zwolle, the capital city of the province, the German authorities had declared *Standrecht* (summary justice).

Team Dudley also reported that the headquarters of the commander of all German forces in the Netherlands, Wehrmachtsbefehlshaber in den Niederlanden, General F. (Friedrich) Christiansen, had reportedly moved his command post to the border city of Denekamp, about 25 kilometres east of their position.

Members of the SD who were stationed in Almelo. They went to great lengths to hamper the resistance in Twente. (C. B. Cornelissen)

The location of the Wehrmachtsbefehlshaber in den Niederlanden, General der Flieger Christiansen, was passed on to England by Jedburgh team Dudley in early September 1944. (Private collection)

Due to the incident with the German trucks the previous day, the Jedburghs' headquarters was moved north that night. The risky journey – all their material was transported in plain sight on a farmhouse cart – went without any incidents. The group reached its destination at midnight. Several hours later, the largest airborne operation of the war would begin.

Sunday, 17 September 1944

On the Sunday morning of 17 September, at around 0930 hours, the first of more than two thousand Allied transport aircraft and gliders took off in England and headed for the Netherlands. At 1300 hours, the first forces of the American 101st Airborne Division arrived above the most southern landing zones – at Son and Veghel. Jedburgh team Daniel II, assigned to the American division, departed from Welford airfield around 1050 hours.

Besides the two aforementioned Dutch BBO agents, Lieutenant Du Bois and Sergeant Faber, the team consisted of two British Jedburghs, Major R. K. (Robert) Wilson and Sergeant G. W. (George) Mason. Wilson, born on 4 November 1911, came from the 12th Medium Regiment Royal Artillery.[30]

Mason, born on 19 December 1922, had served with the 27th Lancers of the Royal Armoured Corps.[31]

Team Daniel II had been placed in the aircraft that transported the 502nd Regiment and divisional staff. Lieutenant Du Bois was in the second plane, along with division commander Major General Taylor. Major Wilson was in the sixth plane, while Sergeants Faber and Mason followed in the ninth. Their flight to the Netherlands went smoothly until the air armada came under heavy flak at approximately 1320 hours. The sixth and ninth planes caught fire, but could maintain formation. All Jedburghs from team Daniel II eventually jumped and landed safely nearby to Son.[32]

Just before their departure of the 82nd Airborne Division, team Clarence's Captain Bestebreurtje was asked by Major General Gavin if he had ever parachuted out of a Douglas C-47 transport aircraft. The Dutchman indicated that this was his first parachute jump from an American plane. Bestebreurtje said about what happened next, 'And right there on the airfield, the commanding general of the 82nd Airborne proceeded to give me a one-minute lesson in how to jump from an American C-47.'[33]

Besides Bestebreurtje, team Clarence consisted of two American Jedburghs, namely Lieutenant Verhaeghe and Sergeant Beynon. G. M. (George) Verhaeghe

A Dutch volunteer transports paratroopers of the 101st Airborne Division. On the very right, a Dutch commando is seen in an American uniform. (NIMH)

was born on 12 March 1918 to Flemish parents who had migrated to the U.S. He still spoke fluent Dutch. Before Verhaeghe signed up in the U.S. Armed Forces, he worked as a security guard. When he was approached by OSS in October 1943, Verhaeghe volunteered immediately.[34] The wireless operator of the team, W. W. (Willard) Beynon, born on 2 June 1923, was the son of a police captain. After the attack on Pearl Harbor, Beynon enlisted and ended up in the U.S. Signal Corps. Next, he voluntarily followed parachute training at Fort Benning, where he was recruited by OSS.[35]

During the flight to the Netherlands Captain Bestebreurtje and Lieutenant Verhaeghe were on board the aircraft of Major General Gavin. Sergeant Beynon was in the third plane, with the team's equipment and radio set. When the formation reached the Netherlands, Bestebreurtje felt a wave of emotions: 'It was a feeling of warmth for the land. I saw the fields and the farmhouses, and I could even see a windmill turning. I remember distinctly thinking to myself: "Well, here is poor old Holland back again and we have come to liberate you". I felt lucky and was proud to be there.'[36]

Just before arriving over the landing zones, the pilots began to watch for the landmarks they had rehearsed in England. Gavin's staff had laughed when Bestebreurtje told them to look for the tallest mountain east of Nijmegen, the

Team Clarence: Verhaeghe, Beynon, and Bestebreurtje. (The Beynon family)

Vlierberg near Berg en Dal.[37] When the Americans approached Nijmegen by air, the Dutchman turned out to be right. Bestebreurtje recalled, 'Now they saw it, rising up ahead of them and looking for the world like Mt Everest in contrast to the almost two-dimensional look of the Dutch countryside.'[38] Despite heavy German anti-aircraft fire, the division's staff and Jedburgh team Clarence made a good landing just after 1300 hours, about two kilometres south-west of Groesbeek.[39]

Team Edward had left England by glider at around 1120 hours with the front elements of the I British Airborne Corps. Besides carrying ƒ 10,500 in cash, the team took a jeep and a trailer with them.[40] The flight of the Jedburghs went smoothly. Around 1410 hours, the men made an excellent landing on the glider landing zone at Groesbeek.[41]

Captain Staal's team Edward consisted of four other members, including the two British officers who were added to his team as reinforcements. Staal's original teammates were two American Jedburghs, Captain M. (McCord) Sollenberger and Sergeant J. R. (James) Billingsley. Sollenberger was born on 24 September 1910, in Baltimore. He visited several private high schools in Europe before the war. In 1942, Sollenberger enlisted in the U. S. Cavalry and was made an officer later that year.[42]

Captain Bestebreurtje (third from left), behind him Major General Gavin, moments after landing near Groesbeek. (S. Bentley)

The original three members of Jedburgh team Edward. Sollenberger in the front, Staal, and Billingsley behind. (The Sollenberger family)

The other American, Sergeant Billingsley, was born on 25 February 1915, the son of a minister in Romney, West Virginia. He worked as a radio technician at a radio station for several years. In July 1943, Billingsley enlisted in the U.S. Armed Forces and was trained as a radio operator.[43]

The fourth Dutch Jedburgh group to be deployed that day was team Claude. It was transported to the Netherlands together with the British 1st Airborne Division. Besides the Dutch officers Captain Groenewoud and Lieutenant Knottenbelt, the team was made up of two Americans. First Lieutenant H. A. (Harvey) Todd had been a teacher before the war. In 1941 Todd enlisted, at age twenty-five, in the U.S. Army. In 1942 he completed Officer Candidate School at Fort Benning and was assigned as a second lieutenant in the 8th Infantry Division. Subsequently, he served with several other units, including the 541st Parachute Infantry Regiment.[44] The wireless operator of the team, Sergeant C. A. (Carl) Scott, was born on 25 December 1922 and grew up in Columbus, Ohio. He joined the U.S. Armed Forces in 1943.

Right: The American Sergeant Billingsley was team Edward's first wireless operator. (The Beynon family)

Below: Team Claude: Scott, Groenewoud, and Todd. Lieutenant Knottenbelt is not included in this photograph. (The Beynon family)

The American Sergeant Scott was team Claude's wireless operator. (The Beynon family)

Team Claude landed by parachute around 1400 hours at Wolfheze. Lieutenant Knottenbelt had been deployed separately from his teammates. He arrived together with the 1st Parachute Brigade and a few other Dutch commandos by glider, also at Wolfheze. In general, the airborne landings went very well that day. Just after 1400 hours, nearly all 16,500 troops of the first wave had landed. These forces had brought 500 vehicles, 300 artillery pieces, and approximately 590 tons of equipment with them.[45]

SFHQ had provided Jedburgh team Daniel II with *f* 5,000 in cash and one radio set. Although the Jedburghs had made a good landing, their radio transmitter was smashed when it hit the ground. Unfortunately, a second set, which was to arrive in a glider in the second transport wave, would not reach the team either. The loss of these sets was a major setback for team Daniel II as it could not establish radio contact with England or the other Jedburgh teams.

Despite shelling by German artillery, Daniel II's members succeeded in reaching the divisional collecting area about two hours after landing.[46] They soon came into contact with local Dutch civilians, who provided them with useful intelligence.[47] Lieutenant Du Bois was now attached to Major General Taylor as an interpreter and liaison officer; he would stay with the general continuously during the first two days. The other members of the team also worked from the divisional headquarters in Son.

British parachutists land amid previously arrived gliders, in the area near Wolfheze. (National Liberation Museum Groesbeek)

Members of the Dutch resistance providing information to an American officer near Veghel. (NIMH)

The 501st Regiment of the 101st Airborne Division had landed west of Veghel and taken the bridges over the Zuid-Willemsvaart Canal and the Aa River around 1500 hours, thereby achieving its initial objectives. The 1st Battalion of the 502nd Regiment marched towards Sint-Oedenrode, where it secured the bridge over the Dommel Stream. A company of this regiment then moved on to the village of Best, just north of Eindhoven, to take the road bridge over the Wilhelmina Canal, but were halted by fierce German resistance. At Son, the men of the 506th Regiment were also unsuccessful in taking the bridge over the Wilhelmina Canal; just before they reached the main bridge, it was blown up by the retreating Germans.

The PAN commander of Son, S. (Sjef) Lavrijssen, who lived right next to the canal, had foreseen the destruction of the bridge. With material that Lavrijssen had prepared, the American forces were able to swiftly construct a temporary bridge and two rafts.[48] However, the bridge could not support heavy traffic, which meant that the Germans created the first obstacle between the 101st Airborne Division and the XXX British Corps. The parachutists could only wait for the engineers of the corps, who had to build a Bailey bridge in order to cross the Wilhelmina Canal.[49]

Tanks of the XXX British Corps in Valkenswaard en route to Eindhoven, 18 September 1944. (NIMH)

When Lieutenant General Horrocks, commander of XXX British Corps, learned that the airborne landings had proceeded as planned, he ordered his units to start the attack. Around 1500 hours, the corps' forward elements passed the Dutch border. Contrary to expectations, they were soon embroiled in heavy battles with German's forces. Only toward the evening did the British vanguard reach the town of Valkenswaard, which was still about ten kilometres removed from that day's objective: the city of Eindhoven.[50]

German *Sprengkommandos* in Eindhoven had started demolitions right after the Allied landings. Critical infrastructure was destroyed, including the boiler house at the Phillips plant and the town's rail yard emplacement. Due to the lack of weapons, the local resistance stood powerless. Still, members of the PAN from Eindhoven and Woensel did get involved in a long battle with German demolition squads near the station.[51]

North of team Daniel II, Captain Bestebreurtje's team had landed near the village of Groesbeek. The Jedburghs soon found out that their equipment and radio transmitter were dropped too early and had actually landed in the German Reichswald, a forest just across the border. Sergeant Beynon, the team's wireless

German Sprengkommandos demolished the railway station of Eindhoven right after the Allied landings. (NIMH)

operator, tried to retrieve the packages but had to give up his attempt due to heavy German fire.[52] This meant that team Clarence, too, had no means to communicate directly with England.

After landing, Major General Gavin and Captain Bestebreurtje moved, followed by the 307th Airborne Engineer Battalion, to the edge of Groesbeek to set up a command post. On the way, the group suddenly stumbled on a hidden enemy machine-gun post, from whence they came under immediate fire. Gavin recalled about this event, 'We had gone for only about five or ten minutes when suddenly a machine gun fired from just over my head on the right ...'[53] Captain Bestebreurtje dealt with the shooter with a sudden and magnificent shot from the hip, hitting him right in the centre of his forehead. A second German in the post then gave himself up immediately. Gavin was very impressed by the actions of the Dutch Jedburgh officer.[54]

Moments later, on the same road to Groesbeek, Bestebreurtje saw a German soldier cycling away hastily. The Dutch captain also managed to shoot him. The German turned out to possess several lists with the names, addresses, and telephone numbers of German soldiers who were stationed in the village. The Dutch resistance later went to these addresses. Most Germans and Dutch collaborators turned out to have already fled the village. Still, several Germans were arrested.

Arriving in Groesbeek, Bestebreurtje came into contact with the local OD leader A. (Anton) Melchers, who pointed out to him that the telephone network was still functioning. Bestebreurtje was then able to connect with civilian informants in Nijmegen and Arnhem. He learned that the British had landed at Arnhem and everything seemed to be going well. An acquaintance of Melchers in Nijmegen, however, reported that many German forces were heading in the direction of Nijmegen.[55] This information was immediately passed on to the American division staff.

Bestebreurtje settled down a little later at the Sionshof Hotel, advantageously located between Groesbeek and Nijmegen. Before long, lots of resistance members and volunteers came in. After vetting these Dutchmen as well as possible, the Jedburghs seconded them to the various American regiments as guides and interpreters. Sergeant Beynon came into contact with a young resistance man named T. (Theo) Smiet. He would stay at Beynon's side throughout Operation Market Garden as his interpreter.[56]

At Sionshof, messages soon reached Bestebreurtje that most Germans had left Nijmegen and that the Waal bridges were barely defended. The Jedburgh officer was convinced that this information was reliable, and advised Major General Gavin to seize the river crossings immediately. However, the division commander was not prepared to do so.[57] He had orders to first secure the higher

Sergeant Beynon was team Clarence's radio operator. (The Beynon family)

Resistance member Theo Smiet, Sergeant Beynon's assistant during Operation Market Garden. (The Beynon family)

Soon after the Allied landings, Groesbeek's resistance leader Anton Melchers came into contact with Captain Bestebreurtje. (J. Melchers)

area between Groesbeek and Berg en Dal. Only two companies and one platoon were sent to Nijmegen.

Later that day, Gavin gave the Dutch captain authorisation to personally carry out reconnaissance in the city. Bestebreurtje was also ordered to try to restore the now broken contact with the American forces that had advanced towards Nijmegen. In the evening, Captain Bestebreurtje and Lieutenant Verhaeghe finally left for Nijmegen in a reconnaissance jeep, accompanied by several American parachutists. They were guided by resistance member J. T. M. (Johannes) Reinders, who had been in hiding in Hotel Sionshof.

Around 2200 hours the group arrived in the centre of Nijmegen. The men failed to find the American troops, but they did manage to approach the road bridge by jeep up to a distance of about 800 metres. From there, they advanced on foot. Before long they walked into an ambush, as Bestebreurtje recounts: 'Suddenly guns opened up on us, machine guns … and small arms fire. A moment before it had been pitch black and now I could see the flashes of fire from the muzzles of guns. They seemed to be all around us …'[58] Lieutenant Verhaeghe was hit by a burst in his upper thigh. Resistance man Reinders was killed instantly.

The bridges over the Waal at Nijmegen were crucial targets for the American 82nd Airborne Division. (National Liberation Museum Groesbeek)

Captain Bestebreurtje was hit in his left elbow and both his hands. He had also taken several rounds to the chest, but these had been deflected by the pair of binoculars strung around his neck. With great difficulty, Bestebreurtje managed to lift the badly wounded Verhaeghe and staggered back to the jeep, finally throwing the American lieutenant in the back. Bestebreurtje then rushed to an American field hospital. After being treated for his injuries, Bestebreurtje returned – with both arms bandaged and without permission of the medical staff – to his headquarters in Hotel Sionshof. His teammate Verhaeghe was out for the rest of Operation Market Garden.[59]

The first day of the offensive went well for the American 82nd Airborne Division; the 504th Regiment took the Maas bridge at Grave and the bridge across the Maas–Waal Canal at Heumen. The 505th and 508th Regiment seized the important sector between Groesbeek and Berg en Dal. It soon became clear to Captain Bestebreurtje that, despite the good will and the cooperation of the civilian population, there was great disagreement between the various local resistance groups. As there was no time to settle these disagreements, Bestebreurtje kept the different underground movements apart as much as possible.

The other Jedburgh team at Groesbeek, Edward, had gone with the airborne corps' staff to establish a command post. At that time, there was hardly any enemy activity in the area. Captain Staal, Edward's commander, left by jeep to the north to contact the resistance. The wireless operators of the team, Billingsley and Willmott, established first contact with SFHQ around 2000 hours.[60] The team now estimated the number of resistance fighters in the immediate area to be around 300 men, of which some already assisted the Allied airborne forces. Besides resistance folk, many citizens had rushed in to volunteer and provided 'outstanding assistance', according to team Edward.

Near Arnhem – the sector of the British 1st Airborne Division – the situation was similar. Team Claude, under command of Captain Groenewoud, had been ordered to establish contact with the local population at the landing zone first, and request their assistance in gathering the dropped divisional supplies. The Jedburghs were also tasked to collect all civil transportation means that could be used to move supplies and equipment into Arnhem.

Immediately after landing, Groenewoud's teammate, the American Lieutenant Todd, went to reconnoitre the area with a Dutch civilian. Captain Groenewoud moved to Oosterbeek to gather volunteers. Todd returned after about an hour, accompanied by approximately thirty Dutchmen. He also brought three cars and a German army truck. He had taken out its owners, two Germans who stood near the vehicle, immediately: 'They might have surrendered but no time for PWs [prisoners of war] here.'[61] Captain Groenewoud, too, managed to enlist helpers. All volunteers were immediately put to work in the British drop zones.

Prior to the drop, the team's wireless operator, Sergeant Scott, had requested the jumpmaster in the aircraft to parachute the radio transmitter first. This enabled him to follow the package on the way down. Unfortunately, the radio set was still dropped after the men, resulting in another lost Jedburgh radio set. After landing, Sergeant Scott was sent out by his officers to search for the lost communications equipment and the containers they had brought with them.[62]

On Sunday, 17 September 1944, the British paratroopers made a good start as well. Losses were minimal and most of the dropped material could be recovered.[63] According to the operation's plan, the British 1st Airlanding Brigade, under command of Brigadier P. H. W. (Philip) Hicks, was to stay at the landing zones to guard them. These areas would be used again the next day for the arrival of reinforcements. The 7th Battalion, The King's Own Scottish Borderers had to occupy the Ginkelse Heide, a heathland at the city of Ede, and secure a new drop zone there. The 1st Parachute Brigade of Brigadier G. W. (Gerald) Lathbury was ordered to seize the bridges over the Rhine at Arnhem. However, the nearby presence of elements of the German II SS-Panzerkorps had not been taken into account by the Allied planners.

In order to quickly reach the bridges, the British had designated a motorised reconnaissance unit to be the first to advance into Arnhem. This unit did not get very far, though; east of Wolfheze they were obstructed by a hastily established German defence line. The 1st and 3rd Battalion of the 1st Parachute Brigade also failed to reach Arnhem. Soon after leaving the landing zones, they became entangled in fierce battles with German units.[64] Just after 1500 hours, the 2nd Parachute Battalion, led by Lieutenant Colonel J. D. (John) Frost, marched towards Arnhem as well. Team Claude's officers, Groenewoud and Todd, decided to join this battalion while Sergeant Scott was ordered to stay behind and continue searching for the missing radio set. The radio operator was to proceed to Arnhem as soon as he had located the team's communication equipment.

The British Lieutenant Colonel Frost was in charge of the paratroopers at the bridge in Arnhem. (Airborne Museum Hartenstein)

Frost's unit took the southern route into the city and experienced little resistance on its way in. According to Todd, Captain Groenewoud quickly made telephone contact with the pre-occupation mayor and the former police chief of the town. Groenewoud learned that the acting mayor, a member of the NSB, had already fled from the city.[65] A bit later, the Jedburgh officers, along with a section of British paratroopers, captured a German command post.[66] Captain Groenewoud obtained some very important documents here, including German demolition plans for the ports of Rotterdam and Amsterdam.[67]

Around 1930 hours Lieutenant Colonel Frost and his forces occupied the buildings at the north end of the Arnhem road bridge. In order to be able to seize the southern end of the bridge too, the 2nd Parachute Battalion urgently needed reinforcements.

Arriving at the road bridge, the Jedburghs went on reconnaissance with several British officers to find a suitable location for battalion headquarters.[68] When the parachutists tried to return to the bridge, they encountered a German armoured unit. After a brief but fierce firefight the Germans retreated, enabling the Jedburghs to rejoin their colleagues at the bridge. Subsequently, the Jedburgh officers settled in the attic of the municipal waterworks building, where a

On the first day of Operation Market Garden, Captain Groenewoud and Lieutenant Todd moved into the attic of the the building of the municipal waterworks in Arnhem, very close to the bridge ramp. (NIMH)

section of the 2nd Parachute Battalion had also taken position. With darkness moving in, the Jedburgh officers decided to spend the night at the bridge. As there was no sign of Sergeant Scott yet, Groenewoud and Todd did not have any means of communication. Lieutenant Colonel Frost, too, was dealing with the communication problems; he had still not yet been able to establish contact with division headquarters with his radio sets.

The Dutch Lieutenant Knottenbelt, attached to team Claude as reinforcement, had landed separately from his colleagues that day. He had been concerned mainly with the selection of citizens who volunteered to assist the British parachutists. Those who were recruited were issued a distinctive orange armband which the team had brought from England. In the course of the evening, the Dutch commando tried to reach his teammates in Arnhem, accompanied by a British sergeant. Unable to break through, Knottenbelt eventually returned to the British divisional headquarters, which at that time was located in Wolfheze. During the rest of the evening, Knottenbelt continued to make contact with the local Dutch population and gathered as much intelligence as he could.

Immediately after the first landings, the Arnhem KP had sought to make contact with the British forces to offer their assistance. To their great surprise, the paratroopers refused their help.[69] Local KP member G. J. (Gijs) Numan

The forged identity papers of resistance member Gijs Numan. He soon found out that the British parachutists did not trust the Dutch underground. (G. Numan Jr)

commented, 'I got the impression that they were afraid of provocateurs and we [the resistance] were just not trusted.'[70] The British airborne division was indeed very sceptical about the Dutch resistance. It later transpired that several senior British officers had been warned not to rely too much on the underground groups, presumably (partly) due to the *Englandspiel* and bad experiences with resistance movements in other European countries.[71] Unfortunately, this meant that British forces barely accepted assistance from the Dutch resistance during Operation Market Garden.

Jedburgh team Dudley, operating sixty-five kilometres north-west of Arnhem, was informed by SFHQ that day of the Allied landings. It was expected that the Allied ground forces would reach them within ten to twelve days. Major Brinkgreve, the team's commander, was already instructed by headquarters to keep the roads free and to protect important bridges in the Overijssel province. The Dutch Jedburgh officer made contact with as many local resistance leaders as he could, and urged them – despite the euphoria about the Allied landings in the South – to delay engaging the Germans. Due to the lack of weapons and training, the resistance could not engage in prolonged battles with German forces.

Commentary

In general, the first day of Operation Market Garden went relatively well. The first wave of forces had successfully arrived in the Netherlands and most of the initial goals were realised. Moreover, the Allies suffered only few casualties. In and around Arnhem, however, clouds had gathered as the Germans had disabled the railway bridge and the pontoon bridge. This meant that only the road bridge over the Rhine in Arnhem was still intact.[72] However, the few British parachutists that had reached Arnhem had only seized the northern end of this bridge. If the paratroopers did not succeed in taking the southern end of the bridge soon, the whole operation could fail.

In the southernmost area of operation, dark clouds appeared on the horizon, too. XXX Corps had only advanced twelve kilometres on the first day, less than half of the planned distance. The Germans had been able to mass much more combat power than Field Marshal Montgomery expected. Moreover, Hitler realised the magnitude of the Allied operation and had already organised a counter-attack. German troops were being directed from the Reich to the Netherlands. Furthermore, German forces stationed in the west of the Netherlands had been ordered to attack the Allied bridgeheads in the Netherlands.[73] The Dutch Jedburgh teams would soon experience Operation Market Garden turn into a bitter fight.

On the first day of Operation Market Garden over 16,000 troops landed on Dutch soil.
(NIMH)

4

THE BRIDGE TOO FAR

Monday, 18 September 1944

Monday was an important day for the American 101st Airborne Division: according to plan, it had to link up with the advancing British XXX Corps. Moreover, the division was to receive the first reinforcements from England.[1] The 2nd and 3rd Battalion of the 502nd Regiment again attacked the town of Best to try to seize the important bridge over the Wilhelmina Canal. Stiff German resistance, however, forced the Americans to wait for XXX Corps's tanks.

The 506th Regiment, with the 3rd Battalion upfront, advanced at dawn in the direction of Eindhoven.[2] At 0900 hours, the battalion was halted by Germans forces in Woensel, near the outskirts of Eindhoven. At that time, Lieutenant Du Bois of Jedburgh team Daniel II had already succeeded in reaching Eindhoven. In a street named Woenselsestraat, Du Bois came into contact with the Roxs family. Eleven-year-old A. (Albert) Roxs witnessed the event, and later commented:

> At approximately 0700 hours, we heard the sound of different military boots and decided to leave our basement. When we opened the front door, we were surprised to see a soldier in an American uniform, who greeted us in Dutch, saying a friendly *goedemorgen* [good morning]. The Allied soldier came into our house and introduced himself as Bram du Bois.[3]

The Roxs family informed the Dutch officer that a large number of German troops were positioned in a nearby school. Du Bois was also warned that German 88mm artillery was located just a bit further off.[4] Upon receiving this important information, Du Bois took position on the roof with a short-range radio set to contact nearby Americans forces.[5]

Shortly after, the 2nd Battalion of the 506th Regiment, led by Lieutenant Colonel R. L. (Robert) Strayer, was ordered to outflank the Germans in Eindhoven. With the help of a resistance fighter who pointed out the German positions, the American parachutists swiftly took out the enemy artillery. The

An American paratrooper next to German 88mm artillery in Eindhoven. Each ring on the barrel represents a destroyed target. (J. Weijers)

bridges over the Dommel Stream were subsequently reached without much further trouble. Thereafter, the American forces commenced clearing the city, receiving assistance from the local underground movement, PAN.[6]

By evening, Eindhoven was completely under Allied control, with all important bridges seized.

In the city, Lieutenant Du Bois would come into contact with Dutch BBO agents K. (Krijn) Buitendijk and J. M. (Jacky) van der Meer. They had been parachuted into the Netherlands in August 1944. After the Allied landings the Dutchmen had immediately crossed the lines. Later, Du Bois sent the BBO agents north, to Captain Bestebreurtje of team Clarence, who was at that time situated near the city of Nijmegen.

At 1215 hours, the American division had established first contact with a British reconnaissance patrol of XXX Corps. When the corps finally entered Eindhoven, it was welcomed most enthusiastically by its citizens. This, however, delayed XXX Corps's advance even more.

A vehicle with PAN members driving through liberated Eindhoven. (I. van der Heijden)

It was not until 2100 hours that the British troops reached the southern bank of the Wilhelmina Canal at the village of Son. Its engineers did not waste any time and built a Bailey bridge immediately. At approximately 0530 hours, the first tanks crossed the Wilhelmina Canal and continued their advance towards Nijmegen.[7]

That Monday, team Edward, under command of Captain Staal, moved with I British Airborne Corps to Malden, just south of Nijmegen. Upon reaching the village, the Jedburgh group quickly liaised with the local resistance. Subsequently, a meeting with several regional OD departments was hastily organised. During this gathering, which was attended by no fewer than 200 resistance members, team Edward noticed that there was internal disagreement within the underground groups. After addressing this issue, the willingness to cooperate with each other improved.[8] Team Edward then handed out fifty orange armbands to specially selected resistance members, who were to function as reconnaissance forces and guides to Allied units.

Later that day, team Edward informed SFHQ that the arrests of collaborators were going well, and that the local resistance had already been employed by

Above: A British tank makes its way through the crowds in Eindhoven. (NIMH)

Below: Dutch resistance members with American paratroopers in Veghel. (S. Bentley)

the airborne forces. As airborne corps still had not heard anything from the 1st Airborne Division, Captain Staal was requested by airborne corps headquarters to ask SFHQ how the battle in and around the city of Arnhem was developing. Subsequently, team Edward sent the following telegram to England:

> Most urgent. Corps needs information concerning military situation Arnhem. Watermark [code name for SFHQ] ask [team] Claude for latest details and send us all information already available.

However, neither airborne corps nor team Edward knew that team Claude's radio equipment had been lost during the drop; SFHQ was thus not in contact with Captain Groenewoud's team. Looking for alternative ways to gather information about the circumstances in Arnhem, team Edward unsuccessfully tried to get into contact with people inside the city through a clandestine telephone line. Captain Staal was eventually able to connect with team Clarence, who did have a telephone connection with Arnhem. Captain Bestebreurtje informed Staal that the British parachutists were under great pressure in Arnhem. This was one of the first messages to reach airborne corps that indicated that the battle in Arnhem was not progressing satisfactorily.[9]

On the night of 17/18 September, Captain Bestebreurtje had sent a large number of resistance members to Nijmegen to scout the city. At first light, the Dutch officer again headed for Nijmegen, this time wearing civilian clothes. Bestebreurtje recollected, 'I went up several streets and across some backyards when I got into Nijmegen. It was almost dusk and at two or three points I saw Germans in positions, stopping Dutch civilians and asking for their identification.'[10]

As he did not possess any identification papers, forged or otherwise, Bestebreurtje had to cancel his infiltration attempt. In the meantime, some 500 resistance civilians had gathered at Hotel Sionshof, Bestebreurtje's headquarters near Groesbeek. This group made a very good impression on Major General Gavin. As opposed to the British, Gavin did deploy the Dutch resistance in his sector during Operation Market Garden. The American general would not regret this decision, as he later commented, 'Their attitude was most reassuring, and ... they [the Dutch population and the resistance] proved to be among the bravest and most patriotic people we had liberated.'[11]

In Hotel Sionshof, rumours reached Bestebreurtje about German forces attaching explosives to the bridges in Nijmegen. It was said that the bridges could be detonated from inside the Nijmegen post office. The Dutch Jedburgh officer subsequently sent a small group of resistance volunteers to Nijmegen to check up on the situation. A few hours later, they returned to the hotel, reporting that no detonation control device had been found in the post office.

A monument remembering Operation Market Garden attached to the wall at Hotel Sionshof. This monument was dedicated on 17 September 1954 by Arie Bestebreurtje. (Private collection)

In the meantime, one of the civilians at Sionshof had informed Bestebreurtje that a car had been hidden by the Germans in a forest nearby. Bestebreurtje did not waste any time and picked up the vehicle right away.[12] From that moment on, he was able to move around much faster. After the loss of his teammate Verhaeghe, the Dutch officer was swamped with work. Captain Bestebreurtje therefore appointed local resistance member R. M. (Rob) Smulders, who had good command of English, as his personal assistant.[13]

That Monday, Major General Gavin ordered the Nijmegen resistance to keep an eye on the city's Waal bridges, day and night. Moreover, the division commander authorised Jedburgh team Clarence to arm the resistance fighters with weapons from wounded and killed American parachutists. Captain Bestebreurtje himself requested two dozen men from OD commander Melchers in Groesbeek, who were to act as armed guards for captured Germans soldiers.

Meanwhile, American forces at Nijmegen were confronted with heavy attacks from the Reichswald. When German troops even infiltrated the landing areas

Post-war photograph of resistance member Rob Smulders. He became Captain Bestebreurtje's adjudant during Operation Market Garden. (S. Bentley)

near Groesbeek – where the second wave of American forces from England were due to arrive – Gavin withdrew a large number of troops from Nijmegen. The Germans were successfully driven from the Groesbeek area around noon.[14] Although the German attacks had been repelled by the American forces, the enemy had been able to send reinforcements to Nijmegen.

Lieutenant Knottenbelt from team Claude had been busy recruiting civilian volunteers in the village of Oosterbeek, just west of Arnhem. At approximately 0900 hours, he was informed by Arnhem KP commander Kruyff that the entire telephone network of Arnhem and Oosterbeek was still operational. Kruyff also apprised the Dutch commando about the British and German positions in Arnhem. According to Kruyff, Knottenbelt was 'unpleasantly surprised' upon learning that a large number of German armoured vehicles were positioned in Arnhem.

Through the resistance, Knottenbelt was also able to contact a British officer, Captain J. E. (John) Killick, who was located near the road bridge in Arnhem.[15] Killick confirmed the precarious situation in the city. Knottenbelt immediately relayed this information to division headquarters. The next day, the Dutch lieutenant rang the same number again, only to have the call answered by a German.[16]

Monday was to be a rough day for the Jedburgh officers and British troops at the road bridge in Arnhem. On Sunday evening, Lieutenant Colonel Frost's battalion had been reinforced by the 1st Parachute Brigade and a section of the division's reconnaissance element. These were the only forces that had succeeded in moving past the German defence lines west of Arnhem. In the meantime, German command ordered elements of the 9th and 10th SS-Panzer Division to Arnhem. At that moment, the British force at the bridge consisted of approximately 750 men. Allied reinforcements were desperately needed in order to conquer the south end of the bridge, which was still in German hands.

At the bridge, Captain Groenewoud desperately attempted to contact division headquarters. At around 0930 hours, a column approached the bridge from the south. This turned out to be a reconnaissance unit from the 9th SS-Panzer-Division, led by Hauptsturmführer V. E. (Victor) Gräbner. The German officer intended to force a pass over the bridge.[17] The column caught the British paratroopers by surprise, and the first few vehicles managed to reach the other side of the bridge. Lieutenant Todd, who was now located in an excellent observatory in the building of the municipal waterworks, was able to direct an anti-tank weapon positioned one floor below.[18]

After the initial surprise, the parachutists quickly succeeded in destroying twelve vehicles of Gräbner's column.[19] A British parachutist who was present at the scene was very much impressed with the Jedburgh officers' marksmanship: 'With me shooting like a wild west cowboy, was a Dutch officer, and a Yankee officer, and boy could they shoot.'[20] Todd was able to take out six Germans on his own.[21] Before long, Gräbner was killed with most of his men. The remaining Germans were forced to withdraw, leaving the bridge blocked with burning wrecks.[22]

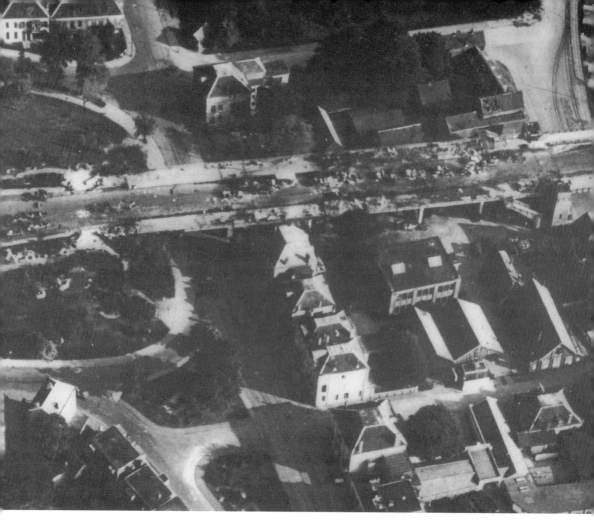

The remnants of Gräbner's reconnaissance unit on the road bridge in Arnhem. Captain Groenewoud and Lieutenant Todd were located in the building partially seen at the bottom left. (Private collection)

Shortly after this attack, Todd was fired at by a German sniper – a bullet even ricocheted off his helmet. Despite his luck, the flying glass shards wounded him in the face. Meanwhile, Captain Groenewoud reported that he had contacted a number of airborne units who were about a kilometre from the bridge. Unfortunately, these forces met with stiff German resistance and could not break through.[23] Although both the British and the Germans suffered great losses, the numerical advantage of the enemy slowly started to prove decisive.[24]

Meanwhile, the British airborne division's performance was also severely hindered by failing communication equipment; its short-range radio sets were distorted strongly by Arnhem's buildings and the hilly landscape surrounding the city. Partly due to the communication problems, division commander Major General Urquhart was hardly able to get a picture of the course of the battle.[25] On the first evening of Market Garden, Urquhart had gone out by jeep – without escort – to locate the commander of the 1st Parachute Brigade, Brigadier Lathbury. Unfortunately, Urquhart was quickly cut off from his troops by the Germans. This subsequently led to confusion about who was in divisional command. It was not until the morning of Tuesday, 19 September that the British general could break out and return to British lines.[26]

Approximately sixty-five kilometres north-east of Arnhem, Jedburgh team Dudley was experiencing its own difficulties. Majors Brinkgreve and Olmsted went into hiding in a forest, as rumours had reached them about upcoming *razzias* (roundups) in Overijssel population centres. Despite the precarious situation, the Jedburgh officers could not resist taking a passing German patrol under fire. The Germans then rushed quickly away – as did the Jedburghs.

According to Major Olmsted, feverish activity among the Germans in Overijssel could be observed by now. An uninterrupted column of German forces and equipment moved through the province towards Arnhem. Resistance fighters in the area tried to hinder the German troop transport as much as possible, carrying out nightly attacks on roads and railways to Germany.

On Monday evening, the Jedburgh officers discussed how they could support the Allied advance with the Overijssel resistance. However, Brinkgreve and Olmsted were already very pessimistic about the chances of the Allies reaching them in the near future. SFHQ informed the Jedburghs that the British SAS wanted to send a special reconnaissance team to the city of Deventer; team Dudley was to prepare the reception of this group. Moreover, at team Edward's request, SFHQ asked team Dudley to report on the military situation in Deventer, and, more specifically, on the German positions at the city's bridges over the IJssel River – an offshoot of the Rhine. These bridges were vital to the Allies as they functioned as key entry points to the Overijssel province.

Tuesday, 19 September 1944

At around 0530 hours, the first units of the Household Cavalry and the Guards Armoured Division crossed the Wilhelmina Canal via the Bailey bridge at the village of Son. At this time, Market Garden had been underway for a good forty hours, and XXX Corps should have been very close to Arnhem. Instead, the corps was still some sixty-five kilometres away. Near the town of Best, elements of the 502nd Regiment, which were supported by British tanks and the PAN, were finally able to drive away the Germans. In the process, hundreds of German soldiers were made prisoners of war.

That day, Lieutenant Du Bois from team Daniel II went to reconnoitre the southern canal dyke at Son together with Lieutenant Colonel N. D. (Ned) Moore

Germans prisoners transported by American paratroopers. (NIMH)

and a group of American parachutists.[27] After having walked merely a few hundred meters, a German tank emerged at less than 300 meters' range – the men took heavy fire immediately.[28] A while later, more enemy tanks advanced from the south-east. These belonged to the Panzerbrigade 107, under command of Major B. F. (Berndt) Freiherr von Maltzahn. This German brigade had originally been on its way to northern France, but due to the Allied landings Von Maltzahn had been redirected to the Netherlands to cut off the Allied corridor to the Rhine.

Besides the Bailey bridge, divisional headquarters – where the other members of Jedburgh team Daniel II were present – came under attack.[29] Although only a small part of the American division was located at Son, the Germans got the impression that this area was heavily defended. After two of his front tanks were destroyed, blocking the road to the bridge, Von Maltzahn withdrew his forces.[30]

According to the operation plan, Tuesday was the day that the 325th Glider Infantry Regiment of the 82nd Airborne Division was to reinforce the American forces at the city of Nijmegen. However, bad weather would keep them in England for four days. Meanwhile, increasing numbers of German troops reached Nijmegen; in just a few days, the number of German battalions in the

Major General Gavin (in the middle) and Captain Bestebreurtje (with his arm in a sling) in consultation with British officers. (S. Bentley)

city had increased from just two to fifteen.[31] Due to the lack of reinforcements and close air support, Gavin decided to postpone the attack on the bridges over the Waal until the arrival of the tanks of XXX Corps.

At around 0800 hours, the corps's vanguard finally contacted the 82nd Airborne Division in the town of Grave. Only in the late afternoon did the Guards Armoured Division reach the southern outskirts of Nijmegen.[32] Meanwhile, Jedburgh teams Clarence and Edward organised a meeting with the local resistance groups to discuss how they could assist in capturing the Nijmegen bridges.[33] At the end of the day, Captain Bestebreurtje had a total of approximately 800 Dutch volunteers at his disposal. Among them was J. J. L. (Jan) van Hoof, a member of the resistance movement Geheime Dienst Nederland (GDN, Secret Service Netherlands).[34] He had come to Sionshof with detailed sketches of the German positions at the Waal bridges.

Again rumours spread that the Germans could detonate the charges on the bridges from within the Nijmegen post office. A renewed plan for the capture of the Nijmegen bridges was swiftly developed by Gavin, Browning, and Horrocks. Three units were to attack the bridges and post office: group 'A' was to conquer the road bridge, group 'B' the railway bridge, and group 'C' was to seize the post office. Captain Bestebreurtje selected the Dutch volunteers who were to guide the Allied forces to their targets.[35]

It was late afternoon when the Allied attack began. The Germans in Nijmegen, however, now had heavy artillery and a range of tanks at their disposal.[36] The British tanks proved to be very vulnerable to anti-tank weapons in the narrow streets of Nijmegen. When night fell, group A gave up its attempt; group B also failed to reach its target. Resistance man Van Hoof, who had guided this group, was captured, tortured, and shot.[37] Group C did reach the post office but no detonation mechanism was discovered there.

In the meantime, team Edward's leader, Captain Staal, had requested SFHQ to drop weapons for the local resistance, as the underground in and around Nijmegen was dealing with a desperate shortage of arms. This request was unfortunately denied – the supply of (infantry) reinforcements was given absolute precedence by Allied headquarters. Team Edward later successfully connected with the city centre of Arnhem, again by telephone. The Jedburghs found that the British parachutists were standing their ground at the bridge but were still involved in heavy battles. This information was immediately relayed to airborne corps headquarters.[38]

On Tuesday evening, Generals Gavin, Browning, and Horrocks met to discuss how to end the now two-day stalemate at Nijmegen. The Allied commanders subsequently prepared a new plan to conquer the bridges over the Waal the next day.[39] Around the same time, Sergeant Beynon, who was driving a jeep south of Nijmegen, lost his way. The Jedburgh almost drove into a minefield but was warned by American paratroopers moments before. He spent the night with this unit, which had dug in near the canal at the village of Mook. The Americans parachutists and Beynon would subsequently prevent two German crossing attempts.[40]

In Oosterbeek, about thirty kilometres north, Lieutenant Knottenbelt had again been in telephone contact with Arnhem's resistance leader, Kruyff. Knottenbelt was informed that the British parachutists at the bridge could not hold out much longer. The Dutch officer apprised division headquarters right away. The civil telephone system kept proving to be extremely useful in getting information reports out of Arnhem. However, around noon – to the great dismay of the Arnhem resistance men and the Jedburghs – British forces destroyed the telephone exchange at Oosterbeek. The parachutists were convinced that the 'resistance members' with whom they were in contact were actually NSB members and Dutch traitors.[41] In truth, a vital communication link from headquarters to Arnhem was destroyed.

For the remainder of the day, Knottenbelt continued recruiting Dutch volunteers.

A Dutch commando instructs members of the resistance at Hotel Hartenstein at Oosterbeek. (Airborne Museum Hartenstein)

According to the Dutch commando, a group of approximately fifty volunteers was assembled by evening.[42] He appointed Lieutenant Douw van der Krap, a member of the local KP, as commandant of this group.[43] Douw van der Krap, in turn, appointed former Cornet J. (Jan) Eijkelhoff deputy commander of the so-called 'Oranje Legioen' (Orange Legion).

Several members of the legion had unsuccessfully tried to drive a jeep into Arnhem that day to deliver supplies to the bridge. The Dutch commando A. F. M. (August) Bakhuis Roozeboom, who had accompanied the men, was killed during the attempt.[44]

The British Colonel Barlow, who was supposed to form resistance groups in cooperation with the aforementioned Dutch Lieutenant Commander Wolters, was also killed in action on Tuesday. Without Barlow, Wolters stood powerless. The Dutchman later recollected, 'While I can say that I had Barlow's fullest confidence, yet unfortunately, that was not so with the others at [British] headquarters.'[45]

The Dutch commando Bakhuis Roozeboom was killed in action on 19 September 1944, in an attempt to reach the British parachutists in Arnhem. (Dutch Commando Museum)

In Arnhem, Lieutenant Todd recovered somewhat from his injuries. A British parachutist, who had taken over his post in the municipal waterworks building near the bridge, was killed by a German sniper. It was to be another day of heavy fighting for the parachutists.[46] Just before dawn, the first German attack began. From his old position, Lieutenant Todd managed to take out several enemies.[47] A bit later an unknown civilian informed Captain Groenewoud that a large column of German armoured vehicles was approaching Arnhem from the west.[48] Due to the continuing problems with the radio transmitters, Lieutenant Colonel Frost was unable to verify this information or relay the intelligence to division headquarters.

At approximately 1000 hours, two German tanks appeared north of the British positions at the bridge. Despite being only lightly armed, the parachutists managed to destroy one of the armoured vehicles.[49] Before long, a much heavier German attack followed. Todd shot five Germans during this attack, but was forced to leave his post when he took heavy machine-gun fire.[50] The American subsequently took over a Bren gun position. To Frost's and the other parachutists' delight, Todd quickly managed to take out the crew of a German 20mm anti-aircraft gun that was firing 'point blank' at the parachutists.[51]

At this time, over fifty wounded paratroopers were treated in the waterworks building. Due to the shortage of medical supplies, it was impossible to take care of them. Captain Groenewoud tried to contact a hospital via telephone, most likely the nearby Sint-Elisabeth Gasthuis, but was unsuccessful. Although the Germans had established a cordon around the British positions at the bridge, Groenewoud and Todd volunteered to try to reach a general medical practice that was located a few streets away. Moreover, a working telephone could be available there, through which contact with division headquarters might be restored.[52]

A British parachutist at the bridge heard of the Jedburghs' risky plan. He later commented, 'I remember saying to them [Groenewoud and Todd] "You are committing suicide". But they were determined to head that way. I saw them sneaking past the wall on the right side. Where the road turned right, they disappeared from my view.'[53]

About halfway, the Jedburgh officers prepared to cross a street. At that moment Captain Groenewoud was hit in the forehead by a German sniper. He was killed instantly.[54] Lieutenant Todd immediately dived in the doorway of a nearby house. Inside the building he stumbled upon a civilian who spoke some English. With the help of this man, Todd was able to contact a Dutch doctor by phone. The American Jedburgh was informed that it was impossible to send medical help as the Germans had threatened to fire irrevocably at ambulances.[55] Lieutenant Todd eventually headed back to his old post at the bridge to rejoin the fighting.

Todd soon found out that the German units in Arnhem, who were also suffering significant losses, had changed their tactics; they were now firing continuously with tanks and heavy artillery at the buildings that housed the paratroopers, causing even more casualties on the British side.[56] For the parachutists at the bridge the only thing left to do was to hold out as long as they could and wait for reinforcements. According to the operation plan, the majority of the 1st Polish Independent Parachute Brigade would land south of the road bridge that day. Unfortunately, this unit, too, was forced to stay on the ground in England, as a result of the bad weather conditions.

After suffering heavy losses, Major General Urquhart concluded that further attempts to reach Arnhem were pointless.[57] His parachutists, who were now

A view of the John Frost bridge in Arnhem, from the Jacobus Groenewoud park beside the Rhine; recent photograph. (Private collection)

attacked from all sides, fell back to positions around the Hotel Hartenstein in Oosterbeek. The general established his headquarters in this hotel. During the battle, the sector at Oosterbeek became known as the 'perimeter'.[58] Urquhart's forces also lost control over the area where the gliders of the Polish brigade were bound to arrive. Consequently, the Polish forces ended up in the middle of a battle. Only a small number of the Polish soldiers were eventually able to join the 1st Airborne Division. To make matters even worse, a large amount of the supplies that were dropped by the RAF fell straight into German hands.[59]

On the night of 18/19 September, the drop of the SAS team in the province of Overijssel had failed. The aircrew of the bomber had been unable to find the landing zone. On Tuesday, Jedburgh team Dudley held a meeting with several resistance leaders, including Captain Lancker and local KP commanders Ter Horst and C. (Cor) Hilbrink. Major Brinkgreve, who was of the opinion that RVV chief Lancker did not have clear plans, noted that he intended to relocate to the headquarters of the Twente KP.[60] As a result, the already bad relationship

Team Dudley relocated to Huize Lidwina in Zenderen on 19 September 1944. (C. Hilbrink)

between the local KP and RVV deteriorated further – just as the collaboration between Brinkgreve and Lancker.

After the troublesome meeting, Ter Horst and Hilbrink left by motorbike. They came back by car at night, to pick up the Jedburgh team. The vehicle, which was painted black, could be easily mistaken for a Gestapo vehicle. On the way back, the car was held up several times by long German convoys en route to Arnhem. In the village of Enter, the men were ordered to stop at a German road block. Instead, the vehicle dashed through an opening meant for bicycles, whilst Ter Horst, Hilbrink and another shooter fired away at the Germans, killing a non-commissioned officer and wounding several others.[61] Without further incidents, the group arrived at the KP headquarters. The next day, a similar vehicle was taken under fire by the Germans at a nearby checkpoint. An SS member and a Gestapo official were killed as a result of this shooting.[62]

The headquarters of the Twente KP was located in a remote villa named 'Huize Lidwina'. It made a good impression on the Jedburghs. Guards were posted and the command post even had an electronic warning system. The KP Twente also had several vehicles at its disposal and turned out to run an extensive intelligence network. Brinkgreve informed SFHQ of this the day that he joined up with the local KP. Furthermore, the team informed SFHQ that the resistance in the Twente region of Overijssel cut railways every night. About 200 resistance men had been armed by the Jedburghs so far. In total, the team was in contact with an estimated 1,000 (unarmed) resistance members in Overijssel. As a result of the many questions from England about the situation at Arnhem, Dudley's radio traffic increased significantly.

Wednesday, 20 September 1944

On Wednesday morning, the German Panzerbrigade 107 again assaulted the sector of the American 101st Airborne Division. With long-range shots, the Germans were able to block all traffic over the Wilhelmina Canal for some time. The Americans countered the German attack on the Bailey bridge at the village of Son with great difficulty. It was only after the arrival of the British 8th Armoured Brigade, who had been called in for assistance, that the Germans were driven away.

As it had been impossible for any vehicle to cross the bridge, the Allies once again lost valuable time.[63] North of Son, the Germans also infiltrated the area between the towns of Veghel and Heeswijk. The 501st Regiment, however, succeeded in trapping the German forces in a pocket, taking hundreds prisoner.[64] Just west of Eindhoven, in the village of Wintelre, the 53rd Welsh Division was also involved in heavy fighting. The division gratefully received backup from local PAN resistance fighters.[65]

On Wednesday, Jedburgh team Edward put XXX Corps in contact with the technical director of the Nijmegen Waterways and Ferries. The Dutchman was able to provide XXX Corps with information about the Nijmegen bridges and other ways to cross the Waal. Later, Jedburgh teams Edward and Clarence again received important intelligence about the situation in and around Arnhem via the civil telephone network. First Allied Airborne Army later commented, 'The Dutch liaison party provided by SFHQ for Airborne Corps HQ did excellent work in establishing telephone communication with the Dutch resistance and getting their reports on the situation at Arnhem.'[66]

That day, team Edward relocated its headquarters to the Sint-Anna Hospital in Nijmegen. There, the Jedburghs notified SFHQ of corps headquarters' satisfaction about the performance of the resistance. According to team Edward, resistance groups in Nijmegen, Arnhem, and Malden were well organised and provided many guides and guards. Captain Staal also reported to headquarters in England that the resistance provided valuable (tactical) intelligence.

On Wednesday, the first contact with team Daniel II after the start of Operation Market Garden was finally established. Coming from Eindhoven, the members of Daniel II reported personally in Nijmegen. It was then that Captain Staal found out that Daniel II had lost its radio set. Later on Wednesday, Captain Staal's team was notified by SFHQ that messengers from occupied areas north and west of Arnhem were on their way. BBO agent L. G. (Leonard) Mulholland – parachuted north of Arnhem in July 1944 – sent several men south. On his way from Overijssel was resistance man D. (Dolf) Fleer. He had been ordered by Major Brinkgreve to head for Arnhem. Within several days, Fleer reached the city. From there he managed to establish telephone contact with Captain Staal.

Meanwhile, team Dudley informed SFHQ that German General Christiansen's headquarters was located on the Singraven estate near the town of Denekamp, in the Twente region of Overijssel. The telegram was relayed to Jedburgh team Edward the same day.[67]

After a two-day stalemate in Nijmegen, the 3rd Battalion of the 504th Regiment crossed the Waal in small canvas boats. The Americans of the 82nd Airborne Division were out in the open, in broad daylight, and suffered heavy losses.[68] Those who managed to cross the river immediately stormed the north end of the bridges. Meanwhile, the 2nd Battalion of the 505th Regiment, and a battalion of the Guards Armoured Division, assaulted the southern ends of the two Nijmegen bridges.

After heavy fighting, the Allied forces seized both bridges. When the first British tanks crossed the road bridge, at around 1900 hours, the Germans tried to blow up the bridge;[69] fortunately for the Allies, the explosives failed to detonate.[70] At the road bridge, Captain Bestebreurtje personally took out a German sniper and arrested another German soldier.[71] When German resistance in the area decreased, Bestebreurtje organised a supply column to get ammunition to the opposite side of the river as quickly as possible.

Shortly after the capture of the bridges, the Dutch Jedburgh officer was notified by the underground that the Germans had plans to destroy the bridges by using combat divers. The resistance claimed that a dive team had already been spotted in Nijmegen the night before. Although the Allies did not take this information very seriously, nets were placed in the water near the bridges. Later in September 1944, German *Kampfschwimmer* would severely damage the railroad bridge in Nijmegen, after all.[72]

After the capture of the bridges over the Waal, the Allies were approximately twenty kilometres away from Arnhem. However, to the surprise and anger of the paratroopers of the 82nd Airborne Division, Lieutenant General Horrocks ordered XXX Corps to halt and wait for reinforcements. He was first focused on the defence of Nijmegen itself.[73] The British parachutists in Arnhem, though, were now on the verge of collapse. The north end of the road bridge was still in their possession but would fall back in German hands if reinforcements did not arrive soon.

Lieutenant Todd, still located in the attic of the building at the bridge ramp, managed to eliminate another German who had been firing continuously at them with a machine gun.[74] Unfortunately, the Germans spotted the American officer; a hail of bullets followed. When a bullet ricocheted off his carbine, the Jedburgh quickly made himself scarce.

Shortly after, two German tanks fired at the paratroopers at very close range, rocking the entire building.[75] Todd was eventually blown out of his post, probably by a German mortar, and lost consciousness for several minutes. When he awoke, he found out that his left ear's eardrum had been damaged and that a mortar shard was embedded in his hand. After swift treatment of his wounds, Todd was back on his feet and assisted in extinguishing the many fires in the building.

In nearby Oosterbeek, the situation was also rapidly deteriorating. On Wednesday, Lieutenant Knottenbelt decided to instruct the resistance members

The building of the municipal waterworks in Arnhem was heavily damaged during the battle of Arnhem. (The Todd family)

of the Oranje Legioen to either go home or go into hiding;[76] indeed, if these resistance fighters were to be captured by the Germans, they would most likely be executed on the spot. Yet a number of men chose to stay.

Late afternoon, Knottenbelt established contact with his team's radio operator, Sergeant Scott. Despite continuous sniper fire, the American Jedburgh had not stopped searching for his radio transmitter. Unfortunately the team's set was still missing.[77]

On Wednesday night, Lieutenant Knottenbelt met up with Canadian paratroop officer Lieutenant L. J. (Leo) Heaps. This Canadian officer, who had been attached to the 1st Airborne Division, was ordered by Major General Urquhart to try to bring supplies to the bridge in Arnhem. Both lieutenants were convinced that it was impossible to move straight from Oosterbeek to Arnhem, as a wall of German troops and tanks was blocking the route.

Instead, Knottenbelt and Heaps developed a plan that involved the ferry at the nearby village of Driel. After crossing, they would try to move east, straight into Arnhem.[78] The officers, accompanied by three soldiers, started their journey near midnight. The group was able to reach the ferry, but upon arrival they

Dutch members of the resistance at Hotel Hartenstein. Lieutenant Knottenbelt ordered them to go into hiding on 20 September 1944. (Airborne Museum Hartenstein)

British paratroopers in a trench in Oosterbeek. (NIMH)

noticed that the boat had already been disabled by the enemy. Subsequently, the men returned to the Oosterbeek perimeter, evading several German patrols in the process.[79]

Thursday, 21 September 1944

On Thursday, the 101st Airborne Division received messages from the local resistance about a forthcoming German attack on the village of Sint-Oedenrode, approximately fifteen kilometres north of Eindhoven. Division commander Maxwell Taylor took this information very seriously and responded by sending four battalions of the 501st Regiment to the area. Meanwhile, Lieutenant Du Bois of team Daniel II had gone ahead of the American forces and liaised with the resistance in the city of Uden, about halfway to Nijmegen.

Further north, teams Clarence and Edward set up an intelligence centre in the power plant in Nijmegen. The plant had been seized in the night from Sunday to Monday by members of the local resistance group called 'De Pandoeren'. The resistance men managed to surprise the German guards and assumed control over the valuable building.[80]

From the power plant, telephone connections were established with most of the large cities in the Netherlands, including Amsterdam, Utrecht, Rotterdam, The Hague, Arnhem, and Zwolle. Through one of the contacts in Amsterdam, team Edward received information about Dutch ports and oil terminals being destroyed by the Germans. The Jedburghs' information centre proved so useful that XXX Corps took it over the next day.[81] Through a telephone line with the village of Elst, just south of Arnhem, the Jedburghs collected eyewitness reports

In the power plant in Nijmegen, the Jedburghs established an important information centre in which telephone connections could be established with most of the large cities in the Netherlands. (National Liberation Museum Groesbeek)

on the progress of the Polish airborne landings near Driel. The Polish forces were originally to be dropped directly south of the Rhine Bridge in Arnhem. As this had been impossible, they landed further west.[82]

As a result of a wrongly interpreted radio message, a number of aircraft carrying Polish soldiers had turned back halfway through the flight to the Netherlands, leaving General Sosabowski with only about a thousand men after landing. In order to reach the British forces, the Poles now had to cross the Rhine by ferry at Driel. However, the ferry was already disabled by the Germans – as Lieutenant Knottenbelt had learned earlier. By now, the Germans had also occupied the strategically located Westerbouwing, a small mound near the river. From this height the Germans were able to pour direct fire onto the Rhine, complicating the situation even further.[83]

Meanwhile, Lieutenant Colonel Frost had been seriously wounded at the bridge in Arnhem. Major C. F. H. (Freddie) Gough, commander of the reconnaissance squadron of the British Airborne Division, took over Frost's command. The paratroopers had already decided the previous day that they would attempt to break out towards the Oosterbeek perimeter. On Thursday, Gough ordered the men at the bridge to prepare to move in small groups towards Oosterbeek. Lieutenant Todd was to lead one of these teams.[84]

When the order to break out finally came, the American Jedburgh officer and his group dashed towards a nearby, burned-out school. When Germans approached the building the paratroopers fled, but soon ran into a German machine-gun post. Todd still had a hand grenade and was able to neutralise the enemy's position.[85] Shortly after, sneaking through the burning city, Todd heard Germans coming and saw no other option than to climb into a tree. The other members of his group either fled or were arrested. The American Jedburgh would remain in the tree until dusk, before desperately relocating to a bush, where he would stay until the next morning.[86]

Although the Allied paratroopers lost the battle at the bridge in Arnhem, they did an outstanding job. It was due to their effort that the German 10th SS-Panzer-Division could not use the bridge over the Rhine before 21 September. This left the Germans less able to build up the defence at Nijmegen during the first days of Operation Market Garden.[87] This was all over now, though, as the road bridge was back in German hands.

The situation for the remainder of the 1st British Airborne Division would grow increasingly troublesome throughout Thursday.[88] Lieutenant Knottenbelt moved into a house at the northern edge of the perimeter in Oosterbeek to repulse heavy German attacks. As the division was suffering heavy losses, Knottenbelt was later ordered to contact the Poles at Driel and request their immediate assistance. The Dutch commando swam across the Rhine and succeeded in reaching the Polish

During Market Garden the headquarters of the German 10. SS Panzer Division was located in Huize Ruurlo. Jedburgh team Dudley sent this information to England on 21 September 1944. (Rijksdienst Cultureel Erfgoed)

troops.[89] He then swam back across the river and rejoined his British colleagues. It was not until Friday night that a small group of Polish parachutists was able to reach the British forces in Oosterbeek. Unfortunately, that was too little and too late to make a real difference in the perimeter.

On Thursday, several resistance leaders from Overijssel visited the headquarters of the KP and the Jedburghs in the village of Zenderen to discuss the amalgamation of the Overijssel underground. In early September 1944, the Dutch government-in-exile had already ordered the KP, OD, and RVV to start working on equal footing and unite into the BS, the Netherlands Forces of the Interior. That day it was decided that the Twente KP would, from then on, be under Colonel Hotz's command. He had been the leader of the OD in Overijssel. A follow-up meeting about the unification of the underground was planned for Sunday, 24 September, which was to be attended by KP, OD, and RVV leaders from Overijssel.

Later that day, team Dudley informed SFHQ that the resistance was putting up roadblocks by felling trees along the roads. Additionally, the Jedburghs reported to England about rumours that the headquarters of the German 9th and 10th SS-Panzer Divisions were located in the castle Huize Ruurlo, to the north-east of Arnhem.[90]

Friday, 22 September 1944

On Friday morning, the 506th Regiment of the American 101st Airborne Division was ordered to occupy the city of Uden, approximately twenty-five kilometres south of Nijmegen. Near 1100 hours, a group of approximately 150 American parachutists reached Uden. Mere minutes later, the first Germans forces arrived.[91] Heavy fighting erupted, but the Americans were able to repulse the German attack. The enemy did manage to cut the road between Uden and Sint-Oedenrode, separating the 506th Regiment and Lieutenant Du Bois from the main force. Other sectors of the 101st Airborne Division also endured fierce German attacks that day.

These continuous German actions concerned Generals Browning and Horrocks. Operation Market Garden was already hanging by a thread and was sure to fail if the enemy kept succeeding in blocking the way to Nijmegen. Consequently, Horrocks sent troops from Grave, just south-west of Nijmegen, to the south again, in order to hold off flanking German attacks.[92] The road between Uden and Sint-Oedenrode would only be opened the next day by an infantry brigade of the British Guards Armoured Division. After having been separated from the

American paratroopers in Veghel on 21 September 1944. Several members of the local resistance are seen near the vehicle. (NIMH)

main force for about forty-eight hours, Lieutenant Du Bois was finally able to rejoin the American 101st Airborne Division.[93]

In Nijmegen, team Edward contacted Captain C. R. (Charles) Strutt of the Special Force Detachment of the Second British Army.[94] In a meeting with Strutt and several Civil Affairs officers from XXX Corps, the deployment of the Dutch resistance was discussed. It became apparent that the army corps was concerned about the armed underground forces now that the Germans were driven out of the city. Presumably, XXX Corps worried about skirmishes, as weapons circulated freely among the civilian population. Still, team Clarence was ordered to put together a group of approximately 300 resistance fighters for clearing German pockets of resistance. However, XXX Corps would revoke this plan the following day: without consulting the Jedburgh teams, it had been decided that that large resistance groups in the area were no longer allowed to carry weapons.[95]

That Friday, Sergeant Beynon from Jedburgh team Clarence was able to contact SFHQ for the first time using team Edward's radio set. The American

Jedburgh immediately requested a new transmitter and informed SFHQ that the situation in the area was under control. Team Clarence also reported that they now had two auxiliary units of resistance fighters at their disposal, each the size of a company. According to the Jedburghs, the units were already fully capable of performing military duties. This transition from resistance forces into military units was the first step towards the establishment of the so-called 'Stoottroepen'. (see p. 128)

Meanwhile, Lieutenant Todd of team Claude was still hiding in the bushes in Arnhem. Despite German troops passing by several times just a few metres away, he was not discovered. Later that day, he took shelter in a nearby burned-out building. The Jedburgh officer managed to hide for several days in Arnhem, but was eventually discovered and arrested.[96] On Friday, the building in Oosterbeek where Lieutenant Knottenbelt stayed was shelled by heavy German artillery. All parachutists inside the complex were killed during this barrage.[97] As if through a miracle, Knottenbelt himself only suffered minor injuries. After things temporarily quieted down, the Dutch officer joined a British company on the eastern edge of the perimeter.

That day, Knottenbelt would see his team member Sergeant Scott for the last time. Due to ongoing German attacks, the size of the perimeter decreased rapidly. That night, about fifty Poles managed to cross the Rhine. They eventually reached Oosterbeek but to no avail. By this time, only a quick relief by XXX Corps could save the British parachutists.

The mechanised army corps, however, was unable to reach them because of continuous German attacks. Near the village of Elst, approximately ten kilometres away, the British Guards Armoured Division was halted by the 10th SS-Panzer Division, which was backed by several other German units. Only a small section of the 43rd Wessex Division succeeded in reaching the Poles in Driel that day.[98] Subsequently, they attempted to take munitions and supplies across the Rhine with two amphibious vehicles. However, the roads were now in a terrible condition and the vehicles kept getting stuck. Moreover, low fog prevented them from keeping sight.[99] Eventually, the attempt was given up.

In the neighbouring province of Overijssel, Jedburgh team Dudley lost an important ally on Friday; that afternoon, local KP commandant Ter Horst was stopped at a German check point and arrested. Before long, the SD began interrogating and torturing the resistance commander. Luckily, team Dudley was informed by the resistance about Ter Horst's arrest within merely twenty minutes. Major Brinkgreve evacuated the KP headquarters in the villa Lidwina in Zenderen immediately.

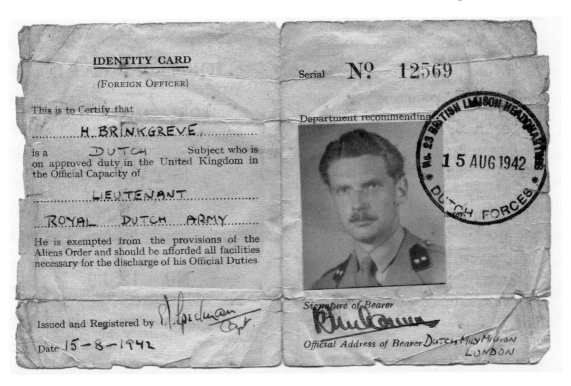

Military ID card of Major Brinkgreve, the commander of Jedburgh team Dudley. (The Brinkgreve family)

Saturday, 23 September 1944

After consultation with XXX Corps on Saturday, Jedburgh team Edward came to the conclusion that its mission was completed. Captain Staal then informed SFHQ that he would consider his assignment fulfilled as soon as he had contacted team Claude, which nobody had heard of since the start of Market Garden. Interestingly enough, the Dutch Jedburgh captain requested a new mission in the Netherlands straightaway; his experiences with the Dutch resistance had been excellent and he could not wait to lead another Jedburgh team.

Later that day, Captain Staal and his American teammate Captain Sollenberger left Nijmegen and headed for Arnhem, taking a radio set with them. The risky journey to Arnhem would take them right through enemy territory. Despite being continuously under enemy machine-gun fire, the officers were – amazingly – able to reach the south shore of the Rhine near Driel.[100] As the Jedburghs saw no possibility of crossing the Rhine that day, they were forced to spend the night near the river. Unfortunately, due to heavy enemy fire, the

Jedburgh officers were not able to cross the Rhine on Sunday either. They returned to Nijmegen that same day.[101]

On Saturday, the Allied air force had showed itself regularly above the encircled British troops at Oosterbeek. Despite Allied air support, German attacks on the British positions continued. Major General Urquhart understood that his heavily battered division could not withstand for much longer.[102] A group of 120 Poles did manage to cross the Rhine that night but this number was much too low to turn the tide in Oosterbeek.

In Overijssel, team Dudley's situation was also precarious. On the night of 22/23 September, the Jedburghs hid in a farm near their former hideout. The local resistance tried to liberate Ter Horst that night, but were unsuccessful as the building where the resistance leader was held was covered with machine guns. Despite the arrest of their leader, several members of the KP Twente went to Lidwina the next day to collect material and supplies that had been left

The remnants of Huize Lidwina. (C. Hilbrink)

behind. Moments after their arrival, a large number of SD members appeared. These forces stormed the building, trapping the resistance fighters.[103] The Jedburghs, who were completely powerless, saw the raid from a distance and could only flee.

The KP fighters at Lidwina desperately tried to shoot their way out. Most resistance fighters were shot on the run, or arrested. The captives were interrogated extremely violently. Before long, they were shot and laid down in the house. Subsequently, the villa was blown up by the Germans.[104]

Much to the Jedburghs' relief, the other local KP leader, Cor Hilbrink, arrived at their new safe house the following day. Hilbrink, who had lost his father and brother in the raid, took over Ter Horst's command.[105] The latter was executed that evening.[106] The resistance in Twente had suffered an enormous blow.

After Ter Horst's death, Cor Hilbrink took command of the Twente KP. (C. Hilbrink)

Sunday, 24 September 1944

On Sunday, the members of team Daniel II gathered in the village of Veghel, north of Eindhoven. The 101st Airborne Division had taken hundreds of prisoners of war by now and had them locked up in an abandoned factory in the village. Major General Taylor, short of hands, ordered the Jedburghs to secure these prisoners. Team Daniel II cleverly used the local resistance to guard the POWs.[107] In the meantime, problems had emerged between the local KP and OD in Uden. A conflict between the resistance groups obstructed the support of American troops in the area, who were still confronted with heavy German attacks. Upon hearing of this, Lieutenant Du Bois returned to Uden to remind the underground who the enemy was, ensuring optimal assistance to the Americans.[108]

Intense battles raged throughout the day. Several resistance fighters of the KP from the village of Kesteren, strategically located between the rivers Waal and

The beret and identity papers of wireless operator Lee Faber of Jedburgh team Daniel II. (Private collection)

German prisoners guarded by American parachutists in Veghel. (Stichting Remember September 1944)

Prince Bernhard visits Eindhoven on 23 September 1944. Behind him, wearing the officer's hat, is BBO staff officer Kas de Graaf. (NIMH)

Rhine, managed to cross the lines on Sunday and deliver valuable intelligence to team Edward. This information concerned enemy positions at the Waal and the nearby city of Tiel. The KP men were sent back by the Jedburghs to gather more information. A resistance member from the Utrecht, a major city located in the centre of the Netherlands, was also able to reach liberated territory. He, too, brought in important information about the situation in the still occupied regions of the country.

Intelligence kept coming in on Sunday. A Dutch intelligence officer, who had been active around occupied Ressen and Bemmel, to the north of Nijmegen, reported to team Edward later that day. This man, most likely a BI agent, indicated that he had access to a network of radio transmitters and intelligence posts throughout the country. Team Edward subsequently sent the officer to the headquarters of the airborne corps and XXX Corps.

That day, the airborne corps's headquarters received a disturbing message from Major General Urquhart: his division was as good as defeated.[109] Meanwhile,

British paratroopers being supplied by air. (NIMH)

Lieutenant Knottenbelt of Jedburgh team Claude was still involved in heavy fighting in Oosterbeek and had taken command of a group of approximately twenty-five British parachutists. The decimated airborne division had to fight fiercely to maintain the perimeter.

The last days of Market Garden

On Monday, 25 September, Captain Staal contacted Major Wilson of team Daniel II in Veghel. As commander of the Dutch Jedburgh teams, Staal instructed him to report to the 3rd Special Force Detachment, which was located in 21st Army Group's headquarters near Brussels. With permission of Major General Taylor, team Daniel II left for Brussels the next day. The team returned to England by airplane on Wednesday. Its Dutch members, Lieutenant Du Bois and Sergeant Faber, were immediately summoned to the Dutch Queen Wilhelmina to report on the situation in the Netherlands.[110]

A group of British paratroopers who were able to reach the Allied lines. Lieutenant Commander Wolters (second from the left) was among the lucky ones. (National Liberation Museum Groesbeek)

Meanwhile, the first German tanks had moved into the British perimeter in Oosterbeek. This put the parachutists at risk of being cut off from the Rhine, thereby losing the possibility of returning to Allied lines. After consultation with corps commanders Browning and Horrocks, Major General Urquhart decided upon evacuating the remainder of his division. The evacuation of the battered 1st Airborne Division to the opposite shore of the Rhine took place in the night from Monday to Tuesday.[111] Ultimately, only one quarter of the division returned to friendly territory. The remainder had either been killed, made prisoner of war, or was missing.[112]

On Tuesday 26 September, team Edward finally succeeded in contacting a member of team Claude. Lieutenant Knottenbelt – now wounded in his thigh by a piece of shrapnel – had again swum across the Rhine and had reached Nijmegen.[113] Only then did Captain Staal learn about the break-up of team Claude and its missing members. Staal then considered his mission complete. He flew back to England with his team the following day.

Captain Bestebreurtje's team Clarence would stay involved in employing the local resistance in Nijmegen for the remainder of September 1944. At the end of the month, Major General Gavin gave Bestebreurtje and Sergeant Beynon permission to temporarily return to England, but only on the condition that they would soon return; the German attacks in the area did not cease.[114] Resistance fighters from Nijmegen and its surroundings were required in the defence line prepared at the Waal by the 82nd Airborne Division. Bestebreurtje would come to play an important role in transforming the former resistance into regular infantry units. As a result of the failure of Market Garden, the Allies now had to maintain an extensive front line along the rivers in the south of the Netherlands. Additional (interior) forces were desperately needed by the Allied units stationed in the area.

Commentary

From a strategic perspective, Operation Market Garden barely contributed to the Allied campaign in north-west Europe. The Germans had only been forced back on a narrow front. For Field Marshal Montgomery, this result was enough, though, to claim that the operation had been 'ninety per cent successful'. The British commander, however, had not succeeded in establishing a bridgehead over the Rhine. This meant that the industrial heart of Germany was still not threatened directly.[115]

The narrow strip that the Allies did conquer in the south of the Netherlands was a very vulnerable point in the frontline. Before the extended flanks of this corridor could be secured, the rest of the provinces of Noord-Brabant and Limburg needed to be conquered first. There was a bright spot, though: the established bridgehead over the Maas and Waal could act as a springboard for a new offensive in the direction of the German Ruhr area.[116]

Market Garden was very costly to the Allies: more than 7,000 men of the 1st Airborne Division had either been killed, injured, or went missing in action. The American 101st Airborne Division suffered 2,100 casualties. The 1st Polish Independent Parachute Brigade lost over 370 men. In total, the Allies lost nearly 12,000 men during the operation.[117]

As regards the Dutch Jedburgh teams, their deployment in the Netherlands had been an experiment for SFHQ. The groups, originally meant to operate independently inside enemy territory, had been deployed jointly with conventional forces for the first time. The Jedburghs, again, proved valuable. Almost immediately after their arrival, they were able to realise effective support from the Dutch resistance and civilians, who were attached to Allied units as guides, guards, scouts, and infantry forces.

Teams Edward and Clarence also managed to provide I British Airborne Corps and SFHQ in England with valuable intelligence about the progress of the battle in and around Arnhem – and at a time when no other sources were available. Airborne corps headquarters later described team Edward's contribution with the Dutch resistance as 'most valuable'.[118] Major General Gavin expressed similar words, describing the resistance's performance as 'exemplary'.[119]

Jedburgh teams Daniel II and Claude were less successful. Team Daniel II lost both radio sets at the start of the operation, while its two British members had trouble contacting the local resistance. Despite these setbacks, the team did have some successes. During the first days of the operation, Lieutenant Du Bois mainly served as an interpreter and liaison officer to division commander Taylor. Later, Du Bois often went ahead of the American forces in order to scout the area and contact resistance groups. The other members of the team made themselves useful by collecting intelligence and organising improvised POW centres.[120]

Although the team played only a modest role in utilising the resistance, the underground groups and local population were a benefit to the American forces. Major General Taylor later declared:

> I must pay tribute to the Dutch civilians for their invaluable assistance throughout the Holland campaign. The members of the underground, identified ... by orange armbands, were everywhere, bringing us information on the Germans and the local situation. They served as a secondary intelligence service throughout the campaign ...[121]

The dangerous tactical situation in Arnhem hindered team Claude in the execution of its mission. The British distrust with regard to the Dutch resistance also obstructed the team's efforts. Due to the heavy German opposition, Groenewoud and Todd were forced to act as infantrymen, leaving them unable to organise the resistance groups in Arnhem in such a way that it could be of benefit to the Allied operation. Both officers did, however, contribute laudably as infantry forces during the fight at the bridge in Arnhem. It must be kept in mind, though, that this had not been the purpose of their deployment.

Lieutenant Knottenbelt, the Dutch commando attached to team Claude, was successful to some degree, organising the spontaneously formed Orange Legion and employing civilians to collect divisional supplies. Knottenbelt, too, managed to gather important intelligence about the developments in Arnhem. The 1st Airborne Division's satisfaction about the Dutch commando is made clear: 'Lieutenant Knottenbelt and his Dutch commandos were first class. Their help was unfailingly efficient, and in very good measure. To them is due the great help received from the civilian population …'[122]

After the end of Operation Market Garden, Knottenbelt was the only member of team Claude to make it back to friendly territory; Captain Groenewoud was killed in action early in the battle, while Lieutenant Todd, after his arrest in Arnhem, was interned in several German POW camps. Early in May 1945, Todd was able to escape. Advancing American troops reached him several days later.[123]

The team's radio operator, the American Sergeant Scott, was declared missing in action after Market Garden. Only after the war was it discovered that he had not survived his mission. Scott's makeshift grave was found near the city of Wageningen, some ten kilometres west of Oosterbeek. OSS concluded that he had died on 2 November 1944, presumably while attempting to cross the Rhine.

The fifth Jedburgh team operational in the Netherlands during Operation Market Garden, team Dudley, was the only group that was parachuted independently into occupied territory. The group was expected to be reached by Allied ground forces within two weeks. As Market Garden failed, the team was now trapped deep behind enemy lines. With the Germans on their heels, the team had attempted to unite the inharmonious Overijssel resistance and organise supply drops.

The delay of the Allied advance in the Netherlands did provide an (unforeseen) opportunity for Dudley's Jedburghs: Major Brinkgreve's group was now able to provide long-term assistance to the Overijssel underground groups. The resistance was still disorganised and, most of all, short of weapons and training. However, the circumstances in the still-occupied regions of the Netherlands would deteriorate in the autumn of 1944. A precarious time lay ahead for the Jedburghs and their Overijssel resistance companions.

The Autumn and Winter of 1944–1945

Establishment of the Stoottroepen and Bewakingstroepen

Already on 22 September 1944, Field Marshal Montgomery had initiated planning the successor operation to Market Garden. This offensive, code-named Gatwick, aimed to advance from the eastern flank of the corridor up to the Rhine. This meant that Montgomery abandoned his plan of advancing north beyond Arnhem even before the British 1st Airborne had withdrawn from the perimeter in Oosterbeek.[1] The first step of Operation Gatwick was to reach the towns of Gennep and Kleef, to the east of Nijmegen. However, the operation could not start before the Nijmegen bridgehead was completely secured. The Germans thus needed to be driven out of the area between the Maas River and the eastern side of the corridor first.[2] Due to the eventual failure of Operation Market Garden and intense enemy activity on the Allied flank, preparations for Operation Gatwick were postponed on 7 October 1944.[3]

During the autumn of 1944, the provinces of Limburg and Noord-Brabant in the south of the Netherlands were only slowly liberated.[4] Around that time, to the west, the First Canadian Army and the German 15th Armee were fighting over access to the port of Antwerp in Zeeland – the banks of the Westerschelde estuary were still in German hands. The battle in Zeeland was eventually decided in the Allies' favour in November 1944, which finally allowed them to clear all mines in the Westerschelde. Thereafter, a long front line ran along the rivers Maas and Waal in Noord-Brabant and Limburg. North of Nijmegen, the front line passed through the Betuwe area – a stretch of land between the Rivers Waal, Rhine, and Lek – which was known by the Allies as 'the Island'.[5]

In the southern regions of the Netherlands that were liberated, BS headquarters decided to militarise the (former) resistance groups and make these available to the Allied units that were stationed along the extensive front line. Former KP commander for the provinces of Zeeland, Noord-Brabant, and Limburg J. J. H. (Johannes) Borghouts was ordered to transform the resistance into so-called 'Stoottroepen' (ST, or Shock Troops) and 'Bewakingstroepen' (BT, Security forces).[6] Borghouts was to cooperate with the Dutch Major C. H. J. F. (Charles) van Houten, who had been installed as special representative to the commander of the BS, Prince Bernhard.[7]

The tasks of the ST would be solely of a military nature. In order to join this unit, resistance members had to have taken part in the armed resistance. Resistance members who had not been involved in (para)military activities were seconded to the BT and would mostly perform security services for the Allies. During Operation Market Garden, the BS had already decided on recruiting 500 men from the local underground to form a 'Shock trooper' unit. In late September 1944, the 1st ST Company was officially established. This unit consisted mainly of former PAN members. Shortly after, the 2nd ST Company was formed in the nearby village of Veghel.[8]

As the liberation of Noord-Brabant, the river area of Gelderland and Zeeland, progressed, the number of ST and BT companies in the southern Netherlands increased. This rapid growth created a great need for experienced instructors. In response, SFHQ appointed a Jedburgh team to assist in organising the training and deployment of the ST and BT. This kind of mission was exceptional, as

Members of the PAN standing in front of their headquarters in Eindhoven. (S. Bentley)

Captain Bestebreurtje
continued his activities
in Nijmegen and
surroundings after
Operation Market Garden.
(The Bestebreurtje family)

Jedburgh groups were normally deployed inside occupied territory.[9] Captain Bestebreurtje's team was appointed to carry out this assignment.

After the termination of Market Garden, team Clarence's Sergeant Beynon had travelled back to England. The American sergeant returned to the Netherlands in early October 1944.[10] He was accompanied by British Jedburgh Captain P. C. H. (Peter) Vickery, who was to replace the badly wounded American Lieutenant Verhaeghe.

Vickery was born on 19 December 1920. Before his time with the Jedburghs, he had been part of the GHQ Liaison Regiment, a special reconnaissance unit also known as Phantom.[11] The assignment in the Netherlands was Vickery's first Jedburgh mission. As part of team Clarence's follow-up mission, Captain Bestebreurtje and Sergeant Beynon were stationed in Nijmegen. Captain Vickery was sent to the village of Boven-Leeuwen, approximately twenty kilometres west of Nijmegen.[12] From that moment on, the Jedburgh team operated under the code name Stanley II.

Early in October 1944, Stanley II started to provide the ST with improvised basic military training. The 1st ST Company was attached to the Second British Army as early as the second week of October.[13] The unit was subsequently stationed along the Waal front, in the area of Boven-Leeuwen, Wamel, and Dreumel (all west of Nijmegen).[14] Over this very disparate area, consisting of many areas of no man's land, small German units crossed the Waal nearly every night to vandalise, take POWs, or collect intelligence.

The 1st ST Company was ordered to clear the area and prevent the Germans from infiltrating. On 10 October 1944, Major van Houten sent the following telegram to Prince Bernhard:

> This morning, 10 October at 1000 hours, 123 Shock Troops, under the command of the C-Brabant, have left on nine English trucks for deployment in the Maas and Waal region ... All last arrangements were made in Eindhoven by the English Commando Captain mentioned in my notes yesterday, Captain Vickery ...[15]

Warning signs along a dyke at the front in the southern Netherlands, autumn 1944. (NIMH)

The 1st ST Company would face difficult conditions – their operational area was under continuous German artillery fire.[16] In spite of these conditions, the men were able to do good work, taking out several German soldiers who attempted to infiltrate the Allied sector. The ST also experienced losses; Captain Vickery suffered minor injuries in an artillery attack. Shortly after the deployment of the 1st ST company, a second group was sent into action. This company was stationed in Dreumel to cover the area along the Waal up to the ancient Fort Sint-Andries, near the village of Heerewaarden. Their task was to keep watch, protect the dykes, and check passersby on important access roads. Around this time, Vickery made a BT company responsible for guarding the villages of Dreumel and Alphen.

At Nijmegen, Captain Bestebreurtje and Sergeant Beynon were involved in the establishment of several training centres for former resistance members. Bestebreurtje deployed a single ST unit along the frontline between Dreumel and Nijmegen. In the third week of October 1944, the British 8th Armoured Brigade, led by Brigadier G. E. (George) Prior-Palmer, was stationed along the Waal.

ST members observe the opposite bank of the Waal. (NIMH)

The brigade was responsible for a front section approximately twenty-five kilometres in length. As this was a considerably large area, the unit was in desperate need of additional troops. Elements of the ST were to reinforce the British brigade.

The Dutch units were, however, dealing with a significant shortage of weapons, clothing and food. Much to their luck, Captain Vickery was acquainted with Prior-Palmer, for he had served under him at the military academy. Brigadier Prior-Palmer was generous and provided the 1st ST Company with much needed supplies. The brigadier took an interest in the Dutch troops and even inspected them personally, which, according to Vickery, made a great impression and boosted morale. Later that month, several of Vickery's forces were attached to the 12th Battalion King's Royal Rifle Corps, which was also stationed in the area. This unit provided the Dutchmen with medical training and instructions in the use of mortars.[17]

At the end of October, the ST under the 'Brabant Command' consisted of six companies, and a seventh was being established. Due to the rise of the number of units, BBO commandant Van Oorschot appointed two Dutch commandos who were to aid the overworked Jedburgh team Stanley II.[18] These were sergeants R. P. P. (Raymond) Westerling and G. H. J. (Dick) Bendien. These commandos, from No.2 (Dutch) Troop, had been part of BBO since September 1944.[19]

Sergeant Westerling, attached to team Stanley II, instructing ST forces in unarmed combat. (NIMH)

At the end of October, Captain Bestebreurtje took part in the liberation of the city of 's-Hertogenbosch. He served as liaison officer between the British 53rd Welsh Division and the local resistance fighters, who were heavily involved in the battle over the city.[20] The 2nd ST Company also took part in the city's liberation. Afterwards, the 8th ST Company was formed out of members of the KP group Margriet. This underground movement had been active in and around 's-Hertogenbosch.[21]

Besides their instruction and liaison activities, captains Vickery and Bestebreurtje were involved in clandestine crossings over the Waal. Canoes and other vessels were used to smuggle weapons and people across the river. Around this time, Captain Vickery was also in contact with a collection of Dutch informants. From inside the city of Tiel in the Betuwe region, located on the opposite side

Sergeant Bendien was also added to team Stanley II, here providing weapon instructions to ST members. (NIMH)

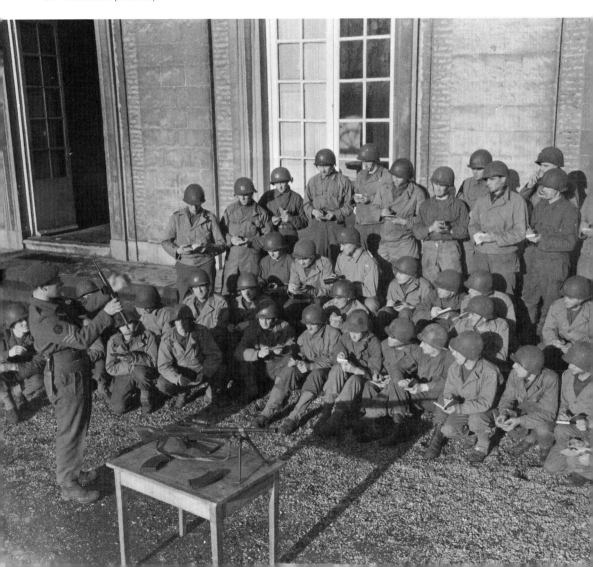

The 8th ST Company was formed out of members of the KP group Margriet. (NIMH)

of the Waal, several resistance members provided Vickery with information on enemy troop positions, command posts, and artillery positions. Thanks to this intelligence, the Allies were able to deliver precise artillery fire onto targets located across the river.[22]

Behind the lines in Overijssel

In the meantime, Jedburgh team Dudley managed to re-establish contacts that had been broken as a result of the raid on the Twente KP headquarters late September 1944. The team also liaised with resistance groups located in several of the larger cities in the province of Overijssel. By their own estimation, they were now in contact with approximately 3,500 resistance members.[23] In their new headquarters, a farm called Erve Juninck near the village of Saasveld, the Jedburghs realised that they might have to wait months for the arrival of the Allies. In view of this prospect, Major Olmsted decided to abandon his military training activities for the time being and, instead, focus on establishing a provincial intelligence circuit. After developing and distributing an 'intelligence circular' for the Overijssel resistance, he swiftly received an 'amazing amount' of information.[24]

Team Dudley moved into the farm at Erve Juninck near Saasveld in the first half of October 1944. (The Brinkgreve family)

Team Dudley's commander, Major Brinkgreve, was still engaged in unifying the Overijssel resistance groups. The Dutch officer viewed unity within the underground as the main prerequisite for effective deployment.[25] He organised the first three-way meeting in Overijssel on 1 October 1944, which included representatives of the KP, OD, and RVV. Unfortunately, Captain Lancker, commandant of the local RVV, was absent during this meeting. He let Brinkgreve know he was ordered by national RVV headquarters not to accept any authority outside his own organisation.[2]

In Lancker's absence, a number of important positions were created for Overijssel. In addition, the groups were each appointed their own sectors within the province. Lancker was given command of a small district – although he possessed limited real authority.[27] From this day, the armed resistance in Overijssel would officially amalgamate into the BS Overijssel and fall under command of (former) provincial OD leader Colonel Hotz;[28] Major Brinkgreve would act as an 'independent' supervisor of the Overijssel BS. After the meeting, the Jedburgh officer reported to SFHQ that the unification of the Overijssel resistance was progressing well. All resistance groups – save the RVV – were very cooperative, according to Brinkgreve.

Colonel Hotz was appointed as commander of all BS forces in the province of Overijssel. (C. B. Cornelissen)

One of the prime objectives of Jedburgh team Dudley was to deliver arms and supplies to the Overijssel resistance. However, after spending nearly three weeks behind enemy lines, the Jedburghs still had not received weapons from England: all dropping attempts had failed. Due to the shortage of weapons and the harsh German security measures, the resistance had been forced to scale down its activities.[29]

Late in September 1944, SFHQ notified team Dudley that it would again try to parachute supplies into Overijssel. Finally, on the night of 1/2 October 1944 two successful supply drops were carried out: the first in the fields code-named 'Arie', near the village of Markelo, the other one in a field code-named 'Paardeslenkte' in Hezingen, a border hamlet in the municipality of Tubbergen.[30] Before long, several more supply loads from England were received. By the end of the month, the Overijssel resistance had a considerable amount of weapons and explosives at its disposal.

The now combined headquarters of the Jedburghs and Overijssel BS would not stay long in Saasveld. SD activity in the immediate surroundings was excessive and the continuous flow of people towards the farm had drawn too much

Drop zone Paardenslenkte in the hamlet of Hezingen, recent photograph. (Private collection)

Several supply containers that were dropped in the Twente region of Overijssel. (C. B. Cornelissen)

attention. It was decided to move the command post to yet another farm, named 'De Paus'. This farm house was well-situated near drop zone Paardenslenkte.[31] It was decided to move headquarters on Friday 6 October.

The dangerous journey towards Hezingen started at dusk. Several hours later, only about five kilometres from their destination, the men stopped at a safe house near the village of Ootmarsum. By midnight, a courier arrived there to inform the Jedburghs that De Paus in Hezingen had been raided by the Landwacht earlier that day.[32] Several resistance fighters and Jewish people in hiding at the farm had been arrested or shot. It soon turned out that one of the captives was a senior resistance member named G. (Geert) Schoonman. He had just been appointed chief inspector of the team's drop zones by Major Brinkgreve. Although the Jedburghs had again been very lucky, they had lost a valuable companion. There was nothing else to do than to return to Saasveld, where the Jedburghs' headquarters would remain until 12 October 1944.[33]

Almost immediately after the end of Operation Market Garden, discussion arose in England about the future deployment of Jedburghs and SAS teams in the occupied Netherlands. On 23 September, the Dutch Jedburgh officer Captain Staal had already requested SFHQ to prepare a new mission, preferably in either

Post-war photograph of the farmhouse at De Paus. Some of the containers that were dropped on the Paardenslenkte can be seen. (C. B. Cornelissen)

Overijssel or the neighbouring province of Drenthe. Besides SFHQ, the SAS intended to deploy additional forces in the Netherlands.

On 3 October 1944, SFHQ instructed team Dudley to organise the reception of an SAS group. They next day, however, the Jedburghs reported that the German security services were very active in the area. Moreover, about 1,500 civilians had been apprehended and deported to Germany. To make matters worse, the Twente region of Overijssel had turned into a training area for German parachutists. These forces belonged to the 3rd Fallschirmjäger Division, which had nearly been annihilated in Normandy. The battered division was sent to Overijssel to recover and rebuild.[34] It later turned out that the German parachutists were preparing for the Battle of the Bulge, which was to commence several months later.[35]

Finally, it became so dangerous in Overijssel that Major Brinkgreve decided to temporarily break off radio contact with SFHQ. His decision to increase safety measures was far from exaggerated. Due to Operation Market Garden, German police, SD, and other security services previously stationed in the south of the Netherlands had fled to the centre and the north of the country. The increased pressure from the German side was also undoubtedly related to the raid on the local KP headquarters two weeks prior. As a result of this event, the Germans had laid their hands on sensitive information, including correspondence between local resistance commanders. These documents told the Germans that resistance man Johannes ter Horst had played an important part within the Twente resistance. Unfortunately, the names of 'Henk' (Brinkgreve) and 'Evert' (Lancker) had also come up.[36]

When radio contact with England was restored, team Dudley received word from SFHQ that the SAS had developed doubts about the deployment of a team in Overijssel. This reluctance was probably the result of the deteriorating situation in the province. Moreover, the Allies had abandoned their plan of advancing north beyond Arnhem for the time being. This meant that the German forces in the northern part of the Netherlands, including Overijssel, would not be directly threatened in the near future. The SAS eventually cancelled the planned mission. SFHQ also postponed the deployment of a new Jedburgh team.[37]

On the night of 7/8 October, *f* 130,000 was dropped for team Dudley. These resources had been requested by Brinkgreve to lessen the strain of the many people in hiding in the province, including the railway strikers. Shortly after, the Jedburghs informed SFHQ that Generalfeldmaschall K. R. G. (Gerd) Von Rundstedt, the supreme commander of the German forces in western Europe, had been spotted in Terborg, approximately thirty-five kilometres north-east of Nijmegen. Interestingly, another Generalfeldmarschall, O. M. W. (Walter) Model, established his headquarters in Huis Wisch – a castle located in Terborg – after he fled from Oosterbeek on 17 September 1944. Model's command post moved to Germany soon after. However, the Germans had maintained a forward operating post in Terborg.[38] A few days after Dudley's message reached England, the castle in Terborg was attacked by the Allied Air Force. Shortly after, a second air raid followed. The owner of the castle, Dutch nobleman R. F. A. A. W. L. (Richard) van Schuylenburg, was killed in the first attack.[39] Regrettably, no high German officer was hit.

On 12 October, the Jedburghs evacuated their headquarters in Saasveld again. The new command post was to be established near the village of Enter, approximately fifteen kilometres to the west. In the dark, on bicycles loaded with weapons, documents, maps, and transmitters, the group moved westwards. The men reached their destination, a farmhouse named De Koerdam, the following day. Before long, about twelve people worked from De Koerdam: the Jedburghs, Hilbrink and five other (former) KP members, and three female couriers.[40] Provincial BS commander Hotz was residing elsewhere but visited the farm regularly.

Castle Huis Wisch was heavily damaged due to Allied airstrikes. (Rijkdienst Cultureel Erfgoed)

In the second half of October 1944 team Dudley moved into farmhouse De Koerdam near Enter. (C. Hilbrink)

Meanwhile, SFHQ had received information that fuel for the much-feared V-weapons was transported from Germany to the west of the Netherlands by rail. At that time, little was known in England about these notorious weapon systems. Team Dudley was subsequently ordered to collect intelligence on these transports. The Jedburghs had already established a solid courier service which enabled them to keep an index of the situation in approximately two hundred Dutch cities and villages. Around this time, the Jedburghs learned, for instance, that the provincial capital, Zwolle, was being transformed into a German bastion.[41]

On 22 October 1944, team Dudley came into contact with a resistance man who worked under the name Fopkonijn (or 'Bogus Bunny'). He claimed to have been sent to the Netherlands by the Dutch BI. Having just been warned by SFHQ that the enemy was actively trying to infiltrate the Dutch resistance, the Jedburghs did not take any unnecessary risk. SFHQ soon validated that Fopkonijn was indeed a Dutch intelligence officer. His true name was G. B. (Gerrit) Buunk. He was parachuted over the province of Utrecht in July 1944 to assist the RVV. After the failure of Operation Market Garden, Buunk was instructed to establish signal stations above the IJssel Line in the east of the Netherlands.[42] Later, he was attached to Captain Lancker's staff as a liaison officer.

After his arrival in Overijssel,
BI agent Buunk became part
of Captain Lancker's staff.
(Streekarchief Epe Hattem Heerde)

From late October 1944, Major Olmsted began coordinating his intelligence activities with Buunk's. Around that time, a resistance member brought in the complete German defence plan for the IJssel Line and the city of Deventer. Intelligence kept pouring in that month. The Jedburghs even got their hands on the German defence plans for the large ports in the west of the Netherlands. Naturally, SFHQ was very interested in these documents.

The Jedburghs were now also in contact with a wounded Allied parachutist officer and several downed Allied Air Force members. Major Brinkgreve saw very little chance of getting them through the lines and requested SFHQ to send a small plane to the Netherlands to evacuate these men. Brinkgreve let headquarters know that the Noordoostpolder was a suitable location for this 'pick-up' operation. This was a large and flat area north-west of Zwolle, adjacent to the Netherlands' largest lake, the IJsselmeer. Brinkgreve proposed that a member of team Dudley was to be evacuated as well; he would take all the gathered intelligence with him and report in England about the situation in occupied Overijssel. SFHQ gave its assent and let the Jedburghs know that preparations in England were to start straight away.

In late October, team Dudley reported that some eight to ten thousand German parachutists were now stationed in Twente. The Jedburghs suspected that a new SS division was being established in the region as well.[43] In the meantime, the Twente BS had informed the Jedburghs of their plan to rob the Almelo branch of the De Nederlandsche Bank (Dutch National Bank). Allegedly, millions of guilders were stored there, destined for Germany.

The rumours turned out to be correct; German State Commissioner of the Netherlands A. (Arthur) Seyss-Inquart had transported an enormous amount of money from Arnhem to Almelo. Via team Dudley, the Twente BS asked the Dutch government-in-exile for permission to raid the bank. The authorities responded via SFHQ the same day:

> K. P. do not require our authority for action other than dealing with the matter of a military nature. If banks Almelo are attacked, it is however most important that the 150 million guilders do not go into circulation for obvious economic reasons. K. P. should stipulate what amount will be used for illegal and the remainder should be safely disposed or destroyed ...[44]

In late 1944, millions of Dutch guilders were stored in the office of the Nederlandsche Bank in Almelo. (C. B. Cornelissen)

SFHQ stressed that neither the Jedburghs nor the local BS commanders were to take part in the operation. On 15 November 1944, the local resistance eventually seized over *f* 46 million – the biggest bank robbery in Dutch history to date.[45] It was an enormous financial boost for the underground. Headquarters in England was so impressed that even British Prime Minister Winston Churchill was informed about the successful bank raid.[46] The euphoria was, however, short lived: the occupier soon arrested most of those involved. Moreover, almost all of the stolen money was retrieved. Again, the Germans proved to be a formidable opponent of the Overijssel underground.

After residing at the farmhouse at De Koerdam for several weeks, the Jedburghs were informed by its owners that it was becoming too dangerous for them. Once more, a new safe house needed to be found. On Monday 30 October, the Jedburghs' headquarters was relocated to a farm in the village of Heeten, in the Salland region of Overijssel, about twenty-five kilometres west of their former location. For the first time, team Dudley established a command

After the successful raid, the Germans offered a reward of *f* 1,000,000 for information leading to the arrest of the bank robbers. (C. B. Cornelissen)

Bekendmaking

In verband met een op 15 November 1944, tusschen 18 en 19 uur plaats gehad hebbende roofoverval op de Nederlandsche Bank aan de Wierdenschestraat te Almelo, wordt een ieder, die inlichtingen kan verschaffen omtrent auto en/of personen, die zich gedurende dien tijd bij de Nederlandsche Bank of omgeving opgehouden hebben, verzocht zich te vervoegen ten Politiebureele te Almelo of den naast bijzijnden Politiepost.

Een belooning van

f 1.000.000 (EEN MILLIOEN GULDEN)

is in uitzicht gesteld voor dengene of degenen die aanwijzingen verstrekt (verstrekken), welke leiden tot opsporing van de daders.

Wanneer meerdere personen aanwijzingen verstrekken, zal de in uitzicht gestelde belooning worden verdeeld in verhouding tot de belangrijkheid van de gegeven inlichtingen.

ALMELO, den 18 November 1944.

post outside of Twente. Sergeant Austin, always in danger of being discovered by German radio detection forces, had already moved to the nearby village of Schoonheten. He subsequently relocated briefly to Heeten and then to the village of Luttenberg, several kilometres north of his Jedburgh colleagues.[47]

Soon, meetings with local resistance leaders were organised in Heeten. According to Major Olmsted, his teammate Major Brinkgreve was very busy at this time; the Dutch Jedburgh officer was the only person who kept the Overijssel resistance united.[48] A resistance man later commented: 'This guy [Brinkgreve] was really it. He was an authority. You just felt: this man is taking charge, he is doing something. You simply had to follow him …'[49] The Dutch Jedburgh officer would eventually become the key figure of the resistance in Overijssel.

At the end of the month, SFHQ notified team Dudley that the Overijssel resistance commanders should prepare to hold all important bridges and prepare themselves to support the Allied advance through the province. Ground forces were to arrive soon – or so it seemed. The Jedburghs and the Overijssel resistance could not know that the liberation of Overijssel was still some six months away.

A code sheet used by Jedburgh team Dudley during the operation in Overijssel. (The Brinkgreve family)

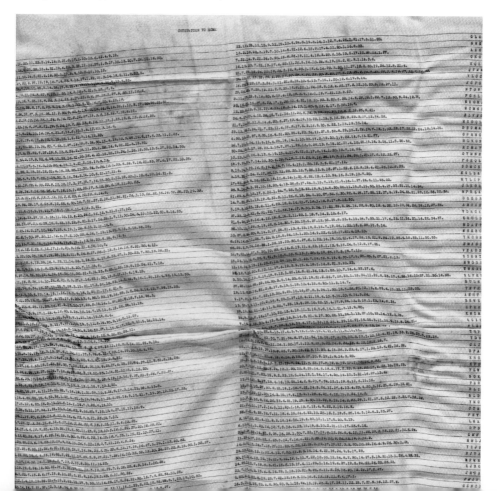

November 1944

Early in November, whilst heavy fights were still ongoing in the south of the Netherlands, Field Marshal Montgomery resumed preparations for Operation Gatwick. This offensive was to commence from the Nijmegen area, and on 2 November 1944 Montgomery ordered the First Canadian Army to ready itself. This army, led by Lieutenant General H. D. G. (Henry) Crerar, was also ordered to prepare a sub-operation that involved capturing the high grounds between Arnhem and Apeldoorn.[50] In this novel set-up, the First Canadian Army and the Second British Army – the armies comprising the 21st Army Group – were appointed several new operating sectors.

A week later, when the battles in Zeeland and West-Brabant had finally been decided, the First Canadian Army was assigned a section of the front line which ran from the island of Walcheren, in Zeeland, to the city of Cuijk, just south of Nijmegen. The sector of the Second British Army was shifted to the south. The four divisions of II Canadian Corps were stationed between Lithoijen and Cuijk. Lieutenant General Crerar declared that these divisions were thus responsible for 'the most important bit of ground' of the 21st Army Group: the bridgehead at Nijmegen.[51]

Meanwhile, Sergeant Beynon of team Stanley II had returned to headquarters in England. Beynon spoke very little Dutch, and his commanding officer, Captain Bestebreurtje, felt that, despite his good work, it was better to have him replaced by a Dutch-speaking instructor.[52] Bestebreurtje himself remained active in the Nijmegen area, training and deploying Dutch ST and BT units. Around that time, the 2nd ST Company was relocated to the vicinity of Oeffelt and Beugen, south of Cuijk, to keep watch at night and prevent German patrols from crossing the Maas.

By then, the BT unit in Dreumel was transformed into an ST company.[53] Slowly but surely, the former resistance groups were issued the necessary supplies and gear. British forces on site proved generous, and Captain Vickery, the second officer of team Stanley II, even managed to provide an entire company with British weapons and personal gear.

By that time, the British Jedburgh officer commanded two companies, the 7th and the 8th. The first was deployed in the area of Wamel, Dreumel, and Alphen.[54] The 8th company, positioned in the town of Boven-Leeuwen, had replaced the 1st Company at the front along the Waal.

The Allied unit stationed in this sector, the British 8th Armoured Brigade, was responsible for a considerable section of the Waal front and in desperate need of reinforcements. At the request of this British brigade, Captain Vickery contacted 21st Army Group's headquarters to ask for more Dutch

The Stootroepen are supplied with much-needed provisions. (NIMH)

forces. The Jedburgh officer was, however, informed that the units were needed elsewhere. After a month of deployment at the Waal's banks, the 8th Armoured Brigade was finally relieved by the Canadian 2nd Armoured Brigade.[55] Its commander, Brigadier J. F. (John) Bingham, was pleasantly surprised by the performance of the ST.[56]

Early in November 1944, SFHQ contacted team Dudley to find out if it had any information about an SAS team that was parachuted into the neighbouring province of Drenthe. Recently, SAS headquarters had lost all communication with the men. This team, code-named Gobbo, consisted of five Belgians and a Dutch sergeant. They had been parachuted near the village of Westerbork at the end of September 1944. Under the command of Lieutenant E. (Emile) Debefve, the team was to liaise with the Drenthe resistance and collect intelligence.[57] Dutch Sergeant R. A. (Rudy) Blatt, originally a member of No. 10 (Inter-Allied) Commando, had been attached to this team by BBO. It later turned out that team Gobbo's hide out had been raided by the Germans. As they had lost all their equipment, the men had decided to move south, hoping to cross the lines into liberated territory.

An ST member is practicing marksmanship under supervision of a British officer, possibly Captain Vickery. (NIMH)

On their way, the SAS group reached northern Overijssel in early November 1944. Luckily, they soon got into contact with the local resistance. BI agent Buunk, then active in that area, moved the parachutists to a shelter near Almelo. Team Dudley then informed England that team Gobbo was safe and sound. Furthermore, the SAS men felt safe enough to stay in Overijssel for the time

Members of Belgian SAS team Gobbo. Sergeant Blatt is not shown in this photograph. Adjutant Groenewoud (with glasses) was not part of team Gobbo. He was later also parachuted in the province of Drenthe. (C. B. Cornelissen)

being. Before long, the Belgian parachutists cooperated with Buunk, gathering intelligence and relaying bombing targets to England. Sergeant Blatt was placed under Major Brinkgreve's command. The Jedburgh officer soon deployed him as a weapon instructor for the resistance in the Twente region of the province. The Dutch commando proved an unexpected but very useful complement to Brinkgreve's team.

During November 1944, the Jedburghs were again experiencing difficulties getting supplies from England to Overijssel. As winter approached, the weather conditions became increasingly unfavourable. Moreover, the low-flying aircraft that delivered the supply containers drew a lot of attention. The metal cylinders, sometimes weighing up to 350 pounds each, often wound up in trees, which considerably delayed the collection process. As a result, several of Dudley's drop zones had to be abandoned due to German activity. Major Olmsted commented on these dangerous supply operations: 'The actual drop itself was very dangerous because of the wide visibility allowed by the Dutch landscape. The heavy concentration of German troops with constant guards each night to locate such clandestine operations also was a sobering factor ...'[58]

After his arrival in Overijssel, the Dutch commando Rudy Blatt was placed under Major Brinkgreve's command. (Dutch Commando Museum)

Deliveries into the occupied Netherlands were also very dangerous for the Allied Air Force. This was proven by the fatal crash of a Short Stirling bomber in early November 1944, destined for team Dudley;[59] it was not until halfway through November that a supply drop on one of team Dudley's zones in Overijssel succeeded.

Meanwhile, Major Brinkgreve tried to select the final location for the planned pick-up operation (see p. 144). Unfortunately, he was unable to find a suitable strip of land in the Noordoostpolder. Brinkgreve did find a location for a seaplane to land, which he relayed to England.[60] The Jedburgh team also informed headquarters that, by now, some 20,000 German forces were stationed east of the IJssel River – many of them in the Overijssel province.[61]

After having spent two months behind the lines and with no Allied forces in sight, team Dudley concluded that it had to cut back its activity; as long as the Germans in Overijssel weren't facing direct military pressure, the situation in the province was simply too dangerous. Time had come for one of Dudley's members personally to deliver the gathered intelligence at headquarters in England.

Converted bombers were used to drop supplies into occupied territory. A Short Stirling is shown here. (A. J. van Hees)

In early November, Major Brinkgreve attended a secret conference of representatives of the resistance from the Achterhoek and Veluwe, two regions in the neighbouring province of Gelderland. During this meeting, which was also attended by Arnhem resistance commander Kruyff, Brinkgreve learned that a mixed escape party of the 1st Airborne Division, downed Allied Air Force personnel, and several Dutchmen were to cross the lines to Allied territory. It was agreed that Major Olmsted would join this party. The American Jedburgh was expected to be gone for about ten days and then return to Overijssel with a supply drop.[62]

On Sunday 12 November 1944, Jedburgh team Dudley gathered for the last time. Afterwards, Sergeant Austin was sent to another safe house. Major Brinkgreve would soon leave for BS headquarters in Amsterdam – which was also coping with internal struggles of its own. Interestingly, the Dutch Jedburgh officer travelled to the nation's capital by car. This vehicle belonged to a wine merchant from the city of Kampen named J. (Jan-Willem) Siebrand. This Dutchman provided the Höhere SS- und Polizeiführer J. B. A. (Hanns) Rauter – the highest SS and police leader in the Netherlands – and other senior German officials with wine and liquors. Though widely regarded as a collaborator, the wine merchant was actually a loyal and active resistance man. Because of his connections with German officials, Siebrand could move freely with his vehicles through the entire nation. Major Brinkgreve possessed excellent forged ID documents, which enabled him to pass German checkpoints while wearing civilian clothes. Together, Siebrand and Brinkgreve were an excellent duo.

Despite visiting family and friends whilst on missions being strictly forbidden by BBO, Brinkgreve, on his way back from Amsterdam, suddenly appeared at his mother's doorstep in Het Gooi, a region in the centre of the Netherlands. They had not seen each other in over four years.[63] It must have been an emotional day for them. The family visit was only a short one, though, since a lot of work was waiting for Major Brinkgreve in Overijssel.

Major Olmsted began his dangerous journey to friendly territory on 16 November 1944. That morning, the American headed to the town of Ede, where he contacted resistance commander Kruyff and, remarkably, BBO agent Bram du Bois.[64] After his Jedburgh mission with team Daniel II, Du Bois had again been deployed in the Netherlands, this time by BBO and MI9 (the latter a secret British organisation tasked with evacuating personnel out of enemy territory). Du Bois' mission, code-named Pegasus II, was to organise the crossing of the group.[65]

From Ede, Major Olmsted and Lieutenant Du Bois moved on to the village of Lunteren. This is where they met Major H. P. (Hugh) Maguire, the intelligence

Major Olmsted managed to reach friendly territory in November 1944. (C. Hilbrink)

officer of the British 1st Airborne Division. Maguire would act as commander of the British escape party. At his arrival in Lunteren, Olmsted was wearing an overall and clogs. His accent and looks raised a lot of suspicion among the British paratroopers.[66] Du Bois experienced quite some trouble that day convincing the men that Major Olmsted was no agent provocateur.

In the early hours of 19 November, the escape party moved without any trouble to the next assembly point. However, when the group reached the main Ede–Arnhem road, they stumbled upon a German sentry; a skirmish and chase followed. Olmsted's precious bag containing all the documents and intelligence was shot to pieces. In the tumult, the group quickly fell apart. The next morning, Olmsted, together with a British flight sergeant and a British lance corporal, still managed to reach the northern banks of the Rhine. Shortly after sunset, the men were picked up by a patrol of the 101st Airborne Division, near the ferry at the village of Heteren, west of Arnhem.[67] Olmsted's escape was very laudable as only seven of approximately 114 men were able to cross the Rhine.[68]

Since the start of the supply drop operations into Overijssel in October 1944, the armed resistance had grown considerably.[69] On 14 November, Brinkgreve had informed SFHQ that he now had some 4,000 BS forces at his disposal, of which 1,500 were armed. Additionally, Brinkgreve let headquarters know that he had divided the BS in the province in three sectors: firstly, the area along the IJssel and the Noordoostpolder; secondly, the Salland region; and, thirdly, the Twente region. Salland was under Captain Lancker's command (former RVV), while the other two sectors belonged to the (former) KP and OD leaders. Brinkgreve also notified London that 'the [German] troops in or coming to Achterhoek [and] Twente number 60,000 men'. According to information provided by the Overijssel BS, the Germans were also establishing yet another infantry division. Furthermore, the enemy was connecting all defence lines in the province.

Around that time, Major Brinkgreve requested an air attack on the barracks in the village of Schalkhaar, near Deventer. The so-called 'Westenbergkazerne' was home to the Dutch Politie Opleidingsbataljon (POB, Police Training battalion). The POB had been established in 1941 by Rauter. Each Dutchman who signed up with the national police was trained here according to German standards and ideology. This institution in Schalkhaar permanently housed some 500 to 800 men, who were deployed to counter the Dutch resistance – including the Overijssel underground. This made the POB buildings attractive targets for Jedburgh team Dudley. Brinkgreve informed England that all personnel were present between 0600 and 0700 hours, implying that an air raid within this time frame would inflict the most damage. More telegrams were sent back and forth about the barracks in Schalkhaar, but, for reasons unknown, the barracks were never bombed by the Allies.

In mid-November, Brinkgreve reported that the German parachutists in Overijssel had gathered in and around the cities of Enschede and Almelo. From there, they started moving in a westward direction. It was also rumoured that some 500 parachutists were now stationed in Kampen, with another 800 in the area between Kampen and Wijhe. The Dutch Jedburgh officer also informed SFHQ that about 20,000 German soldiers had been directed to Gronau, just across the border near Enschede. These forces were destined for deployment along the Ijssel – and for the city of Arnhem.

On 16 November 1944, Brinkgreve informed headquarters that Captain Lancker still refused to cooperate. Moreover, Lancker manifested himself as the provincial resistance commander, according to the Dutch Jedburgh officer. Fearing that the strife between team Dudley and Lancker would grow out of hand, SFHQ emphasised that 'unnecessary friction' was to be obviated. By now, SFHQ felt obliged to converse with Prince Bernhard of the Netherlands, commander of the BS, about the continuing tension between Brinkgreve and Lancker.

Subsequently, Prince Bernhard himself addressed Lancker via the following telegram, which was sent on 20 November 1944: 'From Prince Bernhard to Evert. Have heard that you are commander for Salland repeat Salland. To avoid misunderstanding, it is important that you do not violate boundaries.'[70] Several days later, Lancker informed SFHQ that he suspected team Dudley was 'sabotaging' him, and that he would only take orders that came directly from BS headquarters. Brinkgreve's and Lancker's relationship continued to be cumbersome for now.

After Major Olmsted's evacuation, Brinkgreve's only original teammate was his radio operator, Sergeant Austin. To decrease chances of being detected by Germans, he never signalled from the same location for long. Halfway through November 1944, Austin had moved to Luttenberg, located in the centre of the province. Within a couple of days after his arrival there, the nearby villa Bloemenbos, a resistance safe house, was raided by the Germans. When Major Brinkgreve heard of this attack, he immediately sent one of his couriers, A. (Ank) van der Poll, to Luttenberg to evacuate Austin.[71]

Unfortunately she was unable to get the Irishman to safety in time; when the SD searched Austin's neighbours' house, the occupants lost their calm and fled. Subsequently, the Germans ransacked Sergeant Austin's hideout as well.[72] The Jedburgh radio operator was quickly discovered, together with his KP assistant M. (Chiel) Ploeger. The men were immediately transported to the Zwolle House of Detention – the facility where the Germans interrogated their 'heavy cases'. Austin would soon meet German interrogator Kriminalobersekretar E. G. (Ernst) May, a notorious counterintelligence officer, who, in the early stages of the war, had played an important part in the *Englandspiel*. It was to be a difficult and anxious time for Austin.

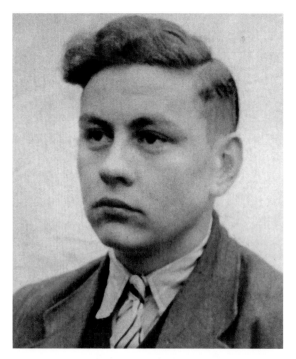

Wireless operator Austin of team Dudley had to relocate constantly to prevent detection by German radio direction-finding units. (The National Archives)

Twente KP member Chiel Ploeger was arrested along with Sergeant Austin in Luttenberg. (C. Hilbrink)

Right after the news about Austin's capture reached Brinkgreve, he evacuated his headquarters and moved to another farm in the village of Heeten. Thereafter, the (combined) command post of Brinkgreve and the Overijssel BS moved to the village of Okkenbroek, in the municipality of Deventer, where it would remain until January 1945. With Austin's arrest, Major Brinkgreve had lost his communication channel with headquarters in England. After a while, Brinkgreve could get some messages to SFHQ via BBO agent Beekman, who operated Captain Lancker's radio set. For the time being, maintaining contact with England would be a challenge for the Dutch Jedburgh officer.

December 1944

In the six months that had passed since the Allied invasion of Normandy, the Germans had suffered heavy losses. Hitler's industry also kept enduring heavy Allied bombings. The Third Reich found itself in a hopeless situation, no longer able to replace its losses. Despite this, the German propaganda machine kept predicting a turn in its favour. Hitler himself hoped to turn the tables with a surprise attack on the Belgian Ardennes, a weakly defended section in the Allied line – by destroying enemy forces north of the defensive line of Antwerp–Brussels–Luxembourg and recapturing Antwerp, Germany hoped to split the enemy front, effectively separating the American forces from the British.[73]

The first blueprints for this plan had already been developed by the Germans in September 1944. As preparations took longer than expected, the 'Battle of the Bulge' did not start until 16 December 1944.[74] This German offensive came as a total surprise to the Allies. Despite severe losses, the Allied forces were able to recover quickly and take the upper hand. All that was achieved by the Germans was a bulge in the front line, which was at its largest on 26 December. By late January 1945, the Germans were driven back completely. Although the enemy's attack was repelled successfully, the Allies were forced to postpone their own attack plans for six weeks.[75]

In early December 1944, unaware of what had happened to Sergeant Austin, SFHQ had asked BBO radio operator Beekman why team Dudley suddenly failed to come on air again. After being informed about Austin's arrest, headquarters in England let Beekman know that a replacement radio operator would be sent to Overijssel as soon as possible. At this time, Belgian SAS Lieutenant Debefve and his teammates, who had arrived in Overijssel in early November 1944, ran into trouble as well. The men were then based in Vroomshoop, north of Almelo, collecting intelligence and acquiring targets for the Allied air force.[76] The trailer from whence the Belgians were operating was attacked by Germans on the evening of 4 December. Debefve was injured during the shootout but he and his colleagues managed to escape;[77] two Dutch resistance fighters who were left behind were arrested and later executed. Fortunately, the Belgians were picked up by the local resistance that same night.[78]

Meanwhile in England, British Jedburgh radio operator H. (Harry) Verlander was selected as replacement for Austin. Verlander had previously been part of Jedburgh team Harold, which had been active in France in the summer and autumn of 1944.[79] By this time, Beekman informed headquarters that he wanted to cross the lines; the pressure of working in occupied Overijssel had become too much. The radio operator explained that German activity in the region was growing stronger each day, and that it was nearly impossible to work.[80] His anxiety had worsened upon hearing from SFHQ that his wife – also an SOE agent – had been arrested by the Germans in occupied France.[81] Headquarters agreed to Beekman's request and selected Dutch BBO agent S. (Sjoerd) Sjoerdsma as his substitute.

The trailer in Vroomshoop that housed SAS team Gobbo was raided in early December 1944. (C. B. Cornelissen)

BBO radio operator Sjoerd
Sjoerdsma replaced Austin
in early January 1945.
(The National Archives)

After Austin's arrest, Major Brinkgreve continued his work in Overijssel to the best of his ability. In addition to organising the resistance, he and Sergeant Blatt developed an integral training programme for the Twente BS. Blatt would take care of instructions in each BS district in this region of Overijssel.[82] Interestingly enough, the Jewish Rudy Blatt was born in Germany in 1912. He moved to the Netherlands in 1933 due to the increasing levels of anti-Semitism prevalent in his home country. After the Dutch capitulation in May 1940, Blatt joined the resistance. When the Germans were on to him, he decided to try to escape to England. Blatt reached his destination and joined the Dutch Irene Brigade, soon volunteering for the Dutch Commando Troop in England. In September 1944, he joined BBO and was subsequently attached to the SAS.

Much to his joy, Blatt encountered highly motivated BS members in Overijssel, who were very eager to learn. When the news of the German Ardennes offensive reached the province, though, everyone was surprised and worried. Sergeant Blatt recounted: 'We just could not comprehend what had happened. Each day, we had been waiting anxiously for the definitive breakthrough of the Allies and the capitulation of the *moffen* [a Dutch offensive term for Germans], but now the tables were turned!'[83] The resistance in Overijssel understood very well that they would have to wait a while longer for the Allies' arrival.[84]

Late in 1944, in the south of the Netherlands, the ST under 'Brabant Command' counted approximately two thousand men.[85] Despite this significant number, their training still had not been standardised. Meanwhile, in the neighbouring province of Limburg, a special school had been established with the help of American forces in the area; all men who joined the Limburg ST received basic training here.

The Dutch intended themselves to take care of all ST and BT training as soon as possible, aiming to establish a basis for the new Netherlands army. Jedburgh Captain Staal, who had been the commander of the Dutch Liaison Mission during Operation Market Garden, was put in charge of the organisation and training of the ST in December 1944. Staal swiftly developed plans for the establishment of a school for instructors, and, subsequently, a general training establishment. Several months later, the Centraal Bureau voor Militaire Opleiding (CBMO, Central Bureau for Military Training) was founded, of which Staal became commander.[86]

Jedburgh officer Jaap Staal, seen bottom right, became head of the Dutch CBMO early 1945. (M. Staal)

Before long, Major Olmsted, former member of team Dudley, was appointed BT's head instructor.[87] In addition, a Dutch commando, Captain C. J. L. (Carel) Ruysch van Dugteren, coming from No. 2 Dutch Troop, was appointed supervisor of the BT. Interestingly, this officer would later be seconded to BBO and, in April 1945, be deployed as a member of Jedburgh team Dicing (see chapter 5).

From the establishment of the CBMO onward, the ST would be officially trained as light infantry forces, maintaining British military rules, organisation, and procedures. In mid-January 1945, the expanding Brabant ST companies would be amalgamated into battalions. The companies that were active in the Land van Maas en Waal, the region between the rivers Maas and Waal, made up the 1st Battalion; the 2nd Battalion consisted of the companies that were active along the Maas; the companies operating in West-Brabant and Zeeland made up the 3rd Battalion.[88]

January 1945

In late December 1944, German forces in the south of the Netherlands surprisingly managed to expand their small bridgehead in the province of Noord-Brabant, more precisely at the Kapelsche Veer on the southern bank of the river Bergsche Maas.[89] Fearing German attacks from this bridgehead, the Allies fought hard to destroy it. Meanwhile, there were two other important nearby German bridgeheads. The one in the triangle formed by Roermond–Susteren–Linnich was the most important. Still shocked by the Ardennes offensive, Field Marshal Montgomery decided that the Allied offensive towards the Rhineland would only commence when the enemy's Roer bridgehead was destroyed.[90] The subsequent Allied operation, code-named Blackcock, started on 16 January 1945. After ten days of fighting, the area was cleared of all German forces.[91]

Jedburgh Captain Vickery's mission with the Dutch ST and BT was terminated by SFHQ on 25 January 1945. Vickery returned to England, from whence he would soon be sent to British India by SOE.[92] Captain Bestebreurtje continued his training activities in the Netherlands for a while. In early March 1945, he would again be seconded to the American 82nd Airborne Division, which was at that time preparing for Operation Eclipse.[93] This offensive involved a massive airborne landing in Berlin, in which several regiments of the American division would participate as well.[94] Bestebreurtje, who had lived in Berlin in his younger years, spoke German fluently and knew the city like the back of his hand. However, the Allied plan was eventually cancelled. In April 1945, Captain Bestebreurtje returned to England to prepare for a new Jedburgh mission.

During early January 1945, British Jedburgh radio operator Verlander was on standby to be parachuted into Overijssel. Shortly before departing, the flight was cancelled due to bad weather conditions.[95] In the meantime, BBO agent Beekman had changed his mind and decided to continue his work behind enemy lines after all. SFHQ subsequently replaced Verlander – who did not speak Dutch – with Dutch BBO agent and radio operator Sjoerd Sjoerdsma. This Dutchman was born in Schagen on 17 April 1921 and had been an apprentice mate in the merchant navy. He escaped from the occupied Netherlands in 1944 and reached England via Sweden in September of that year. He then volunteered for service with BBO and was trained by SOE as a radio operator.[96]

The first attempt to drop Sjoerdsma failed as the aircrew of the bomber could not locate the reception committee on the ground. The second attempt, on the night of 5/6 January 1945, was successful. After landing, Sjoerdsma hid for several days in a farmhouse in the village of Losser, north-east of Enschede. Soon he would operate his radio set from the nearby Lutterzand, a nature reserve right along the German border.[97] Major Brinkgreve's new radio operator sent his first telegram to SFHQ on 13 January. From then on, Sjoerdsma would handle all radio traffic for Brinkgreve and the Overijssel BS headquarters.

Having had no direct communication link with England for over a month, Brinkgreve firstly requested SFHQ to repeat all important messages that had failed to reach him. One of the first telegrams that Sjoerdsma received concerned the deployment of the Overijssel resistance in the sabotaging of German V-weapons. Near the end of 1944, many German launch sites for V-1 missiles and V-2 rockets had been established in forested areas throughout the province.[98]

Brinkgreve replied to headquarters that it was essential that the Overijssel resistance continued to operate cautiously; former (offensive) actions had resulted in heavy losses and disorganisation. Coming out in the open with no Allied forces in sight was simply too risky for the BS. The Dutch Jedburgh rightly stressed that the resistance was only capable of offensive actions over a short period of time. Brinkgreve subsequently requested further instructions and informed headquarters that he would pass on the locations of the German launch sites in the province in any case.[99]

In anticipation of the Allied crossing of the Rhine and the long expected arrival of ground forces in Overijssel, SFHQ passed its so-called 'Special Orders' to the provincial BS in late January 1945. It was emphasised that the resistance should only go into action when explicitly ordered by Allied headquarters. Additional instructions followed specifying which targets to attack, such as rocket fuel depots and German petrol and oil dumps. Moreover, the Overijssel BS was ordered to prepare for rail and motorway sabotage. Brinkgreve and instructor Sergeant Blatt swiftly developed plans to form a special 'commando' group, consisting of Overijssel resistance men who had extensive experience with sabotage and other offensive actions. These forces would have to support the local district commanders when the Allies – finally – entered the province.[100]

A destroyed German V-1 launch ramp in a forest in Almelo is inspected by Canadian soldiers. (Library and Archives Canada)

Team Dudley cornered

On 8 February 1945, south-east of Nijmegen, Operation Veritable commenced the Allied invasion of the Rhineland.[101] This offensive, which was one of the successors of Operation Gatwick, had been assigned to the First Canadian Army. Parts of this army had secretly moved to a gathering point near Nijmegen, where they commenced a frontal attack from a twelve-kilometre-wide strip between the rivers Maas and Waal.[102] Simultaneously, the Ninth U.S. Army was to execute

Operation Grenade – the invasion of the Rhineland from the south. However, this American advance was delayed due to the flooding of the Roer Valley by the Germans.[103] Growing German resistance further slowed the battle for the Rhine. Only on 11 March 1945 was the battle of the Rhineland won. This victory meant that the Allies now lined the west bank of the Rhine from Düsseldorf to Nijmegen.[104] This vast river was the last major barrier to the heart of the Reich.

Meanwhile, the Allied Air force continued carrying out dozens of air raids in the east of the Netherlands. The cities of Enschede, Hengelo and Deventer were hit in particular.[105] On 14 February 1945, Overijssel BS headquarters felt compelled to report to SFHQ that many bombs were missing their targets, inflicting many civilian casualties. In the week before, for instance, sixty-one civilians had been killed in an Allied air attack on Deventer.[106]

Despite the imprecision of the bombings and random strafing runs, the Overijssel BS continued to designate targets for the Allied Air Force, such as SD and Gestapo offices and German troop concentrations. The resistance did let SFHQ know that it was very sceptical, as the bombings proved hardly effective.[107] In February 1945, SFHQ was notified by the Overijssel BS that some 3,000 German parachutists were moving from the Achterhoek region, in the neighbouring province of Gelderland, towards to the German town of Emmerich, just east of the city of Nijmegen.[108] This was important information as Operation Plunder – the crossing of the Rhine by the 21st Army Group – was executed in this region about a month later.

By now, it had been months since Major Brinkgreve had last received weapons and supplies from England. Fortunately for the Overijssel resistance, BBO agents Beekman and Hinderink had been able to continue organising supply drops in the province. In early February 1945, SFHQ informed Major Brinkgreve that the Dutch BI intended to deploy an intelligence agent in the east of the Netherlands. It was decided that this agent would be dropped – together with a large number of supplies and money – on drop zone Willow, an area near the German border that Brinkgreve himself had recently selected. Unfortunately, several dropping attempts failed. Finally, on the night of 24/25 February, BI agent P. (Pieter) Bouman was parachuted in carrying a considerable amount of weapons and supplies, and over *f* 200,000 in cash. BI was thankful for the reception of this agent by Brinkgreve: Bouman would collect useful intelligence for the Allies until being overrun several months later.[109]

In the meantime, Brinkgreve's relationship with resistance commander Lancker had not improved. Their bickering came to a sudden end on 11 February 1945. That day, Lancker was killed in a fight with the SD. The resistance commandant was arrested in his headquarters in the hamlet of Hoge Hexel. He managed to pull a hidden gun from his jacket and shoot two men before he himself was

One of the signal lamps used by the reception committee on drop zone Willow. (Private collection)

A basket with a parachute that came down on drop zone Willow in February 1945. (Private collection)

hit. Subsequently, Lancker shot himself in the head; he would not let them take him alive.[110] That month, the Overijssel resistance would lose many other men, including BI agent Buunk, due to an intensive German counter-resistance offensive.[111]

After Lancker's death, resistance man H. (Herman) Doppen took over command of the BS in the Salland region of Overijssel. The collaboration between the Salland BS and provincial BS headquarters would improve in the last months of the war.[112] Meanwhile, Major Brinkgreve had moved his headquarters from Okkenbroek to the city of Enschede. He soon concluded, however, that it was too difficult for him to move about freely in the city. After learning that his radio operator Sjoerdsma had left the safe house in nearby Losser, the Jedburgh officer moved to the farm with a courier.[113]

Not long after, in the evening of 5 March 1945, a Dutch Landwachter, together with a Dutch SS member, appeared at Brinkgreve's hideout. Unfortunately, he was discovered quickly. After assaulting one of the men with his bare hands, thus allowing other resistance members to escape, Brinkgreve tried to flee.[114] Tragically, he was then shot in the head from close range. The critically wounded Jedburgh major died soon after.

The farm in Losser where Major Brinkgreve died on 5 March 1945. In March 2013 a monument was unveiled at this location. (Historische Kring Losser)

At that time, Brinkgreve's original radio operator, Sergeant Austin, was still incarcerated in the House of Detention in Zwolle. German interrogation reports prove that Austin never once gave up his real name: his captors only knew him as 'Bunny Wyatt'.[115] Apparently, the Germans did somehow link Austin to Brinkgreve; after the event in Losser, the Jedburgh sergeant was asked to identify a man in a photo – his former Jedburgh team commander – which he refused. Early in April 1945, about a week before the liberation of Zwolle, the commander of the prison was ordered to select a number of prisoners, or Todeskandidaten, to be shot as a reprisal for a recent act of sabotage. Early in the morning of 4 April 1945, Austin and five other prisoners, including BI agent Buunk, were executed on the IJssel Dike in the nearby city of Hattem.[116] Austin's death marked the end of the long deployment of team Dudley.

The headstone of Sergeant Austin, Hattem General Cemetery. (Private collection)

Commentary

In the months between Operation Market Garden and March 1945, the front line in the Netherlands barely moved. Though the southern provinces of the Netherlands were almost completely liberated, German offensive operations, including the Battle of the Bulge, severely disrupted Allied liberation plans. As Montgomery had abandoned his plan of advancing north beyond Arnhem at the end of 1944, the liberation of the north of the Netherlands was significantly delayed – a delay which team Dudley experienced at first hand.

Instead of being overrun in a matter of weeks, Dudley operated almost seven months behind enemy lines. In the early phase of the mission, Major Brinkgreve spent much time unifying the disharmonious Overijssel resistance. At the same time, the Jedburghs received a considerable amount of weapons and explosives from England. Large sums of money were parachuted, too, intended for the many people in hiding, including railway strikers.

When it became clear that the Allies would not reach the province soon, team Dudley and the Jedburghs focused on establishing an extensive intelligence network in the east of the Netherlands. The high concentration of German military units and security forces hindered the Jedburghs and the resistance greatly. Team Dudley was constantly forced to move its headquarters, and continuous German counter-resistance operations caused many casualties. In the autumn of 1944, Major Brinkgreve restricted sabotage operations and the harassment of the German forces by the Overijssel resistance, for the time being.

After Major Olmsted's evacuation and Sergeant Austin's arrest in November 1944, Brinkgreve found himself temporarily isolated. However, from January 1945 until his death in March 1945, Brinkgreve was able to resume his Jedburgh assignments. Now assisted by a new radio operator and a sergeant instructor, the Dutch officer was able to strengthen the armed resistance, especially in the Twente region of the province. It was (partly) thanks to team Dudley that the Overijssel BS could play a useful role during the liberation of the province in April 1945 (see p. 172).

Last of all, it should be noted that it had not been SFHQ's intention to keep team Dudley behind enemy lines for such a long period. Due to the failure of Operation Market Garden and the delay of the liberation of the northern Netherlands, the Jedburghs were accidentally able to provide long term, and thereby truly effective, assistance to the resistance. The impressive accomplishments of team Dudley, however, did cost the lives of two of its three original members.

Jedburgh team Stanley II's training mission with the ST and BT units in the liberated south was exceptional. Indeed, the Jedburgh team was not deployed behind enemy lines but in friendly territory. This team's activities also proved valuable: within a short time frame, the Jedburghs transformed former resistance groups into light infantry units and organised their deployment along the Waal. The British and Canadian units stationed in the region gratefully absorbed these Dutch units into their long and undermanned front line.

Moreover, Captains Bestebreurtje and Vickery were in constant contact with occupied regions across the river, thereby collecting useful intelligence. In addition, the Jedburghs participated in organising crossings whereby people were smuggled to and from occupied territory. The same clandestine routes were also used to deliver much-needed weapons and supplies to resistance groups across the Waal.

THE FINAL MISSIONS

New (special) operations in the Netherlands

On 23 March 1945, Field Marshal Montgomery finally launched Operation Plunder, his assault on the Rhine. In the meantime, the Allies had already crossed the river elsewhere: a bridge over the Rhine had been captured by General Patton at Remagen. Montgomery's bridgehead, though, remained the point of main Allied effort. Montgomery's crossing of the Rhine went well: five days after the start of Operation Plunder, the field marshal declared that the battle of the Rhine was won.[1] The long-awaited Allied advance towards Germany's industrial heartlands could then commence.

This final thrust into Germany also directly affected the still-occupied regions of the Netherlands: at the end of March, the First Canadian Army was ordered to protect the eastern Allied flank of the main Allied advance and to 'open up the supply route to the north through Arnhem, and to operate to clear north-east Holland, the coastal belt eastwards to the Elbe [River], and West Holland'.[2] This logistical artery on the left flank of the Allies was to nourish the main Allied offensive towards the east. Concretely, it meant that the Canadians had to establish a supply line which would pass the Rhine at Arnhem and, subsequently, the IJssel to the latitude of Zutphen.

The First Canadian Army's commander, Lieutenant General Crerar, planned to accomplish this task from two directions.[3]

The II Canadian Corps was to enter the Achterhoek region (in the province of Gelderland) and advance towards Twente in southern Overijssel. It then had to move westwards and, upon arrival in Deventer, cross the IJssel and clear the area east of the city of Apeldoorn. Finally, II Canadian Corps had to liberate the northern provinces of the Netherlands. Simultaneously, the I Canadian Corps was to conquer the Over-Betuwe ('the Island'), cross the Rhine, and, subsequently, enter the Veluwe from the south.[4]

Generally speaking, these Allied offensives went according to plan. While I Canadian Corps cleared the Over-Betuwe, the other corps liberated the south-eastern part of Gelderland and thereafter the Twente region of Overijssel.

Lieutenant General Crerar was
the commander of the First
Canadian Army. (Library and
Archives Canada)

The eastern part of the Achterhoek and Twente were liberated by units of the
XXX British Corps. The British forces advanced from Ruurlo to Lochem, east
of Zutphen, without facing much German resistance. On 1 April 1945, they
reached the city of Enschede in Twente. Two days later, the city of Hengelo was
conquered. Hereafter, the Canadian forces took over the British positions in the
front line.

In Twente, as well as in other parts of Overijssel, the resistance went into
action, smoothing the way for the Allied advance.[5] From the last week of March
1945, the Overijssel resistance started a sabotage campaign, hindering German
troop movements and supply transports. The BS also attacked isolated enemy
positions, taking many prisoners in the process. Moreover, the resistance was
able to provide the Canadians with valuable intelligence about the strength and
locations of the enemy.[6]

The resistance in the Salland area of the province also assisted the Allied
advance. A Canadian battalion involved in the speedy liberation of the city
of Deventer, for instance, declared that it was grateful to be backed by the

Canadian infantry marching towards Deventer, 9 April 1945. (Library and Archives Canada)

Members of the resistance of Twente pose shortly after the liberation. (C. B. Cornelissen)

'extremely well organised Dutch Underground'.[7] Unfortunately, the Deventer BS could not prevent the bridges over the IJssel from being destroyed by the retreating Germans.

Already in February 1945, new plans for the deployment of SAS and Jedburgh teams were developed in England. These special forces teams were to further accelerate the Allied advance through the middle and northern Netherlands. At the end of March 1945, SAS Brigade commander Brigadier J. M. (Jim) Calvert had a meeting with Lieutenant General Crerar to discuss how his troops could assist the progress of the Canadian ground forces in the Netherlands.[8] Calvert explained that the SAS would be able to cause confusion behind enemy lines, prevent the destruction of vital bridges and airfields by the Germans, and raise the Dutch resistance.

Calvert's proposals were well received by Crerar. Three separate SAS operations were eventually developed: Keystone, Amherst, and Larkswood.[9] Operation Keystone would be launched in the Veluwe area and Operation Amherst in the province of Drenthe. The third operation, Larkswood, would involve Belgian SAS units equipped with armoured jeeps; these forces were to infiltrate the north of the Netherlands. In the airborne operations Keystone and Amherst, Jedburgh teams were incorporated, as well.

Operation Keystone

After the liberation of Deventer, Lieutenant General Crerar was eager to start two new sub-operations that were to accomplish his main goal: creating a supply route via Arnhem and Zutphen. The first offensive, Operation Anger, was to get the forces of the I Canadian Corps, who had seized the Over-Betuwe without much difficulty, to the opposite bank of the Rhine.[10] The second offensive, Operation Cannonshot, involved the 1st Canadian Infantry Division, which was to move from an area south of Deventer to the opposite bank of the IJssel and, thereafter, head towards Apeldoorn. This city was an important communication centre in the Netherlands, connected by main roads and railways with Amersfoort, Arnhem, Zutphen, and Deventer.[11] The other three divisions of the II Canadian Corps were to continue their advance towards the most northern provinces of the nation.[12]

The main goal of SAS Operation Keystone was to accelerate the Canadians' advance across the Veluwe, a forested stretch of land running approximately from Arnhem to Zwolle. The Apeldoorn Canal, of some fifty kilometres' length, that ran across the Veluwe parallel to the IJssel – from Dieren to Hattem – could, however, turn into an obstacle for the Canadian ground forces. A section of the SAS and two Jedburgh teams were subsequently made responsible for the preservation of river and canal bridges, as well as widespread harassing of German troops in and around Apeldoorn. In addition, they were to provide guides and the passing of intelligence for the use of advancing Allied troops. Finally, the special forces were to prevent the destruction or removal of transport (either road, water, rail) vehicles.[13]

Approximately seventy men of the 2nd SAS Regiment were to execute Operation Keystone. As soon as the Canadians crossed the IJssel, the SAS would go into action. The first SAS group ('A') would be parachuted north of Apeldoorn, and the second group ('B') south of the city. Several special armoured jeeps would be dropped with them as well. The third group ('C') was to advance over the ground with jeeps – out of the Arnhem bridgehead – and make contact with groups A and B as quickly as possible.[14]

Two Jedburgh teams with attached SAS personnel were to infiltrate the area a few days ahead of the start of Operation Keystone.[15] The Jedburgh groups, code-named Gambling and Dicing, were ordered to reconnoitre the area, report on enemy units, and organise the reception of Keystone parties A and B. The teams were also tasked to select an appropriate assembly point for SAS party C. Following the arrival of the Keystone units, team Gambling would liaise with group A north of Apeldoorn, while team Dicing contacted party B to the south.[16] Subsequently, the teams would were to ensure coordination between the local resistance and the Keystone parties while the Veluwe was being liberated by Canadian ground forces.

The armed resistance in the Veluwe

After the failure of Operation Market Garden, the Veluwe resistance had gone through very difficult times. The Germans were well aware that many Dutch *onderduikers* ('people in hiding'), resistance fighters, and British parachutists who had failed to reach Allied lines found refuge in the forested Veluwe area. This was met by increasing German efforts to tackle underground activity. The many sabotage acts of September also led to an increase in German reprisals in the autumn of 1944. One of the most horrible acts of vengeance enacted by the Germans in the Netherlands took place in the Veluwe village of Putten on 1 October 1944. As a result of a resistance attack that killed a German officer and wounded another, 660 men and boys were deported to concentration camps, while the village was burnt to the ground.[17]

During the summer and autumn of 1944, BBO had sent several agents to the Veluwe to support the resistance. These missions were severely hindered by German counter-resistance operations. BBO agent J. (Joop) Luykenaar, parachuted near the village of Voorthuizen in late August 1944, caught the Germans' attention soon after his arrival. He was eventually forced to leave the area. Two other BBO agents, S. (Seerp) Postma and radio operator G. H. (Gerrit) Reisiger, were sent to Apeldoorn in early October 1944.[18] Before long, another BBO agent, M. (Maarten) Cieremans, began working from the Veluwe as well.[19]

In October 1944, more agents became operational in the area. Lieutenant Du Bois, who before had been deployed around Eindhoven with Jedburgh team Daniel II, was dropped near the town of Garderen on the night of 16/17 October. Assisted by an SAS radio operator, the Belgian R. (Raymond) Holvoet, Du Bois was to evacuate the airbornes that had stayed behind after Market Garden. Unfortunately, this operation failed the following month (see p. 154). Many involved were eventually arrested. Radio operator Holvoet had already been captured in late October 1944.[20]

Agents Postma and Reisiger found themselves in a perilous situation when their resistance meeting was abruptly ended by a German raid. Many were arrested but both agents managed to escape and subsequently left the Veluwe. However, both agents were captured soon after.[21]

Lieutenant Du Bois was parachuted above the Veluwe in mid-October 1944, with a Belgian radio operator named Raymond Holvoet. (Archive De Roever)

Du Bois's radio operator
from the SAS, the Belgian
Raymond Holvoet.
(Archive De Roever)

According to Arnhem KP commander Kruyff, who later was to lead all resistance in the Veluwe, November 1944 was a 'disastrous month'.[22] Halfway through the month, B. (Berend) Dijkman, resistance commander of a large section of the Veluwe, was arrested.[23]

BBO agent Postma was imprisoned in the Willem III barracks in Apeldoorn with a large number of resistance members facing execution. National sabotage commander and LKP man J. A. (Johannes) van Bijnen subsequently planned to raid the prison. While personally scouting the area, Van Bijnen was discovered by the Germans and shot, dying from his injuries several days later. Postma, along with twelve other resistance members, was executed without trial.[24] Fellow BBO agent Cieremans only just escaped the Germans on several occasions. He relocated to the province of Utrecht in late 1944.[25]

Berend Dijkman was a key figure within the Veluwe resistance until his arrest. (Personal archive)

According to Kruyff, the Veluwe resistance was forced to scale down its activities at the end of 1944 and lay low until 'better times'.[26] In December 1944, Lieutenant Du Bois was trapped by a Dutch traitor. After Pegasus II, he had been ordered to stay active behind enemy lines and assist and train the Veluwe resistance. With Du Bois's arrest, the resistance lost another important asset. Fortunately, the Belgian SAS team Fabian, led by Lieutenant Kirschen, remained active. These parachutists had worked in the Veluwe from September 1944 onwards, occupied mainly with collecting intelligence. (see p. 46). However, early in 1945 the team was ordered to end the mission and cross the lines into liberated territory.[27]

The Veluwe BS resumed a great deal of its activities in the early months of 1945, focusing on sabotaging German communication lines and the establishment of an extensive intelligence network. On the night of 2/3 March 1945, two new

BBO agents arrived: R. L. (Reindert) Bangma and J. L. (Jan) van der Weijden. They were parachuted near the town of Lunteren to arm and organise the local resistance. Several days later, the SS and police commander for the Netherlands, Rauter, was injured in an attack by the resistance near Woeste Hoeve, a small village in the county of Apeldoorn. As a reprisal, 117 prisoners were executed on 8 March – among them Lieutenant Du Bois.

Despite increased German activity, Van der Weijden was able to keep operating in the area. He relocated to the village of Barneveld and directed the reception committee that would later receive Jedburgh team Gambling.[28]

Rauter's bullet-riddled car after the attack at Woeste Hoeve. This act of resistance led to heavy German reprisals in the Netherlands. (Personal archive)

The execution monument at the
Woeste Hoeve. (Personal archive)

Team Gambling in action

Team Gambling was a combined Jedburgh/SAS team that was specially formed
for Operation Keystone. Its Jedburgh members were British Major A. H. (Arthur)
Clutton, British radio operator J. S. S. (James) Menzies, and Dutch commando
Martin Knottenbelt. He had been part of Jedburgh team Claude during
Operation Market Garden and was now temporarily promoted to captain.[29]

Major Clutton was born on 5 August 1898 and was one of the older Jedburgh
officers. He served with the Royal Field Artillery during the First World War;
between the wars he owned a fruit farm in South Africa.[30] In August of 1944,
Clutton was deployed as commander of Jedburgh team Julian in France.

Sergeant Menzies was born on 1 June 1919 and was originally enlisted with
the British Royal Corps of Signals. In April 1941, SOE sent him on a mission to
Gibraltar.[31] From August 1944 on, Menzies served as Clutton's radio operator.

The other half of team Gambling was made up by the following SAS members:
British Captain P. N. Stuart, Dutch Lieutenant J. A. (Johan) de Stoppelaar
Blijdestein, and British radio telegraphist Sergeant F. (Frank) Herring-Sweet. De

Major Clutton of
Jedburgh team Gambling.
(The National Archives)

Sergeant Menzies was team
Gambling's radio operator.
(The National Archives)

Stoppelaar Blijdestein was part of a small detachment of Dutchmen that been seconded to the SAS Brigade.[32]

On Tuesday, 3 April 1945, teams Gambling and Dicing were notified that they would be parachuted over the Netherlands that night: all members would be wearing their military uniforms during the drop but would also take civilian clothes with them. In addition, all Jedburghs were issued *f* 5,000 as operational money. Interestingly, the Dutch officers were provided a cover by SFHQ: if taken prisoner, they would pose as a British officer, for which they were issued forged identity tags. There was a good chance that if Knottenbelt – as a Dutchman – was taken prisoner during the operation, he would be regarded by the Germans as an illegitimate fighter – and summarily executed.

Team Gambling was parachuted on 4 April 1945, at around 0045 hours near the town of Appel, east of the city of Amersfoort.[33] All members made a good landing, together with a large number of supply containers and packages.

After clearing the drop zone, the team moved to a nearby hideout of the Veluwe resistance. Before long, Veluwe BS commander Kruyff arrived to meet the parachutists. He informed them that he had approximately 300 armed men at his disposal, but that these had had no military training. Kruyff also informed team Gambling that he operated a reliable telephone network, including a direct line to the First Canadian Army's headquarters.[34] The BS commander estimated the number of Germans in the surroundings of the Apeldoorn Channel to be around 4,000. This information was quickly relayed to SFHQ via one of the team's wireless sets.

Team Gambling also reported to headquarters that, due to the high concentration of German troops in the area, it was 'almost impossible' to move around in uniform. Later that day, the Jedburghs were informed by SFHQ that team Dicing, unfortunately, had not been able to leave the aircraft the previous night. Kruyff soon found out what had happened: the Germans had occupied Dicing's drop zone at the very last moment, forcing the reception committee to leave the area. Headquarters subsequently requested team Gambling to select a new terrain on which team Dicing could be parachuted.

Kruyff, accompanied by Captain Stuart and Lieutenant De Stoppelaar Blijdestein, left for Apeldoorn on bicycle – wearing civilian clothes – to reconnoitre the area and look for a drop zone for the Keystone forces in the vicinity of the Apeldoorn Canal. Before long, contact was lost with the three men. At night, the team learned that Captain Stuart and his two companions had been stopped by the Germans and their bicycles confiscated. De Stoppelaar Blijdestein reached a safe address in the city of Apeldoorn later that day but did not know what had happened to the others.

<u>GUEUZE 2</u> (Vervolg)

```
     3 Carbine magazine pouches
     3 Mess Tins
     4 Lyons 48 hr rations
     3 prs binoculars
 2,500 cigarettes
    94 lbs Mixed Food and Comforts
    70 Tins Corned Beef
     6 Tins Margarine
     5 Tins Biscuits and Chocolate
    10 Tins Tobacco
     1 Microprint, plan "YEALM"            )
     1 Silk N/YEALM                        )%
    16 Crystals plan YEALM                 )
       Instructional microprints, plan "SALCOMBE")
     4 Silks plan "SALCOMBE"               )  For AAT
    18 Crystals plan "SALCOMBE"            )
     4 Codebooks                           )
     1 Silk Substitution square            )

     4 Codebooks                           )  For FRED
     1 Silk Substitution square            )

     1 Eureka
     2 Jedburgh W/T Sets in webbing equipment

     3 Face Veils
     3 Smocks, Denison
     3 Belts, web
     3 Braces, web (1 shoulder Holster)
     3 Haversacks, web
     3 Pouches, web, for compass
     3 Rolls toilet paper
     3 First Aid Kits, pocket
     3 Pullovers, Ribbed, U.S.A.
     3 Leg Bags (S.O.E. Type)
     9 prs Army Socks (Grey woollen)
     3 flasks, 8 oz. of Brandy
     3 Jackets, Parachutist
     3 Spare batteries
     6 Field dressings
     3 Housewives
     3 Gas Capes
     6 Candles
     3 Sets Oil and flannellette
     3 Torches, U.S.A. Type
    12 Batteries for above
     6 Pencils, chinagraph
     3 pads, army field message AB 153
     9 'B' Capsules
     1 W/T Set B Mk II No. 44530
     1 Accumulator 6 volt/40 uncharged
     1 Hydrometer
```

Team Gambling was parachuted behind German lines with a large amount of supplies. Some of the material is listed here. (Personal archive)

Members of the Dutch resistance wore orange bracelets. The one shown here belonged to a member of the Apeldoorn BS. (Private collection)

Since it was unknown whether Stuart and Kruyff had been detained, combined with the unwillingness of the owners of the house (where the Jedburghs were staying) to allow wireless communication, the team moved to a deserted factory in nearby Barneveld. To their luck, contact with Captain Stuart and Kruyff was restored the next day.[35]

On Thursday, 5 April, resistance leader Kruyff reported to the Jedburghs that he had not yet been able to find a suitable drop zone for the SAS groups near the Apeldoorn Canal. De Stoppelaar Blijdestein was more successful; he had found a suitable terrain, east of Uddel, about ten kilometres from Apeldoorn. This drop zone was code-named Fox. A bit later, team Gambling informed SFHQ of a second site: this drop zone was located near the village of Putten, approximately thirty kilometres from Apeldoorn. This drop zone was given the code name Napier. Apparently, safe drop zones located nearer to the Apeldoorn Canal were not readily available at that time.

That day, the Jedburghs reported to England that all large bridges in and near Apeldoorn had been rigged with explosives by the Germans. Smaller bridges, however, were left untouched. SFHQ, in turn, informed the Jedburghs the following day that supplies for the resistance would be dropped over the upcoming nights. Unfortunately, headquarters deemed drop zone Napier too far away from the Apeldoorn Canal; the SAS parties would not be able to reach the bridges fast enough. A 'blind' drop – thus one without a reception committee – near the bridges was subsequently proposed by SFHQ. Gambling responded by noting that a drop at Fox was a better option, as this terrain was also suitable for receiving jeeps.

Shortly after, headquarters in England notified team Gambling that Napier had been found suitable for Operation Keystone after all. According to the original plan, Operation Keystone was to start on the night of 10/11 April or the night thereafter. Headquarters in England also informed team Gambling that additional SAS forces were standing by to assist them reconnoitring the area. Gambling replied that it did not need any reinforcements; due to the dangerous situation, it was already nearly impossible to operate in the area. Thankfully, the SAS agreed to this. SFHQ subsequently abandoned the plan to deploy team Dicing as part of Operation Keystone. Another assignment would soon follow, though, for this Jedburgh group.

In the afternoon of Sunday 8 April, Captain Knottenbelt left Barneveld to contact resistance leader Kruyff in Apeldoorn. From this point onwards, Clutton and Knottenbelt operated in separate areas, maintaining contact via couriers and telephone. That evening, the Dutch commando spoke on the telephone with a senior intelligence officer of the I Canadian Corps and elaborated on the situation in the area. Knottenbelt stressed that the Germans were expecting an Allied attack from the south and had mined all bridges on that side of the city. Those located north of Apeldoorn were left untouched and, importantly, only loosely guarded by the enemy.

Around that time, the number of Germans south of the city was estimated at 12,000, while only some 2,000 were positioned north of Apeldoorn.[36] This made team Gambling decide to focus on the preservation of the bridges over the Apeldoorn Canal north of the city, more specifically, the bridges in the triangle of the villages of Epe, Oene, and Heerde. SFHQ concurred with this plan.

The next day, whilst contacting as many resistance groups as possible, team Gambling continued their explorations of the area. On Tuesday, 10 April, Major Clutton also left Barneveld for Apeldoorn to contact BS commander Kruyff. Meanwhile, Captain Knottenbelt liaised with the resistance in Heerde to make plans for the preservation of the bridges in that area. That evening, Knottenbelt went out looking for a suitable drop zone for SAS forces in Heerde's vicinity. An attractive heathland that he found west of the nearby village of Epe was unfortunately occupied by the Germans. Knottenbelt eventually found another field close to Epe, which he code-named Renault.

Sergeant Menzies, the Jedburgh team's radio operator, had now almost spent a week in Barneveld. To reduce the risk of him being located by Germans with radio direction-finding equipment, he moved to a safe house in Apeldoorn the next day.

On Wednesday, 11 April, the 1st Canadian Infantry Division launched Operation Cannonshot – the crossing of the IJssel – near the village of Gorssel, just south

Men from the 1st Canadian Infantry Division cross the IJssel River during Operation Cannonshot, 11 April 1945. (Library and Archives Canada)

of Deventer. It would take two days before the entire division had reached the opposite side of the IJssel.

On Wednesday afternoon, SFHQ informed the Jedburghs that the SAS intended to parachute their Keystone units over Fox and Napier that night. Headquarters also informed the Jedburghs that the SAS planned to deploy two extra groups. These would probably be dropped blind on two predetermined fields south of Apeldoorn.

However, team Gambling replied that they considered any SAS operation in the areas south of the city 'suicidal'. As team Gambling's reply was sent late in the day, the Jedburghs asked BS commander Kruyff to arrange for resistance parties to be sent to the drop zones in order to render all possible assistance, should the SAS groups arrive. Luckily, team Gambling's reaction was received in good time and taken seriously at the SAS headquarters: no men were parachuted south of Apeldoorn during Operation Keystone.

Upon hearing that Operation Keystone would commence the next day, Captain Knottenbelt, then located in Heerde, immediately ordered the resistance to focus on the preservation of four bridges: the Olst Bridge, also known as the Klement Bridge, and three smaller bridges north of Apeldoorn.[37] The Dutch officer planned to have thirty men positioned at the Klement Bridge – capable of taking forty tons – and fifteen BS forces at each of the other bridges. Knottenbelt also assigned a commander to each bridge, who all received strict orders to keep the BS men concealed and quiet in their positions until either the SAS or the Canadian ground forces arrived. At this time, the bridges were still not prepared for demolition and were only lightly guarded by the Germans.

On Tuesday night and into the early morning of Wednesday, an SAS party of seventeen men was parachuted on drop zone Napier. Captain Stuart was present on the ground, accompanied by a Dutch reception committee. The drop was successful, and the parachutists were quickly moved to a nearby sheep shed. The SAS group was led by British Captain R. J. (Richard) Holland and British Lieutenant J. (John) Wardley. The group also included two Dutchmen, Sergeants van Beek and Kuypers. Having landed near the village of Putten, the group was now some thirty kilometres removed from the Apeldoorn Canal. As it was impossible to reach the bridge before daylight, the SAS party decided to spend the rest of the night in their hideout.

In the meantime, the planned infiltration of the second SAS group on drop zone Fox, which was located much closer to the Apeldoorn Canal, had unfortunately failed. Shortly before the expected arrival of the parachutists, an unknown plane dropped a flare over the drop zone, which resulted in an exchange of fire between German soldiers and the resistance. The reception committee then wisely left. The resistance groups at the bridges north of Apeldoorn had stayed in place until about 0500 hours. Captain Knottenbelt had been at the Klement Bridge throughout the night. They had great luck escaping detection by German patrols several times.[38] As neither the SAS nor the Canadians put in an appearance, the men scattered to nearby farms, as was foreseen in orders for this eventuality.

That same night, SFHQ had instructed Jedburgh team Gambling to bring the Veluwe BS into overt action soonest after daylight.[39] The Canadian advance was to be supported in every possible way, such as harassing attacks, sabotage of communication lines, occupying and defending bridges, the provision of guides, the prevention of enemy demolitions (particularly on roads) and, finally, the provision of information as to enemy movements and dispositions. SFHQ was ambitious and appeared convinced that the Canadian ground forces would enter the area the following day.

Resistance commander Kruyff, however, was very sceptical and unwilling to commit his forces to any widespread offensive action – at least not until the Canadians had actually reached the Apeldoorn Canal. His untrained resistance men were, after all, surrounded by thousands of German forces. Team Gambling wholeheartedly agreed with the resistance commander. Kruyff subsequently ordered his men to limit their offensive operations to attacks on isolated German troops and vehicles in the immediate vicinity of the canal.[40]

Kruyff's assessment of the situation turned out to be excellent, as the first Canadians would not reach the Apeldoorn Canal until the early morning of 14 April. The Allied ground forces would only reach the opposite banks several days later. Kruyff had, most probably, prevented a massacre of the Veluwe resistance.

Thursday morning, 12 April, broke with no news of the arrival of the Canadian ground forces nor of the jeeps of Keystone party 'C'. At about 1200 hours, Major Clutton spoke to an intelligence officer of the First Canadian Army to find out when ground forces might be expected in the Epe–Oene area. A reply was promised in an hour's time. Eventually a message was received that the answer to his question would be sent by radio.

Team Gambling also contacted SFHQ and proposed to drop SAS forces on drop zones Renault and Napier that night. Captain Knottenbelt had, in the meantime, come to the conclusion that it was not desirable to have the BS forces occupying the same positions near the bridges for a second night. He sent orders by courier to the bridge commanders that they should not position their men around the bridges that night, but instead assemble them at specified collection points, some 500 meters away. There, the BS forces were to be held in readiness should any Allied forces appear. At 1600 hours that day, the Jedburghs received instructions from SFHQ to arrange the reception of an SAS group on drop zone Renault.[41]

Further to the south, Operation Anger had begun that day. Instead of crossing the Rhine, the British 49th Infantry Division had crossed another nearby water way, the IJssel at Westervoort, just east of Arnhem.

The British forces would liberate Arnhem in just several days.[42] Thereafter they moved northwards, in the direction of Apeldoorn. This meant that the Germans would soon be directly threatened from two sides: British forces coming in from the south, whilst the 1st Canadian Infantry Division was advancing towards Apeldoorn from the east.

That night, the reception of SAS forces on drop zone Renault could not be laid on. According to Captain Knottenbelt, the bombers carrying the forces were

British soldiers from the 49th Infantry Division get ready for Operation Anger, 12 April 1945. (National Liberation Museum Groesbeek)

heard overhead, but the presence of German forces near the location prevented the drop from taking place. To make matters worse, the BS commander at the Klement Bridge did not receive Knottenbelt's orders and took positions as previously. As Knottenbelt had feared, the resistance forces were detected and fired upon by a patrol of German parachutists in the early hours of Friday 13 April. The resisters that survived the initial assault were executed soon after; as a reprisal, several civilians were shot as well.[43] In total, twelve Dutchmen lost their lives at the Klement Bridge that morning.

Approximately thirty kilometres south-west, the Keystone party that had landed the day before near Putten had split into three groups to reconnoitre the area and harass the Germans. Team Gambling, tasked to ensure coordination between the local resistance and the Keystone forces, was, however, surprised by the attitude of the SAS men. According to the Jedburghs, the parachutists were acting as 'lone wolves' and did not seem to be interested at all in cooperating with the local resistance.[44] Several days later, SAS sapper J. W. (Jack) Keeble was accidently shot during a firefight with the Dutch resistance, killing one BS man as well.[45]

On Friday 13 April, the Canadians reached the village of Teuge, just six kilometres east of Apeldoorn. Major Clutton soon established telephone contact

The monument at the Klement Bridge, recent photograph. On 13 April 1945, several members of the resistance and civilians were executed at this location by the Germans. The wall behind the cross still shows the bullet holes. (P. Reinders)

with headquarters of the 1st Canadian Infantry Brigade.[46] The Jedburgh officer informed the Canadians that all bridges were still intact and asked when ground forces could be expected in the Epe–Oene area, where about eighty BS forces were still covering the canal bridges. Clutton stressed that, up to that moment, the numbers of enemy forces near the bridges were still relatively small, and that these bridges were not mined. Speed was of the essence, though, as the number of Germans in the area was increasing.

Unfortunately, the Canadians replied to Clutton that they were not (yet) willing to advance that far north. In spite of the Jedburghs' important information, the ground forces held on to their original (frontal) attack plan to enter Apeldoorn from the east. They rather preferred that the resistance would 'do what they could' to prevent the Apeldoornse Bridge, in the centre of Apeldoorn, and the Broeks Bridge, located in the north of the city, from being destroyed. The Canadian ground forces expected to reach the city that afternoon.[47]

However, the Germans were able to repulse the first Canadian attack on the Apeldoorn Canal that day. Surprisingly, the Canadians responded by sending one brigade to the south.[48] This decision was contrary to Jedburgh team Gambling's

The Apeldoornse Bridge in the centre of Apeldoorn. This photograph dates from the 1930s. (Stichting Apeldoorns Kanaal)

advice, which had repeatedly stated that the ground forces should head north. Eventually, this Canadian brigade reached the town of Dieren, approximately fifteen kilometres north-east of Arnhem, on 16 April, where it liaised with units of the British 49th Infantry Division that had just advanced from Arnhem. It must be mentioned that team Gambling had 'no doubt' that, if the Canadians had moved north on Friday afternoon, the city would have been captured that night.[49]

Following the contact with the Canadian brigade, Major Clutton held a meeting with BS commander Kruyff that same day. The situation was quite difficult in Apeldoorn, as all civilians seen in the vicinity of the canal were certain to be seized by the Germans and forced to erect fortifications. After careful deliberation, Kruyff agreed to the Canadian proposal to focus on the Apeldoornse Bridge and the Broeks Bridge.

The resistance commander subsequently developed a plan via telephone with the commanding officer of the Royal Canadian Regiment: if there appeared to be any chance, the resistance would rush to the bridges in a synchronised attack with Canadian ground forces;[50] the BS would come into action when the first gun was fired by the Canadians.

However, this meant that the bridges in the Epe–Oene area had to be abandoned by the resistance. Not surprisingly, all bridges in that area were blown up by the Germans after the resistance left the area.

The remnants of the Klement Bridge. (Stichting Apeldoorns Kanaal)

From 13 April onwards, Captain Knottenbelt was having trouble keeping the resistance groups intact. The BS men were very disappointed about the course of events, in particular the failure of their plan to preserve the bridges. Some small resistance parties were successfully sent east by Knottenbelt to contact the Canadians and provide them with intelligence. Around that time, the Dutch officer also carried out several ambushes on German soldiers with the local resistance. On the morning of 17 April, Knottenbelt would cross the lines himself.

In the night of Friday to Saturday, Canadian forces finally rushed towards the Apeldoornse bridge.[51] The Apeldoorn BS forces had positioned themselves, as coordinated with the Canadians, at the western side of the canal, ready to eliminate the German *Sprengkommando*.[52] Unfortunately, the two Canadian tanks leading the attack were disabled and the attempt had to be abandoned.[53] Meanwhile, another Canadian unit had tried to conquer the Broeks bridge. Just before they reached it, the Germans blew up the bridge.[54] Thereafter, the Canadian forces retreated to their old positions. Now that the Broeks Bridge was blown, only the Apeldoornse Bridge and a small bridge, located 400 metres to the south, remained intact.

After two failed crossing attempts, Brigadier J. D. B. (Desmond) Smith, commander of the 1st Canadian Infantry Brigade, ordered his forces to halt the attack for the time being. At 2300 hours a new attack commenced. The 48th Highlanders then reached the canal in the neighbourhood of Zevenhuizen, in the north-east of Apeldoorn.[55] Simultaneously, another Canadian formation advanced towards the two bridges in the city centre. Unfortunately, this attack was repulsed by the Germans.[56] The bridges over the Apeldoorn Canal remained in German hands for now.

On Sunday 15 April the jeep-borne SAS group 'C' from the original Keystone plan left the newly established bridgehead in Arnhem in ten armoured jeeps, heading for their colleagues who had been parachuted over the Veluwe several days before.[57] The group was commanded by the British Major H. C. (Henry) Druce. Interestingly, this SAS officer was born in the Netherlands to a Dutch mother.[58] Druce's party consisted of thirty-two men, including one Dutchman, Sergeant G. W. E. (Gerardus) Nieuwhof.

On their way north, the group ambushed German forces between Otterlo and Hoenderloo, killing approximately twenty-five soldiers. The SAS party also captured several small groups of German soldiers. Overall, this jeep party would not achieve much. As a result of the orderly German withdrawal, the men were unable to really break through.[59] Moreover, the group was caught up by Canadian ground forces several times. Three days later, Druce would liaise with his SAS colleague Captain Holland, who was in the village of Barneveld at that time, approximately twenty-seven kilometres west of Apeldoorn. Meanwhile, west of Apeldoorn the SAS forces from the dropped Keystone party tried to hinder German troop transports by sabotaging several important roads and railways. At least one successful cut was made by them, blocking all railway traffic between Putten and Nijkerk.

The 1st Canadian Infantry Division prepared for the decisive attack on Apeldoorn on Monday 16 April. The Canadians did not know that, by now, most German forces had left the city; the enemy felt threatened from the south by the 5th Canadian Armoured Division (part of I Canadian Corps), which had advanced from Arnhem and headed north, soon passing Apeldoorn to the west.[60] However, the Germans did leave behind a *Sprengkommando* at the Apeldoornse Bridge.

The bold Apeldoorn BS commander, G. J. (Gijs) Numan, accompanied by resistance man A. (Albert) van der Scheur, decided to go to the Apeldoornse Bridge to try to convince the Germans to give up.[61]

After drinking some *Jenever* (Dutch gin) with the young soldiers, the BS men were able to make a strange kind of a deal: the soldiers would remove the explosives from the bridge, detonate these in the water, and then hand themselves

Gijs Numan was the commander of the BS forces in Apeldoorn. (G. Numan Jr)

over to the BS.[62] The explosion later damaged the bridge but it remained partly intact. Thereafter, the Germans laid down their weapons and surrendered to the Apeldoorn BS.

That Monday night, Numan and Van der Scheur crept over a lock just north of the Apeldoornse Bridge to establish contact with the nearby Royal Canadian Regiment.

The BS men informed its commanding officer, Lieutenant Colonel W. W. Reid, that the majority of German forces had already left the city and that the bridge was in the hands of the resistance.[63] This information was received with great scepticism by the Canadians; they were under the impression that Apeldoorn still held some 3,000 German soldiers.

In order to substantiate their claims, the resistance men offered to hand over the *Sprengkommando* that had surrendered to them. Lieutenant Colonel Reid agreed to this and sent three of his soldiers, together with Numan and Van

Post-war photograph of resistance men Numan and Van der Scheur, standing on the lock they used to reach the Canadians. (G. Numan Jr)

der Scheur, to the opposite side of the canal.[64] When they returned with their prisoners, the Canadians lost their suspicion to some extent. Subsequently, Numan and Van der Scheur returned to the Apeldoornse Bridge, now accompanied by approximately one hundred Canadian soldiers. Before long, more Canadian forces followed.

On the Tuesday morning of 17 April, the Apeldoorn BS commandant fired three flares: the signal for the main force that the coast was clear.[65] Except for some snipers, the Germans were indeed gone. The damaged Apeldoornse Bridge was swiftly reinforced by the Canadians with a Bailey bridge. Apeldoorn was subsequently liberated with hardly any further bloodshed.

Meanwhile, Captain Knottenbelt had reported to the Special Force Detachment at the headquarters of the First Canadian Army.[66] Major Clutton, who had just crossed the lines, was also there.

Around that time, Lieutenant De Stoppelaar Blijdestein and the local BS were liberating the village of Epe. They welcomed the Canadians there on Wednesday.[67] Operation Keystone's last action was carried out by Major Druce's

The damaged Apeldoornse Bridge was quickly reinforced by the Canadian forces with a Bailey bridge. (National Liberation Museum Groesbeek)

Above: A member of the resistance hitches a ride on a Canadian tank in Apeldoorn. (NIMH)

Left: Major Clutton (left) and Sergeant Menzies with a Dutch family who provided them shelter during their mission in the Netherlands. (S. Kippax)

and Captain Holland's SAS groups. Together with the local resistance, they attacked German positions in the city of Nijkerk and took approximately twenty Germans prisoners.[68]

Operation Amherst

When SAS commander Calvert was preparing Operation Amherst, he assumed that his forces would not be parachuted any sooner than 14 April 1945. However, the Canadian advance from Overijssel northward progressed faster than expected. Already on 5 April, the 4th Canadian Armoured Division reached the border of Amherst's planned landing area. Still, the Canadian 2nd Infantry Division and 3rd Infantry Division were some fifty kilometres removed from the western flank. It was then decided to speed up Operation Amherst and to let it commence oxn the night of 7/8 April.[69]

The intention of this SAS offensive was to cause as much confusion behind enemy lines as possible and to prevent the Germans from establishing a solid defence line, thereby paving the way for the Canadian ground forces. The SAS was also ordered to seize several important intersections, canal bridges, and airfields.[70] The French assumed the additional task of encouraging the local resistance groups to undertake action against their occupier.

Some 700 parachutists of the French branch of the SAS were to execute Amherst. These forces belonged to the 2e and 3e Régiment de Chasseurs Parachutistes (RCP) and were divided over fifty groups consisting of ten to fifteen men each. Eighteen armoured jeeps would be dropped with them. These vehicles, equipped with machine guns, provided the forces with greater mobility and were expected to have much effect on the enemy's morale.[71] Interestingly, this massive SAS deployment was rather unusual; it was the first time that these forces were deployed on such a great scale.[72]

The French would be parachuted 'blind' over the province of Drenthe, roughly along the axis of Zwolle–Groningen. To make the operation appear more extensive than it actually was, the forces would be parachuted over a large area, and their parachutes were to be left behind on the drop zone rather than burying them. To further deceive the enemy, puppets would be parachuted across Drenthe.[73] Moreover, Britain's BBC radio service would announce that Allied parachutists had been dropped all over the northern Netherlands. To reduce the chance that the Germans learned about the operation prematurely, the Drenthe resistance would only be informed about Amherst through a radio message after all parachutists had landed. This was also to prevent the resistance from going into action too soon.[74]

Brigadier Calvert was of the opinion that the operational area was totally inadequate for long-term guerrilla-type activities.[75] However, SAS headquarters assumed that the Germans would not be willing to put up much resistance, which would reduce the time span of the operation.[76] It was expected that the advancing Canadian ground forces would reach the French in about seventy-two hours. The enemy did have the 'Assener-Stellungen', though, a defence line in the north of the Netherlands past several canals, connecting the cities of Meppel, Assen, Groningen, and Delfzijl;[77] this was recognised as a potential obstacle for the Allied forces. Another barrier was the Oranje Canal, an approximately forty-eight-kilometre-long canal, running diagonally through a large part of the province and ultimately flowing into the Drentse Hoofdvaart Canal – a section of the Assener-Stellungen.

After the cancellation of the Veluwe mission (see p. 185), Jedburgh team Dicing was hastily assigned to Operation Amherst by SFHQ. However, after several briefings, the team concluded that a mission in Drenthe would be unfeasible. The Jedburghs felt that Amherst was certainly not a Jedburgh operation, and that the state of the resistance in the province did not allow the opportunities that Operation Keystone had.[78] Despite their reservations and low expectations, the members of team Dicing were of the opinion, though, that if anything was to be achieved with the resistance, Jedburgh forces were 'better equipped to do it than any officers the SAS could provide'.[79]

Team Dicing's mission would eventually be to liaise with the local resistance groups and to ensure that their services were made available to the SAS forces – very much similar to their cancelled Keystone mission. Moreover, the Jedburghs were to supply the Drenthe BS with arms that they would bring with them. An additional task consisted of sending BS couriers to meet advancing troops and provide their intelligence officers with tactical information. Interestingly, team Dicing was also ordered to make their 'W/T contact' available to the commander of the dropped SAS forces – should he wish to use it.[80]

Just as the SAS units, the Jedburghs would be parachuted blind, wearing military uniforms. Immediately after landing, team Dicing was to search for resistance groups in the direct surroundings. Contradictory to the setup of Operation Keystone, the Jedburghs were to be deployed simultaneously with the SAS forces. This meant that the team could not establish contact with the resistance ahead of the deployment of the SAS forces, as was the case in Operation Keystone. Team Dicing thus had little time to realise its difficult mission.

The armed resistance in Drenthe

The Drenthe resistance had to operate under extraordinarily difficult circumstances. This was mainly the result of the very many Dutch SD members, Landwachters, NSB followers, and other traitors that resided in the province.[81] Drenthe was at that time referred to by many Dutch as 'Little Germany'. Within the Drenthe resistance, the KP played the most important role. In late 1942 and early 1943, two KP squads were established in the cities of Meppel and Hoogeveen, both located in south Drenthe. Three more squads emerged during the spring of 1944; the groups of Noord-Drenthe, Kerkenveld, and Smilde.

At the outset, J. (Johannes) Post was the provincial KP leader. Under Post, the KP conducted many successful raids on coupon distribution offices. Post himself was arrested several times but managed to escape repeatedly. With the Germans on his tail he was forced to move to other parts of the Netherlands. While pursuing his underground activities, Post was eventually captured and executed in July 1944. After the establishment of the Dutch Interior Forces (BS) in September 1944, Dutch Reserve Captain, H. (Harm) Ketelaar was appointed regional commander for Drenthe.[82] Throughout 1944, Ketelaar would delegate many of his tasks to active resistance man K. (Kees) Veldman, a member of the KP Noord-Drenthe.[83] Towards the end of the war, Veldman assumed responsibility for most of the armed resistance groups in Drenthe.[84]

From the summer and autumn of 1944 on, the Allies sent weapons, supplies, special forces and agents to the province. The already mentioned SAS team Gobbo (see p. 149) was sent to Drenthe at the end of September 1944. A week later, two BI agents were parachuted: G. (Gerard) Kouwenhoven and C. H. (Cornelis) van Bemmel. Kouwenhoven moved to the city of Groningen (in the neighbouring province of the same name), while van Bemmel went to work in city of Assen, located in the north of Drenthe.[85]

As per team Gobbo's request, a four-men instructor team was dropped in Drenthe in the second week of October 1944. This team consisted of three Dutch commandos seconded to BBO and a Belgian SAS adjutant. These were Sergeant Major W. (Willem) van der Veer, Sergeants R. C. (Bob) Michels, N. J. (Niek) de Koning, and lastly Belgian Adjutant R. H. A. (Raymond) Groenewout.[86]

Michels left the province to join the resistance in Groningen, while De Koning and Groenewout became instructors for the resistance in the neighbouring province of Friesland. Van der Veer was the only one to remain almost permanently in Drenthe. De Koning would eventually return to Drenthe in the final months of the war.

Above: Sergeants Blatt (left) and De Koning were dropped into Drenthe by BBO. (Dutch Commando Museum)

Left: Willem van der Veer as a corporal in 1941. He was sent to Drenthe by BBO in October 1944. (Archive De Roever)

The Dutch commando Captain Ruysch
van Dugteren was added to team Dicing.
(Archive De Roever)

Team Gobbo was forced to leave Drenthe in October 1944, due to the failure
of Operation Market Garden and a raid by the Germans on their hideout.
Around that time, BBO instructor Van der Veer had to postpone his tasks due to
the dangerous situation and went into hiding for the time being.[87] The Drenthe
resistance also lay low in the final months of 1944, save a spectacular KP raid
on the Assen prison. Twenty-nine prisoners, among whom were many resistance
fighters, were freed. After this successful action, the Drenthe resistance cut down
its activities until the Allies resumed their advance in the Netherlands.[88]

Some weeks prior to the start of Operation Amherst, BI radio operator Van
Bemmel was discovered by the Germans and killed in the gunfight that followed.[89]
Subsequently, a series of arrests within the Drenthe resistance followed.[90] In
anticipation of the arrival of the Allies, BBO agent Van der Veer resumed his
instruction activities around February 1945, preparing the underground for the
arrival of the Allies.

Team Dicing in action

Originally, team Dicing was a combined Jedburgh/SAS team. During the planning
for Operation Amherst, the team's composition changed: its SAS members were

withdrawn, while Jedburgh Captain Bestebreurtje was added. Team Dicing consisted initially – apart from its SAS members – of two British Jedburghs and a Dutch commando, Captain C. J. L. (Carel) Ruysch van Dugteren. The British members were Major R. A. F. (Robert) Harcourt and Sergeant C. C. (Claude) Somers.

Captain Ruysch van Dugteren, originally a member of the Dutch commandos, was born on 2 August 1910. He fulfilled his compulsory military service in 1930 with the Dutch 14th Infantry Regiment.

Later, he migrated to South Africa and became a farmer in Transvaal. He arrived in England in April 1942 as a volunteer and quickly joined the Commandos. Right before Market Garden, Ruysch van Dugteren became one of Prince Bernhard's bodyguards. In late 1944, he started acting as supervisor

Major Harcourt of team Dicing. (The National Archives)

of the newly formed Dutch ST (see p. 162).[91] Around March 1945, Ruysch van Dugteren was seconded to BBO and subsequently attached to Jedburgh team Dicing, presumably at the request of Prince Bernhard.

Major Harcourt, born on 16 January, 1920, was originally part of the British Royal Armoured Corps and had served as a staff officer and signals specialist in Sicily in 1943.

He also spent some time with the SAS. After volunteering for the Jedburghs, Harcourt was sent to occupied France in August 1944. His drop was not a success as he broke both legs on landing.[92] Sergeant Somers, born in France on 21 October 1923, originally served with the RAF. Before his mission in Drenthe, he had been deployed as a Jedburgh radio operator in France in late September 1944.[93]

In the afternoon of Saturday 7 April 1945, team Dicing was instructed to prepare for their departure to the Netherlands. SFHQ provided the Jedburgh group with two radio transmitters and civilian clothing. Every member was issued ƒ 5,000 operational money; Captain Bestebreurtje, who had been added

French paratroopers shortly before their departure to the Netherlands. (Private collection)

to the team at the last moment, received ƒ 2,500.[94] The Dutch members of the team also received forged identity tags and a cover story: they would declare to be British officers in case they fell in German hands.

Team Dicing was assigned to a bomber that would transport one of the SAS groups to the Netherlands.

The airplane left England at 2000 hours. All forces inside were parachuted blindly near the village of Hooghalen at approximately 2130 hours. At the time of the drop, the weather conditions were exceptionally bad; it was extremely cloudy and windy, while thick fog covered the ground. To make matters worse, the jumpmaster on board 'did not know his job', which resulted in a very slow drop; the Jedburghs subsequently landed very far removed from each other.[95]

After landing, Major Harcourt tried to move to the predetermined meeting point but soon discovered that they were dropped at the wrong location. He did locate some of the team's supply containers. After having waited for his teammates in vain for some time, Harcourt headed south. Before long, he found Captain Bestebreurtje lying on the ground, unable to get up. His Dutch teammate turned out to have landed very badly, severely hurting his right ankle and knee. When Bestebreurtje had left the airplane, the rope of his leg bag swung around his neck. The Dutch captain later commented, 'The whole way down, I was trying to free my neck. I had only just succeeded in doing so when I slammed into the ground.'[96] Major Harcourt brought Bestebreurtje to some nearby woods and then left the area, looking for a better hiding place for his colleague.

That night, the majority of the French parachutists landed some two to five kilometres from the planned landing zones. Some groups even landed on German convoys and fell apart immediately.[97] Moreover, the armoured jeeps were not dropped at all – the short preparation time, the bad weather conditions, and the lack of guidance from the ground were mostly to blame.[98] Those SAS groups that were able to regroup after landing then set up ambushes and carried out small-scale sabotage actions immediately.[99]

In the early morning of Sunday 8 April, Major Harcourt stumbled upon many enemy patrols. Unfortunately, there appeared to be no farm or other building that Harcourt could get Bestebreurtje to before daylight. Upon his return, Harcourt moved the wounded Jedburgh captain to the densest part of the woods and covered as many traces of the containers as possible.

By now, Captain Bestebreurtje had realised that he could not participate in the mission. Harcourt reconnoitred the area again but kept happening upon enemy patrols. The British officer barely escaped detection on several occasions; a German soldier even passed within three yards of him in the woods. When Harcourt thought to have just avoided another enemy patrol, he was detected.

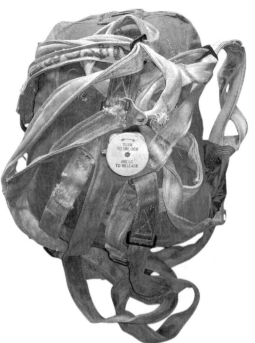

A parachute and leg bag left behind
in Drenthe after Operation Amherst.
(E. Zwiggelaar)

A slight skirmish and chase followed. The British Jedburgh major was eventually cornered and captured at about 1430 hours.

Captain Ruysch van Dugteren had landed the night before in an overgrown stretch of woods. Unfortunately, he had lost his leg bag when he left the airplane. After searching for his teammates for several hours, he left the area to try to establish contact with the local resistance. At around 0600 hours on Sunday he came into contact with T. (Teun) Leever, local gamekeeper and resistance leader in the village of Amen. Just before dawn, Leever brought the Dutch captain to a hiding place in some nearby woods. Leever was subsequently ordered to search for the other Jedburghs and the team's containers and baskets.

At around 1000 hours the resistance man returned to inform Ruysch van Dugteren that he had found Sergeant Somers. The Jedburgh operator was hiding in some bushes in a heathland several kilometres away.[100] Not able to find the collecting point, Somers decided to lay low during the night. Somers, too, lost his leg bag, which contained his radio transmitter.[101] There was a silver lining, though: Leever had located several of the Jedburghs' packages.

A while later, a group of approximately forty members of the Grüne Polizei entered the woods in which Captain Ruysch van Dugteren was hiding. By some miracle, they did not discover the Dutch commando. After the Germans had left, Ruysch van Dugteren ordered Leever to go and look for Major Harcourt, unaware of the fact that the British Jedburgh had already been arrested. As Captain Ruysch van Dugteren had no time to lose, he also instructed Leever to contact all local BS leaders as soon as possible.

The resistance fighter returned at approximately 1700 hours with bad news: some eighty Germans with search dogs were quickly approaching. Subsequently, Ruysch van Dugteren moved deeper into the woods while Leever circled the woods with a bitch in heat. When the German dogs reached the area, they were interested in anything but tracking a human being.[102] This act of Leever most likely saved the Dutch captain from being detected by the enemy.

Several hours later, Sergeant Somers and Captain Ruysch van Dugteren were finally reunited. Unfortunately, the packages that Leever had stashed away that afternoon were discovered by the Germans. Much to the Jedburghs' delight, a basket containing an additional radio transmitter was overlooked. Somers immediately attempted to contact SFHQ through an emergency frequency, but got no response. When night came, Leever brought the two Jedburghs to a nearby shelter and provided them with food and blankets. The Jedburghs spent the rest of the night in this hideout, catching up on some sleep and contemplating what action to undertake the next day.

The aforementioned Dutch BBO agent, Sergeant Major Van der Veer, had quickly established contact with French SAS forces on the night of 7/8 April 1945.

On Sunday, he led a group of Frenchmen to Generalmajor K. (Karl) Böttger's abode in the village of Westerbork. A great many Germans were killed in the subsequent attack. Böttger – commandant of the 674 Feldkommandantur – was severely injured. Before long, the French forces were forced to retreat due to the arrival of German reinforcements.[103] Elsewhere in Drenthe, the French also conducted offensive actions, including a raid on the parsonage in the village of Gasselte, where an office of the German Nationalsozialistisches Kraftfahrkorps (NSKK) was located.[104]

The Germans in Drenthe, who believed that the civil population was aiding the French paratroopers on a large scale, swiftly turned to heavy reprisals. About eight resistance fighters were shot in the village of Norg that Sunday, and another eleven men were executed in the woods near the villages of Anloo and Eext. Some days after, fourteen civilians would be shot in Hoogeveen. In total, the Germans would take the lives of over seventy civilians in Drenthe in April 1945 alone. Shamefully, several captured French parachutists were also executed by German forces during Operation Amherst.[105]

Advancing Allied ground forces reached the first French parachutists on Monday 9 April. Meanwhile, as part of Operation Larkswood, a Belgian

SAS forces at a barn in the village of Gasselte. (J. Bruggink)

jeep-borne SAS unit had reached the city of Coevorden, in the south-east of Drenthe. A reconnaissance element of the II Canadian Corps managed to contact an SAS party in south-west Drenthe. The Canadian main force, however, was still a great distance removed from the French forces.[106]

Leever, the Jedburgh teams' main contact within the Drenthe resistance, was reconnoitring all day and contacted several other nearby resistance elements. He even managed to find a suitable drop zone for the delivery of weapons and supplies. According to Captain Ruysch van Dugteren, Leever was 'invaluable', as he knew the area like his own pocket and gathered much valuable military intelligence. During Operation Amherst, Leever would continue to collect important information, which was gratefully relayed to headquarters in England by the Jedburghs.[107]

On Monday morning, the chief of the local police had reported to the Jedburghs. Based on his information, it was concluded that the number of resistance fighters in the area was minimal – just as the Jedburghs had expected. There were no active BS units in the direct vicinity. The resistance elements that were active appeared to be poorly organised and desperately short of weapons, while there were a great many NSB members and other traitors around.[108] Fortunately, at that time the number of Germans active in the area was relatively low. The few enemy forces around were 'rather jumpy' due to the omnipresent SAS forces.[109]

Sergeant Somers sent his first telegram to headquarters in England at Monday noon. A supply drop was immediately requested: 'All equipment lost. No news Harcourt hit field. Please arrange dropping […] for local resistance tomorrow morning zero two zero hours. Sheet 12 location 216837. Only two torches available.' This drop zone was code-named 'Joyce'. In the meantime, Leever informed Captain Ruysch van Dugteren that thirteen SAS soldiers had been captured by the Germans. At that time, heavy fighting was taking place in the woods to the north-east of their position. Soon, the Dutch captain heard the Germans blowing up several bridges across the Oranje Canal.

That evening, the Jedburghs received SFHQ's reply: 'Your one received. Regret unable drop tonight owing weather. Will try Tuesday night [meaning from 10 to 11 April] if you consider this still in time. What additional equipment do you require. Flash letter D for Dicing.' With a supply drop coming up, Leever went out to arrange a reception committee of about twenty people. Meanwhile, the Jedburghs developed plans for the preservation of the bridges and the telephone exchange in the nearby city of Assen. This city was of great importance to the Canadian ground forces, as two of their three main advance routes ran through it.[110]

A motorised column of the Belgian SAS in Drenthe. (NIMH)

On Tuesday, 10 April, SAS commander Brigadier Calvert realised that the advancing ground forces would not reach the majority of troops within the planned seventy-two hours. The Canadians had indeed been confronted with fierce German resistance. Their advance was further hindered by blown up bridges and crowds of cheering people celebrating their liberation.[111] In response to this delay, Calvert requested Lieutenant General Crerar, commander of the First Canadian Army, to adapt the original advance plan.

The brigadier suggested letting the 1st Polish Armoured Division (part of II Canadian Corps), positioned in the Allied vanguard, advance via a more westward route. Crerar, however, was not willing to alter his original plans for the benefit of the French forces.[112] In the end, most of the French troops would only be relieved between 10 and 14 April. Some of the parachutists operating further north were not even reached before 17 April.[113]

On Tuesday, the Fuseliers Mont Royal of the 6th Canadian Infantry Brigade conquered a bridge over the Beilervaart, a waterway running through the centre

A tank from the 1st Polish Armoured Division making its way through a crowd in Drenthe. (NIMH)

of the province. An attack out of this bridgehead on the village of Beilen would commence the following day.[114] Meanwhile, an SAS patrol reached the airfield at the town of Steenwijk. Regrettably, this installation had been largely destroyed by Allied bombardments – apparently unbeknownst to the SAS. Everything that had survived the bombings was destroyed by the retreating Germans, making the airfield completely useless to the Allies.[115]

That evening, members of the resistance from the city of Assen and its surroundings gathered for the upcoming supply drop.[116] The reception committee took position a mere two kilometres from the notorious Westerbork Detention and Transit Camp. Well over 100,000 Dutch Jews were assembled at Westerbork during the war for transport to concentration camps. The camp also functioned as a secret execution facility for apprehended resistance fighters. At that time,

A British Short Stirling drops supply containers to the resistance. (Personal archive)

there were still quite some German forces in and around Westerbork, making team Dicing's supply operation very risky.

Near 2200 hours, the entire reception committee was complete.[117] At exactly 2300 hours, an Allied aircraft passed and parachuted twenty-two supply containers.

Unfortunately, three containers opened up in the air, breaking and bending some of the weapons. Around 0500 hours all the containers and (scattered) weapons were collected and hidden. To the resistance's satisfaction, they had now approximately a hundred machine guns and rifles, with a similar number of hand grenades at their disposal.

Stores dropped to N.B.S. on the night 10/11th April 1945.

DICING 1

32 Stens
165 Magazines for Stens
33 Loaders for Stens
9,900 rds ammunition, 9 mm Parabellum for Stens
14 Brens
112 Magazines for Brens
14,000 rds ammunition, cal. 303 for Brens
99 Rifles
14,850 rds Rifle Ammunition
5 Pistols
250 rds Pistol Ammunition
2 Carbines, cal. 30
600 rds Carbine Ammunition, cal. 30
106 Grenades Mills No. 36
10 Grenades No. 82
1 Set Reception Committee Torches
10 British 24 hr Rations
4 Khaki Shirts (Officer's)
4 Vests
4 prs Pants, short
1 American type sleeping bag
6 prs Socks
2 Flasks, 8-oz. (filled with whisky)

Containers: Package:

1 x H.25   2583
7 x C.1
11 x C.3
3 x C.8
22

Overview of the weapons and supplies dropped at Jedburgh team Dicing's request. (Personal archive)

A consignment of the weapons was immediately transported to Assen by horse and cart – hidden beneath straw – while Captain Ruysch van Dugteren and Sergeant Somers began instructing the men in the use of the firearms. Leever and two other resistance men stayed behind at the drop zone until daylight to erase all traces. After a quick training session, the Assen resistance men returned to their city to guard two important bridges and prevent the Germans from destroying the telephone exchange. Ruysch van Dugteren had wanted to join them too, but he was advised against it: without (forged) identity papers he would not have a chance to get through.

On Wednesday, the Jedburghs continued their weapon training. Several resistance members went into action immediately, strewing roads with small mines and attacking isolated Germans. Ruysch van Dugteren recounted: 'Tyrebursters did their job delaying plenty [of] retreating vehicles, making the lives of many rather miserable. The number of resisters was low but the ones that were there, lived up to their name.'[118]

In the meantime, two bridges had been seized by the SAS several kilometres to the south-west of Assen. [119] At just about the same time, a Belgian SAS patrol reached the city of Hoogeveen with jeeps.

SAS troops with jeeps amid the people of Drenthe. (J. Bruggink)

At the Oranje Canal, the Belgians evacuated several wounded French parachutists. After having constructed an emergency bridge, the Belgian forces moved on to the village of Schoonloo to reinforce a French group that was engaged in heavy fighting.[120] The Jedburghs reported to SFHQ that day that the important road to Assen was still in German hands. At night, Ruysch van Dugteren covered this path to the city with a band of resisters, inflicting upon the enemy 'some damage' with Bren machine guns.[121]

On Thursday, 12 April, Leever ventured out with the local resistance to attack isolated German positions in the surroundings of Hooghalen. Meanwhile, rumours reached Captain Ruysch van Dugteren that Major Harcourt was arrested. He also learned that Assen was best reached via the villages of Ekehaar and Rolde, south-west of the city, as the Germans were expecting the Allies to attack Assen (straight) from the south via the main road through Hooghalen. The Dutch captain then moved south, crossing the lines. Before long, he reached a Canadian reconnaissance unit, most likely belonging to the 4th

Canadian infantry involved in a battle near the Oranje Canal. (Library and Archives Canada)

Canadian Infantry Brigade. According to Ruysch van Dugteren, the Canadians subsequently acted on the information presented by him.[122]

Before long, heavy fighting erupted in Hooghalen. The Germans destroyed the bridges over the Oranje Canal before retreating. At approximately 1730 hours, the Canadians had liberated the entire village. It was also around this time that Ruysch van Dugteren arrested his first Germans; an officer and his batman who were hiding in a ditch.[123] The town and camp of Westerbork were also

Prince Bernhard of the Netherlands meets freed prisoners from the Westerbork Detention and Transit Camp. (NIMH)

liberated. Captain Ruysch van Dugteren was among the first to enter the camp. He recalled, 'We were the first to walk into the Jew concentration camp, where there were 800 completely mad people. Was glad to get out again.'[124]

On Thursday evening, the first Canadian ground troops reached the edge of Assen, which also marked the start of the attack on the city. Interestingly, Dutch Jedburgh officer Staal – born in Assen – had joined the Canadians to take part in the liberation of the city. The next morning, Ruysch van Dugteren took several Germans, who were hiding in a neighbouring farm, into custody. Later that morning, the Jedburgh officer moved to Assen with several men in order to support the resistance fighters in Assen.

By Friday morning all German forces were driven out of the city.[125] Still, many collaborators were arrested by the resistance. The local resistance also seized two of the city's bridges, including the Groninger Bridge. These overpasses were important for the Allied advance out of Assen towards the city of Groningen.[126] Impressively, the underground had also saved the city's telephone exchange. The Canadians declared:

Captured Germans are transported by French paratroopers. (J. Bruggink)

French parachutists surrounded by elated people in Drenthe. (J. Bruggink)

> One of the most obliging of them [POWs brought in by the resistance] was a German officer who had been charged with the task of blowing up the very modern telephone exchange in Assen. He was bribed by the Dutch underground however and was quietly awaiting our FS [Field Security] in civ[ilian] clothes when they arrived.[127]

From this moment on, things moved fast. Already on Friday evening, a brigade of the 2nd Canadian Infantry Division reached the suburbs of the city of Groningen. In the following days, the Canadians were engaged in heavy street fighting in several parts of the city.[128]

The Allies were severely hampered, though, by German snipers. Ruysch van Dugteren arrived on Saturday in Groningen, where he soon met the local resistance commander. According to the Dutch captain, the Groningen BS was doing good work, sniping German positions and guiding Allied forces.

Subsequently, the Dutch commando offered help wherever he could. Amusingly, Ruysch van Dugteren seized one of Reichskommissar Seyss-Inquart's official limousines, an armour-plated Mercedes-Benz.

On Monday 16 April, the city was completely in Allied hands.

Two days later, Ruysch van Dugteren went to the south to report at the Special Force Detachment at the Canadian field headquarters. Thereafter, he reported

Canadian infantry moves through the city of Groningen. (NIMH)

Members of the BS of Groningen are patrolling their city. (NIMH)

Captain Ruysch van Dugteren in front of Seyss-Inquart's limousine. The German markings on the vehicle have been replaced by Allied white stars; post-liberation photograph. (The Ruysch van Dugteren family)

at Prince Bernhard's headquarters. Sergeant Somers, who had stayed behind in Assen, left the province around the same time.

Heading to the south of the Netherlands, he was arrested by the military police in the city of 's-Hertogenbosch as he could not identify himself. Only after SFHQ intervened was Somers released. The following day, both Somers and Ruysch van Dugteren were flown to headquarters in London.

After his failed landing near Hooghalen, Captain Bestebreurtje hid in the woods for two days. In complete desperation, he then crept to a nearby farm, approximately one kilometre from the village of Hooghalen. To his great relief and happiness, he was welcomed there by farmer J. (Jan) Schutten and his family. They hid the wounded captain and cared for him in the following days.[129]

On Thursday 12 April, Bestebreurtje was overrun by the Canadians – nota bene on his birthday. He was moved to Nijmegen the next day and admitted to the 1st Canadian General Hospital.[130] Major Harcourt, captured on the second day of Operation Amherst, had barely escaped execution twice.[131] He

Teun Leever (on the left) and Sergeant Sommers (second from the left) with members of the Drenthe resistance, just after the liberation. (Rolder Historisch Gezelschap)

Captain Bestebreurtje found shelter at the farm of the Schutten family in Hooghalen, recent photograph. (Private collection)

was eventually transported to Germany and penned up in a camp in Bremen (in northern Germany). Harcourt was liberated by the Allies near the end of April 1945.

Commentary

The missions of Jedburgh teams Gambling and Dicing in Operation Keystone and Amherst respectively were remarkable. Originally, both teams were tasked to prepare the arrival of SAS forces as part of Operation Keystone. After the reception of the Keystone parties, the Jedburghs were to ensure coordination between the local resistance and the SAS, paving the way on the Veluwe for the advancing Canadian ground forces. When team Dicing's Veluwe mission became superfluous, it was switched to Operation Amherst.

Commencing with team Gambling, it can be concluded that Operation Keystone was not a success. The SAS made a bad start when several of their parties could not be parachuted due to adverse ground conditions. The one party that was able to land was parachuted too far from the Apeldoorn Canal to reach the bridges on time. The third SAS element of Keystone, advancing over ground, could not achieve much result either.

Team Gambling's accomplishments in Operation Keystone, however, were impressive. Although a great many German forces were active in the area, the team was able to reconnoitre the surroundings of Apeldoorn and select several drop zones for the SAS forces. The Jedburghs also provided SFHQ and the advancing Canadian ground forces with important and accurate intelligence. Its other goal – widespread harassment of the German troops in the area – was not achieved, though. The local resistance and the Jedburghs did conduct small-scale offensive actions but to not much effect.

Due to the high concentration of enemy forces and the absence of SAS reinforcements, the Jedburghs and the local resistance could not save any bridges. In their attempt to retain the Klement Bridge north of Apeldoorn, the resistance suffered heavy losses. The Apeldoornse Bridge in the centre of the city, however, was seized partly intact. An important factor that limited the outcome of the Jedburghs' efforts was the fact that the Canadian ground forces were not willing to adapt their original attack plans based on the intelligence that team Gambling provided. Instead of sending units to the Epe–Oene area and trapping the German forces from the north – as team Gambling suggested – the Canadians held on to a frontal attack from the east of Apeldoorn. According to the Jedburghs, the liberation of Apeldoorn was subsequently unnecessarily delayed for several days.[132]

Regarding Operation Amherst, it is difficult to make an unequivocal assessment of its effects on the liberation of Drenthe. The necessity of the operation remains controversial to this day, as only relatively few German forces were left in the province by April 1945. The headquarters of I British Airborne Corps was of the opinion that the effect of Operation Amherst on the Germans' morale in Drenthe was 'considerable'.[133] The SAS forces forced the Germans to spread out over the province while enemy headquarters and communication lines had been continuously attacked. This kept the Germans from forming a solid defence line, or organising an orderly withdrawal.[134]

Though the French did not reach all their objectives, Lieutenant General Crerar was of the opinion that his ground forces actually benefited from Operation Amherst.[135] The French were, in any case, able to capture several bridges.[136] The French estimated to have killed 269 Germans, wounding 187 and arresting another 187. At present, this estimate appears to be highly exaggerated. Conversely, the French lost twenty-nine men, with thirty-five wounded, and ninety-six missing in action.[137]

Team Dicing was deployed in much the same manner as the Jedburgh teams in Market Garden had been. The team was deployed simultaneously with other forces, acting as liaison between the military units and the local resistance. Jedburgh team Dicing's performance was greatly affected by setbacks at the time of the infiltration and the accidental break-up of the team. Moreover, the number of resistance fighters in the Jedburghs' immediate surroundings was very low.

The team was infiltrated too late to be able to effectively serve as an intermediary between the SAS and the BS active in the province. The latter group did make itself useful, though. According to I British Airborne Corps, the Drenthe resistance furnished 'considerable assistance' as it 'provided guides and information about enemy dispositions, attended to the wounded, and supplied [SAS] parties with food'.[138] The Drenthe underground even supplied weapons and ammunition – including bazookas – to the lightly armed SAS parties.[139]

In conclusion, Dicing's Jedburghs were able to provide SFHQ and the advancing Canadians with useful intelligence. After arranging a supply drop for the local resistance, the Jedburghs organised small-scale raids and ambushes in the surroundings of the city of Assen. The band of resisters that was directed by the team managed to capture several bridges in Assen and prevent the city's telephone exchange from being destroyed. Team Dicing thus made a humble but noteworthy contribution to the liberation of Drenthe.

Conclusion and Epilogue

The deployment of teams Gambling and Dicing in April 1945 marked the final Jedburgh operations in the Netherlands. In early May 1945, the war in the Netherlands came to an end. The unconditional surrender of all German forces to the Allies was signed in Berlin several days later. The battle of the Allies against the Japanese Empire, however, was still not settled. Assuming that the war with Japan would go on for a long time, the British commander of the Jedburghs, Lieutenant Colonel G. R. (George) Musgrave, had already visited SOE's headquarters for operations in the Far East, Force 136 in British India, in September 1944.

After discussions about the deployment of Jedburgh teams in the Far East, it was concluded that Java and Sumatra, two major islands in the Japanese occupied Dutch East Indies, were suitable areas for the deployment of Dutch Jedburgh teams.[1] Such operations were eventually never executed in the Dutch East Indies, however, as Japan capitulated sooner than expected. Jedburgh forces did see action in others parts of Southeast Asia in 1945, but these teams did not include Dutch personnel.

Looking back, it can be concluded that the Jedburghs were exceptional soldiers. These special forces were the first to be specially trained, equipped, and deployed to strengthen resistance groups in occupied territory. The Jedburghs were created at a time when the use of resistance fighters and militias (in support of large, regular military operations) was not yet standard military practice.[2] Equally unusual were the risks the Jedburghs took by volunteering to operate far behind enemy lines.[3]

It should be emphasised that the Jedburghs were not sent out as 'strike forces'. They operated primarily as all-round advisors to the resistance. By providing training, advice, communication and leadership, they were to reinforce the capabilities of the armed underground movements. This modus operandi distinguished the Jedburghs from other Second World War special operations forces such as the Commandos and the SAS, whose main focus was carrying out raids and offensive actions – in the first place on their own – with precise and limited objectives.[4] Moreover, the latter were not designed for clandestine

Lieutenant Colonel Musgrave, the commander of Milton Hall, addresses Jedburghs at Milton Hall. A map of the Netherlands is noticeable in the background. (NARA)

operations or to operate in civilian clothes, and were an entirely 'military formation'.[5] The Jedburgh were thus more similar to SOE's long term 'circuit organiser' agents, also sent out clandestinely to contact and organise the underground, without taking part in any offensive actions.

There were, however, also noticeable differences between Jedburghs and 'regular' agents. To apply as a Jedburgh candidate, the recruit needed to have already completed full military training. By contrast, regular agents could be recruited as civilians. Moreover, as opposed to agents, Jedburghs were expected to wear a military uniform during their mission – if the situation allowed for it, of course. After all, the presence of uniformed Allied soldiers behind enemy lines was to encourage the resistance to undertake (increased) action against their occupier. In addition, the Jedburghs always acted in teams of at least three men, while agents often operated in pairs (an organiser accompanied by a radio operator).

Jedburgh teams offered a 'total package' to a resistance group: a communication channel to Allied headquarters which allowed the supply of weapons and

Jedburghs climb an obstacle at Milton Hall. (NARA)

explosives, and military assistance from professional soldiers trained in both conventional and guerrilla warfare. In addition, in contrast to organiser agents, Jedburgh teams would only be sent to an area where it was known, or expected, that armed resistance movements were active. Ideally, organisers made sure that underground circuits were formed and assembled, whereupon the Jedburghs strengthened these circuits, ultimately deploying them as effective paramilitary forces in conjunction with Allied military operations.

It should be noted that, contrary to many French teams, the Dutch Jedburgh teams barely had time to give military training or perform much preparatory work. Often, the Dutch groups commenced coordinating the resistance's actions immediately upon arrival behind enemy lines – operations in which the Jedburghs themselves also took part.

Although conditions in occupied France and the occupied Netherlands strongly differed, the French and Dutch Jedburgh teams still largely received the same training. After the teams were formed, the Dutch section did concentrate its efforts fully on the Netherlands, though. Contrary to the conditions in the Netherlands, the French landscape contained extensive forests that provided concealment; France also offered mountainous areas, beyond the Germans' direct reach. In various parts of France the resistance was therefore able to conduct a long and fierce guerrilla war, in which the French teams could play an important (long-term) role.

This type of irregular warfare was impossible in the Netherlands, as the occupier was much better able to exercise control and combat the resistance. Moreover, as a result of the *Englandspiel* in the first years of occupation, the Dutch resistance had suffered significant setbacks and delays with regards to its organisation and armament. Because the situation in the Netherlands differed considerably, and due to the Allied expectation that the country would be liberated rather quickly, most Dutch Jedburgh teams were deployed in an alternative manner.

Four Dutch Jedburgh groups were deployed together with regular forces in Operation Market Garden. After this failed offensive, a Dutch team was given the exceptional task to train and transform former resistance groups – in already liberated areas – into conventional military units. Another team was deployed in the province of Drenthe in the spring of 1945, together with hundreds of other parachutists. An additional, noticeable difference with the French was that the Dutch groups were also sent on mission to collect intelligence; information gathering had merely been an (unexpected) accessory task of most French Jedburgh groups.

Two of the Dutch teams were used in a very similar way to the French. Jedburgh team Dudley was deployed prior to Operation Market Garden, deep in occupied territory to mobilise the resistance, organise sabotage, and preserve bridges. Team Gambling was parachuted in April 1945 with a similar mission in the Veluwe area. Still, the assignments of these two Jedburgh teams differed from the trend. They were expected to be reached by the Allied ground forces in a matter of weeks, thus operating relatively shortly behind enemy lines. In the end, only team Dudley worked long term in occupied territory. That was, however, mainly due to the unexpected failure of Market Garden and had certainly not been SFHQ's intention.

In assessing the results of the Jedburgh teams, it should be noted that the effects of special operations cannot always be measured precisely, especially if these take place within the context of a large and complex operation.[6] Several factors limited the possibilities of the Dutch Jedburgh teams. Firstly, that the incongruous resistance was to be brought into a unified state military effort, which was hardly possible within the extremely short time frame. Some degree of amalgamation was still needed, though, in order to be able to effectively

Major Brinkgreve (centre) and Major Olmsted (right), shown here during an exercise, were able to strengthen the Overijssel resistance. (C. B. Cornelissen)

distribute weapons and coordinate the actions of the resistance. Furthermore, the Dutch resistance was confronted with large numbers of German soldiers, security forces, and collaborators dispersed throughout the entire nation. The enemy was therefore able to fiercely and effectively battle the Dutch underground, limiting the possibilities of the Dutch Jedburgh teams even further.

Did the Jedburghs, despite the aforementioned limiting factors, strengthen the Dutch resistance? And did they manage to mobilise the resistance in conjunction with Allied operations in the Netherlands? When judging the results, it can be concluded that the Dutch Jedburghs' overall performance was valuable. Team Dudley came to be of great significance in the eastern Netherlands, its team leader even evolving into one of the main figures within the Overijssel resistance. Ultimately, the Overijssel resistance contributed effectively to the liberation of the province – partly thanks to team Dudley. The results of the teams deployed during Operation Market Garden differed widely. Teams Edward and Clarence were extremely successful in making the resistance's services available to the Allied forces in their operating sectors. These groups also fulfilled an important intelligence collecting role for the Allied airborne divisions and I British Airborne Corps.

In contrast, teams Daniel II and Claude only made a slight contribution to the organisation and deployment of the local resistance groups during Market Garden. This was mostly due to the dangerous tactical situation in their sectors. Moreover, team Claude was attached to an airborne division that, largely due to distrust, only wanted to make very limited use of the services of the Dutch resistance.

The members of Daniel II and Claude did provide a laudable contribution as scouts and infantrymen, gathering important intelligence in the process. Team Stanley II, which commenced its mission after the end of Market Garden, transformed former resistance groups into regular military units. These were made available to Allied units deployed along the long and undermanned front line in the south of the Netherlands. The respective units gratefully absorbed these Dutch infantry forces into their operational sectors.

The last two Jedburgh teams that were sent on mission in the Netherlands performed well, although they could only make a relatively small contribution in the short time period in which they were operational. Furthermore, the Dutch Jedburgh teams encouraged restraint and prevented untimely resistance activities. Most likely, the Jedburghs thereby prevented unnecessary casualties not only within the underground but also German reprisals on the civilian population.

Although the performance of the Dutch Jedburgh teams can generally be considered a success, there are some question marks regarding the timeframe and manner of their deployment. The first question that arises is whether the Jedburghs were sent in too late. For instance, in team Dicing's operational report it is noted that 'more and better results would have been obtained if more time had been available'.[7] The French teams generally agreed that they, too, should have been deployed earlier.[8] Team Dudley demonstrated that a Jedburgh group could hold out much longer than just a few weeks.

It begs the question what the other Jedburgh teams could have meant to the resistance groups in the south of the Netherlands, had they been sent to the Netherlands prior to Operation Market Garden. In this context, it should be noted that as early as the spring of 1944 BBO agents had been sent to the nation. Yet SFHQ decided to deploy the Dutch Jedburgh teams from September of that year – when the liberation of the Netherlands seemed more and more to be imminent. The teams that were sent to the Netherlands in April 1945 experienced the same conditions: they commenced their operations merely a week – two at the most – in advance of the expected liberation of the area concerned.

How can it be explained that these valuable and highly trained special forces, who wanted to get into action as fast as possible, were deployed this late by SFHQ? The fact that the Jedburgh teams consisted partly of foreign members,

Under team Stanley II's guidance, the ST and BT forces made themselves useful at the front along the rivers in the south of the Netherlands. (NIMH)

who spoke little to no Dutch, likely played a major role in this. After all, it was already very difficult for Dutch-speaking personnel to work in the occupied Netherlands, let alone for foreign soldiers and agents. A fact that bears out this presumption is a passage from team Gambling's operational report: 'Any non-Dutch member of the party [the Jedburgh-team] was a liability to the resistance movement unless his presence there had some absolute justification.'[9]

That foreign Jedburghs could cause problems for the Dutch resistance can also be deduced from a telegram from Major Brinkgreve to headquarters in England, in which he recommended to provide new Jedburgh teams with Dutch-speaking radio operators.[10] A second factor that most likely affected the decision of sending the Jedburghs to the Netherlands at a very late stage was the intention of having them operate in military uniforms. It was expected that this would positively affect the resistance's morale and prevent the Jedburghs from being regarded as unlawful combatants by the enemy. Quite a number of Jedburghs swapped their uniforms for civilian clothes soon after arrival, though, as it was the only way for them to move around without directly endangering themselves and the resistance forces with which they were in contact.

It is very likely that SFHQ reasoned that such small and independent (uniformed) units could only operate for a short time behind the lines in occupied Netherlands. Only when enemy control was collapsing could the Jedburghs operate in relative safety. The risk of capture and execution remained, even under those circumstances, very significant.[11] Although most Jedburghs in the Netherlands were only operational for a short time, they suffered much heavier losses than the Jedburghs sent to France; in proportion, the number of Jedburghs taken prisoner, wounded, killed, or executed in the Netherlands was approximately three times higher.

Another question that arises is whether the Jedburgh teams were large enough. After all, when one of the members was lost, the team was substantially limited in performance. It should be noted, however, that from the perspective of security, small(er) teams were naturally preferred, as larger groups had a higher chance of being detected by the enemy. Still, in the case of Operation Market Garden, the Jedburghs' performance, as well as the resistance's, might have been even more extensive had the Dutch commandos – who were assigned to the various airborne units – been placed under their command.

Barring all criticisms, it can without question be stated that the Jedburghs were part of a bold and successful experiment. They were the first soldiers in the history of war to be especially trained and sent on mission to mobilise and support armed resistance. Ultimately, a small number of Jedburgh forces increased the 'total force' at the Allies' disposal. With the Jedburghs' assistance and that of other special forces units and agents, the resistance in France, Belgium, and the Netherlands was better able to aid their own liberation from Nazi oppression.

After the war, the fallen Dutch Jedburgh Captain Jaap Groenewoud was given his final resting place at the Arnhem Oosterbeek War Cemetery. He was posthumously endowed with the Knight's Cross of the Military Order of William 4th Class by Royal Decree – the Netherlands' highest military award. His citation reads as follows:

Great courage and tact shown at the landing at Arnhem on 17 September 1944 by being commander of an infantry section which penetrated a German headquarters and there confiscated key documents, including the demolition plan of the ports of Rotterdam and Amsterdam. After having returned from this, and being cut off from the main force with some British troops, voluntarily made himself available to try to break through the strong line in order to restore the lost contact. He was killed in that attempt.

Captain Jaap Groenewoud's headstone, Arnhem Oosterbeek War Cemetery. (Private collection)

In recognition of distinguished operational services rendered to the Allied cause at Arnhem, Groenewoud was Mentioned in Despatches by the British government. In 1994, at the north bank of the Rhine in Arnhem, a park was created and named after him.

Major Henk Brinkgreve was also posthumously awarded the Knight's Cross of the Military Order of William 4th Class. He was reburied at the Ooster Cemetery in Enschede. During the funeral ceremony, on 12 June 1945, the Overijssel BS commander Colonel Hotz spoke the following words of praise:

Henk Brinkgreve was a very special man of great stature. With him a distinguished, characterful, and gifted man passed away. Humble and contemplative of nature, he accomplished the very heavy task he had set himself, brilliantly ... His organisational talent, policy, tact, initiative, adaptability, patience, and endearing character enabled him to be the lynchpin of the active resistance and in an exemplary manner inspire and lead his armed companions of the BS to a supreme effort ... Henk ... Therefore, I completely realise that your death is a painful loss to your parents and your fiancé. May they find comfort and support in the conviction that you considered it a sacred duty, the battle to fight for the liberation of our fatherland and for the build-up of a better world, also for your family and your fiancé.[12]

From the British side, Henk Brinkgreve was awarded the King's Commendation for Brave Conduct. The description of the activities for which he was commended reads, 'It is not too much to say that his was the greatest individual contribution to the build-up of the resistance forces in Eastern Holland which, subsequently, in the Mar[ch]/Apr[il] 45 operations, did recognised good work in support of [the Allied] army ...'[13]

Major Henk Brinkgreve's posthumously awarded Knight's Cross of the Military Order of William 4th Class. (The Brinkgreve family)

Captain Arie Bestebreurtje, who took part in three Jedburgh missions, left the Dutch armed forces after the Second World War and moved to New York to work as a lawyer. Before long, Bestebreurtje became a naturalised American citizen. He was initially awarded with the Bronze Cross, the third highest Dutch military decoration, in 1945. However, this award was upgraded to the Military Order of William 4th Class, which was presented to him by Prince Bernhard in 1953 in New York. His foreign decorations include the Order of the British Empire, the U.S. Legion of Merit, and the U.S. Purple Heart.

To the surprise of many, Bestebreurtje became a pastor later in the 1950s. According to Bestebreurtje, his experiences in Drenthe in April 1945 played an important role in his decision to devote his life to the Church. In the 1977 movie *A Bridge Too Far*, the Dutch actor Peter Faber played the role of Captain

Various belongings of Arie Bestebreurtje are on display in the 82nd Airborne Division War Memorial Museum. (82nd Airborne Division War Memorial Museum)

Bestebreurtje. The former Jedburgh officer died in 1983, two years after his retirement, at the age of sixty, after falling through the ice while skating. His Service uniform, Military Order of William and fighting knife are displayed in the National Liberation Museum 1944–1945 in Groesbeek, near Nijmegen. The 82nd Airborne Division War Memorial Museum in Fort Bragg (North Carolina), home of the U.S. Airborne and Special Operations Forces, also exhibits several of Bestebreurtje's possessions.

Jedburgh officer Jaap Staal was awarded the Dutch Bronze Cross for gallantry. In addition, Staal was honoured with the U.S. Medal of Freedom and the Order of the British Empire. At the end of December 1945 Staal was transferred to the headquarters of the General Staff in The Hague, attaining the rank of Lieutenant Colonel. He would play an important role in the early post-war reconstruction of the Dutch army. In 1947 he returned to South Africa, building a career in the construction industry. Staal died in 1981.[14]

Maarten Knottenbelt, the fifth Dutch officer involved in Jedburgh operations, was awarded with the Knight's Cross of the Military Order of William 4th Class. The British government awarded him a Certificate of Commendation for his distinguished services. After VE Day, he voluntarily transferred to the Far East. There he joined a group of BBO and BI agents under command of SOE's Force 136. These Dutch forces were to be parachuted in small teams in the Dutch East Indies at Allied headquarters' request.

Following the capitulation of Japan and the subsequent Proclamation of Indonesian Independence by the nationalist Soekarno, thus marking the start of the Indonesian national revolution, supreme (British) command decided to keep the deployment of Dutch military forces in the region to a minimum. Knottenbelt, however, still carried out a successful intelligence mission in North Sumatra in October 1945.[15] In October 1960 he was honourably discharged from Dutch military service and migrated to Australia. Later, Knottenbelt – now a convinced pacifist – put his life at the service of peacekeeping. He spread his message primarily in Europe and the United States.[16] He returned to the Netherlands in the nineties. Knottenbelt died in August 2004 in The Hague, at the age of eighty-three.

Lieutenant Bram du Bois, the Dutch BBO officer attached to Jedburgh team Daniel II, was posthumously awarded with the Bronze Lion, the Netherlands' second highest award for bravery. He was also posthumously decorated with the U.S. Medal of Freedom. Du Bois was laid to rest in the mausoleum for resistance fighters in the town of Ede, near Arnhem. In Heiloo, where Du Bois had lived before the war, a courtyard was named after him in March 1995. Some of his personal belongings are on display in the Brigade and Guards Regiment Princess Irene Museum in Oirschot.

Jacob Staal being decorated, post-war picture. (M. Staal)

Monument with the names of the fallen Jedburghs in Peterborough Cathedral. (C. Bassett)

In 1945, Carel Ruysch van Dugteren, the Dutch commando attached to Jedburgh team Dicing, was appointed commander of the aforementioned group of BBO and BI agents belonging to Force 136. For his military operations during the Second World War he was awarded the Dutch Bronze Cross. Ruysch van Dugteren eventually returned to South Africa and resumed his farming activities. He died in 1984 at the age of seventy-four.

Lee Faber, the BBO radio operator attached to Jedburgh team Daniel II, was deployed on a second BBO mission in November 1944. Together with BBO agent P. (Peter) Tazelaar, he was parachuted into the province of Friesland to support the resistance in the northern Netherlands. Both survived this successful mission. Faber was also voluntarily transferred to Force 136 in 1945. He would not see action again.

For his performance during Operation Market Garden, Faber was awarded the Dutch Cross of Merit – his second one. For his second BBO mission in the occupied Netherlands, he received the Bronze Cross. The British government awarded him the King's Medal for Courage in the Cause of Freedom. After the war, Faber migrated to Canada, where he worked with his family in the horse trade. He died in October 2009 in Vernon, at the age of ninety.

Lykele Faber, May 2007. (Private collection)

Towards the end of the Second World War, Lord Selborne, as Minister of Economic Warfare responsible for SOE, advised Churchill to keep the organisation going after the war. According to Selborne, this was needed in order to counter 'the Russian menace' and the 'smouldering volcanoes' of the Middle East.[17] After Churchill lost the 1945 elections, the issue of the continuation of SOE came into the hands of the new British Prime Minister, C. R. (Clement) Attlee.[18] SOE was eventually dissolved in January of 1946. After the war, 280 employees were relocated to the Secret Intelligence Service (also known as MI6), which continued to exist after the war.[19] These days, the special forces' role in the British armed forces is primarily executed by the SAS, the Special Boat Service (SBS), and the Special Reconnaissance Regiment (SRR).

The American OSS was dissolved in September 1945. Two years later, the Central Intelligence Agency (CIA) was established, which took over most of OSS's tasks. The U.S. Army Special Forces, also known as the 'Green Berets', were founded in 1952, as advised by former American Jedburgh officer A. (Aaron) Bank. This unit was to perform unconventional warfare, which included Jedburgh-like assignments. According to Bank, who became the very first commander of the Green Berets, the Jedburghs were the U.S. Army Special Forces' predecessors.[20]

The Dutch BBO and BI were both dissolved in 1946. Various former members of these organisations felt the need to continue some of the activities due to the perceived danger of communism and the threat of a new war. Out of BBO and BI, two stay-behind organisations developed in total secrecy. BBO was turned into Dienst Operaties ('O', for Operation Service), which, in case of a Soviet Russian occupation of Western Europe, was to become the backbone of the armed resistance in the Netherlands. Its sister service 'I', for Intelligence, was to provide information to the government-in-exile during a new occupation. Both organisations were formally terminated in 1992, shortly after the end of the Cold War.[21]

Within the Dutch armed forces, the special operations tasks, which were formerly conducted by the Jedburghs and other special units in the Second World War, are presently carried out by the Korps Commandotroepen (KCT) and the Netherlands Maritime Special Forces (NLMARSOF). The largest Dutch special operations unit, the KCT – also known as the Royal Netherlands Army Special Forces Regiment – is tasked with special reconnaissance, direct action, and military assistance in enemy territory. Its operators cooperate closely with special operations forces from many other countries in conflict hotspots all around the world.[22] These days, the typical Jedburgh mission of training, advising, and assisting local or domestic forces and militias, is still incorporated within the KCT.[23]

NOTES

Abbreviations

BBC	British Broadcasting Corporation
Bijl.	Bijlage
Cdn	Canadian
DHH	Directorate of History and Heritage (Canada)
CMHQ	Canadian Military Headquarters
EO	Evangelische Omroep
Inv.	Inventaris
NA	Nationaal Archief (National Archive of the Netherlands)
NARA	National Archives and Records Administration (United States)
NCRV	Nederlandse Christelijke Radio-Vereniging
NIOD	Institute for War, Holocaust and Genocide Studies (The Netherlands)
N.d.	Not dated
No.	Number
Nr(s).	Number(s)
TNA	The National Archives (United Kingdom)
PAEdR	Personal Archive Eddie de Roever (The Netherlands)
PAJvD	Personal Archive Johan van Doorn (The Netherlands)
PIVOT	Project Invoering Verkorting Overbrengingstermijn
POD	Politieke Opsporingsdienst
RG	Record Group
SvD	Staat van Dienst
USASOC	United States Army Special Operations Command
Vol.	Volume
WO	War Office

1. The Jedburgh Concept

1   Foot, *The Special Operations Executive*, pp. 20–21.

2   NARA, National Archives Microfilm Publications, Microfilm Publication m1623, History of the Office of Strategic Services in London 1942–1945 (1989), roll 10, target 4, vol. 12, Special Operations Branch: Basic Documents, 'Coordination of activities of resistance groups behind the enemy lines with allied military operations in an opposed invasion of northwest Europe', n.d., pp. 52–68; *A conversation with General Singlaub*, by Ben Tedore, KNPB production. Available at http://vimeo.com/16545128 (consulted 13 March 2016).

3   SOE staff officer R. E. (Robin) Brook was also involved in the Jedburgh project. At that time, he oversaw SOE operations in France and several other countries.

4   Lewis, *Jedburgh Team Operations*, p. 4.

5   NARA, National Archives Microfilm Publications, Microfilm Publication m1623, Roll 8, Target 1, Vol. 4, Book 1, Special Operations Branch: 'Jedburghs', n.d., p. 1.

6   Mackenzie, *The Secret History of SOE: The Special Operations Executive, 1940–1946*, 603.

7   OSS was placed under the U.S. Joint Chiefs of Staff. Its primary functions were intelligence gathering and operations (sabotage and psychological warfare). OSS' Special Operations Branch (SO) formed SOE's counterpart.

8   For convenience purposes, no distinction is made between the different sergeant ranks. All non-commissioned Jedburgh radio operators are henceforth referred to as 'sergeant'.

9   NARA, Microfilm Publication m1623, Roll 10, Target 4, Vol. 12, Special Operations Branch: Basic Documents, 'Basic Directive on Jedburghs prepared jointly by SOE/SO', December 1943, pp. 36–47. Interestingly, the plan did not include the recruitment of Dutch radio operators.

10 Irwin, *The Jedburghs*, pp. 57–58.

11 A. Brown, 'The Jedburghs: A Short History', April 1991, p. 7.

12 Ibid.

13 J. M. Olmsted, 'Team Dudley', p. 8.

14 Colby, *Honorable men*, pp. 35–36.

15 Gutjahr, 'The Role of Jedburgh teams in Operation Market Garden', p. 30.

16 The author has not been able to find any details regarding the recruitment of Belgian and Canadian Jedburghs.

17 NA, 2.13.71, Inv. Ministerie van Defensie in Londen, annex. 3, Inv.nrs. 185–273, nr. 747 P, letter from M. R. de Bruyne to the Minister of War, 29 September 1943.

18 NA 2.13.71, Bijl. 3, Inv.nrs. 185–273, nr. 1028 P, letter from M. R. de Bruyne to the Minister of War, concerning officieren bestemd voor Staf BNS bijzondere opdrachten, 14 December 1943.

19 Dutch SvD Brinkgreve; TNA, HS 9/210/7; Kemp 1958, pp. 55–56; correspondence with Mrs A. Niessen-Brinkgreve (The Netherlands), March 2011.

20 Correspondence with Mr M. Koolhaas (the Netherlands), November 2011 and August 2012.

21 Report of interview with A. D. Bestebreurtje 1966, p. 1.

22 Ibid., p. 2.

23 Correspondence with Mr A. Bestebreurtje (USA), December 2005; Dutch SvD Bestebreurtje; TNA, HS 9/141/1; K. Bestebreurtje, 'Arie Dirk Bestebreurtje 1916-1983: een bijzonder mens', January 2006.

24 Peelen and Van Vliet, *Zwevend naar de dood*, p. 88.

25 Ibid.

26 Dutch SvD record Staal; Simpson, *The Quiet Operator*, p. 94; Van Ojen, *De Binnenlandse Strijdkrachten*, pp. 483–84.

27 See annex to letter from De Bruyne 14 December 1943: letter from the Minister of War to the head of the Bureau MVT, subject Commando-Toelage, 28 December 1943.

28 Bank, *From OSS to Green Berets*, p. 25.

29 Brown, *The Jedburghs: A Short History*, p. 9.

30 Correspondence with Major General (ret.) J. K. Singlaub (USA), September 2007.

31 Olmsted, 'Team Dudley', p. 15.

32 See 'Weekly training report' (in SOE personnel file Brinkgreve).

33 NARA, Roll 8, Target 1, Vol. 4, Book 1, Special Operations Branch: 'Jedburghs', p. 9.

34 Olmsted, 'Team Dudley', p. 21.

35 The British Major E. A. (Eric) Sykes, co-designer of the Fairbairn & Sykes fighting knife, was also an instructor at Milton Hall.

36 Gutjahr, 'The Role of Jedburgh teams', p. 35.

37 Report of interview with A. D. Bestebreurtje 1966, p. 2.

38 Bank, *From OSS to Green Berets*, pp. 31–32.

39 Colby, *Honorable men*, p. 36.

40 NARA, Roll 8, Target 1, Vol. 4, Book 1, Special Operations Branch: 'Jedburghs', p. 10.

41 Colby, *Honorable men*, p. 38; Interview Singlaub (*A conversation with General Singlaub*).

42 Olmsted, 'Team Dudley', pp. 22–23.

43 Olmsted 'Team Dudley', p. 23; correspondence with W. Beynon and B. Donahue (USA), September 2010–February 2011.

44 Olmsted, Team Dudley, p. 27.

45 For a long time many assumed that the Germans cleverly made use of the mistakes and inaccuracies on British and Dutch sides. Dutch researcher Jo Wolters suggested an alternative theory in 2003. In his Ph.D. dissertation, Wolters concludes that the Englandspiel can, in fact, be called a '*Deutschlandspiel*'. His theory is that the

Germans did not deceive the English, but vice versa. By sacrificing a large number of Dutch agents, the Germans were kept confused about Allied military intentions. Wolters's research was published in a Dutch book titled *Dossier Nordpol: Het Englandspiel onder de loep*. It contains an English summary.

46 Klep and Schoenmaker, *De bevrijding van Nederland 1944–1945. Oorlog op de flank*, p. 80.

47 Parlementaire enquête regeringsbeleid 1940–1945, 'Verslag houdende de uitkomsten van het onderzoek, part 4A en B, De Nederlandse geheime diensten te Londen, de verbinding met het bezette gebied' (published in 1949), p. 533. Although MVT no longer had contact with SOE after the establishment of BBO, the Dutch Jedburghs were formally assigned to BBO only mid-July 1944.

48 Payne Best, *The Venlo Incident: A True Story of Double-Dealing, Captivity, and a Murderous Nazi Plot*, p. 9.

49 Parlementaire enquête regeringsbeleid 1940–1945, 561.

50 NARA, Roll 10, Target 4, Vol. 12, Special Operations Branch: Basic Documents, Supreme Headquarters Allies Expeditionary Force, 'Operational Directive to SOE/SO', 23 March 1944, p. 75.

51 Johns, *Within two cloaks*, p. 12 and p. 178.

52 Visser, *De bezetter bespied*, p. 384.

53 Archive PAEdR, Jedburghs, box 1, map 1 and box 4, letter from Dobson concerning 'Conference - Jedburghs' to De Graaf, n.d.

54 TNA, HS 6/755 'Operation Report Jedburgh team Gambling', p. 10; Foot, *The Special Operations Executive*, pp. 211–12.

55 PAEdR, letter from Major General J. W. van Oorschot concerning the Dutch Jedburgh teams to Colonel Carlton Smith, 25 August 1944.

56 PAEdR, report De Graaf concerning Operation Poaching to the Minister of War, n.d., p.1.

57 Ibid., p. 2.

58 Olmsted, 'Team Dudley', p. 26.

59 Ibid.

60 Ibid., p. 29.

61 NARA, Roll 8, Target 1, Vol 4, Book 1, Special Operations Branch: 'Jedburghs', p. 14.

62 Olmsted, 'Team Dudley', p. 33.

63 Ibid., p. 27.

64 The British commander of Milton Hall, Lieutenant Colonel G. R. (George) Musgrave, decided that the Jedburghs needed to have a common emblem and organised a design competition for this purpose. This was won by the British Captain V. A. (Victor) Gough, who was later captured and executed.

65 Irwin, *Abundance of Valor*, p. 45.

66 Olmsted, 'Team Dudley', p. 37.

2. The Situation in the Occupied Netherlands

1 Cammaert, Het verborgen front, p. 839.
2 Van Ojen, *De Binnenlandse Strijdkrachten*, p. 85.
3 Cammaert, Het verborgen front, p. 763.
4 Van Ojen, *De Binnenlandse Strijdkrachten*, p. 72.
5 De Roever, *Londen roept Amsterdam*, p. 56; Cammaert, Het verborgen front, p. 842.
6 De Roever, *Zij sprongen bij maanlicht*, p. 83.
7 Ibid.
8 Ausems, 'The "Bureau Inlichtingen" (Intelligence Service) of the Netherlands Government in London, November 1942–May 1945: An Overview of its mission, agents and undercover radio traffic'.
9 Riessen e.a., *Het grote gebod*, p. 415. Available at www.lo-lkp.nl.
10 Cammaert, Het verborgen front, p. 847
11 LoFaro, *The sword of St. Michael*, p. 282.
12 NARA, RG 226, 'Appendix B, SF representation on formation HQ in Force Linnet, SFHQ preliminary instructions, Operation Linnet', 29 August 1944.
13 LoFaro, *The sword*, p. 283. It would still take months before the Allies could put the harbor into operation.
14 NA, 2.13.71, nr. 1889A, 30 August 1944.
15 NARA, RG 226, 'Report of Jedburgh team Dudley', n.d., p.1. Henceforth referred to as 'Report team Dudley'.
16 Report interview A. D. Bestebreurtje 1966, p. 3.
17 Huston, *Out of the blue*, p. 197.
18 Like the Dutch, the Polish government-in-exile raised a military force in the UK, including this brigade.
19 In detail, this team had the following tasks: organising and supplying the resistance, ensuring liaison between the resistance and the Allied headquarters, selection and training of resistance members to form reception committees and to support airborne operations, committing active sabotage in Overijssel, establishing a provincial intelligence system, prepare for the defence of bridges that were of interest to the advancing Allied ground forces, and, finally, reporting on (military) developments that were important to the Allied headquarters.
20 NARA, RG 226, documents concerning Olmsted; Irwin 2010, pp. 14–15.
21 TNA, HS 9/65/6.
22 Olmsted, 'Team Dudley', p. 39.
23 Ibid., p. 41.
24 The plane which transported them crashed in the dunes of Texel (northern Netherlands) on the way back to England; De Roever, *Londen roept Amsterdam*, p. 83.

25 Olmsted, 'Team Dudley', p. 42.

26 Telephone conversation with Second Lieutenant (ret.) J. Hinderink (the Netherlands), 8 June 2007.

27 Hilbrink, *De Illegalen*, p. 226.

28 Ibid., p. 174.

29 Hilbrink e.a., *De Pruus komt!*, p. 117.

30 Strawson, *A History of the S.A.S. Regiment*, pp. 1–19.

31 Kirschen, *Zes vrienden komen heden avond*, p. 98.

32 Pogue, *United States Army in World War II*, p. 281.

33 Ryan, *Een brug te ver*, p. 68.

3. The Start of Operation Market Garden

1 Pogue, *United States Army in World War II*, p. 282; Klep and Schoenmaker, *Oorlog op de flank*, p. 108; Horne and Montgomery, *Monty : the lonely leader, 1944–1945*, pp. 280–81.

2 Ellis, *Victory in the West*, II, p. 34; Klep and Schoenmaker, *Oorlog op de flank*, p. 110.

3 Ellis, *Victory in the West*, II, p. 30.

4 Ibid.

5 Klep and Schoenmaker, *Oorlog op de flank*, p. 112.

6 Pogue, *United States Army in World War II*, p. 282.

7 Pogue, *United States Army in World War II*, p. 286; Klep and Schoenmaker, *Oorlog op de flank*, p. 113.

8 Klep and Schoenmaker, *Oorlog op de flank*, p. 113.

9 Dutch SvD Du Bois; TNA, HS 9/451/4; Foot, *SOE in the Low Countries*, 199; Berends, *Woeste Hoeve: 8 maart 1945*, p. 171; www.prinsesirenebrigade.nl/omgekomen%20pib%27er%20Du%20Bois.htm (consulted 13 March 2016).

10 Interview with Lieutenant (ret.) L. Faber, 2 May 2007; 'This is my story', n.d. (written by L. Faber); TNA, HS 9/493/1.

11 Gavin, *On to Berlin*, p. 147.

12 NARA, RG 226, OSS e182, Paris, Box 11, Folder 102, Jedburgh team Edward, 'Dutch Liaison Mission with Airborne Corps. Mission HQ. 'Edward'. Report of activities on Operation Market.', n.d., p. 2. Henceforth referred to as 'Report team Edward'.

13 Ibid.

14 TNA, HS 9/1037/9.

15 Peelen and Van Vliet, *Zwevend naar de dood*, p. 94.

16 A Civil Affairs detachment was also assigned to the American 101st Airborne Division. Shortly after landing, this detachment had to carry out the military administration and handle the contact with the local population. This group consisted of Dutch Lieutenant A. Tigler-Wybrandi and two Britons.

17 Margry, *De Bevrijding van Eindhoven*, pp. 18–20.

18 Correspondence with Mr E. Janssen (the Netherlands), November 2015.

19 See 'De slag om Nijmegen', available at www.noviomagus.nl/Gastredactie/Meijer/Pandoeren/Pandoeren.htm (consulted 20 March 2016).

20 Kruyff, 'Ontstaan en overzicht van de activiteiten van de LKP-groep Arnhem', p. 3.

21 Douw van der Krap, *Contra de Swastika*, p. 249.

22 Van Ojen, *De Binnenlandse Strijdkrachten*, p. 365.

23 Riessen e.a., *Het grote gebod*, p. 461.

24 Hilbrink, *De Illegalen*, pp. 184–85.

25 Klep and Schoenmaker, *Oorlog op de flank*, p. 151.

26 Van Nie, 'Bericht', p. 80.

27 Olmsted, 'Team Dudley', p. 46.

28 Cornelissen, *SIPO en SD in Twente*, p. 107.

29 Ibid., p. 105.

30 TNA, HS 9/1607/1; Loosemore, 'A postscript, to Arthur Brown's The Jedburghs', Muster roll, p. 34.

31 TNA, HS 9/999/6.

32 Interview with L. Faber. He never found out whether the air crew survived.

33 Report of interview with A. D. Bestebreurtje 1966, p. 5.

34 NARA, RG 226, documents concerning Verhaeghe; Irwin 2010, pp. 21–22.

35 NARA, RG 226, documents concerning Beynon; correspondence with W. Beynon; Irwin 2010, 40.

36 Report of interview with A. D. Bestebreurtje 1966, p. 6.

37 Ibid.

38 Ibid.

39 De Groot, *Als sterren van de hemel*, p. 44.

40 These vehicles were lent from the SAS.

41 It should be noted that in the operational reports of the Jedburgh missions, some contradictions can be found. For example, some dates on which the teams met in the field are not corresponding. In this book, the dates of the mission report are followed where possible. Moreover, the author was not always able to determine the date on which telegrams were sent by team Edward to SFHQ and vice versa. The telegrams can be found in NARA, RG 226, OSS e182, Paris, Box 11, Folder 102, Jedburgh team Edward.

42 NARA, RG 226, documents concerning Sollenberger; archive Sollenberger; Irwin 2010, p. 38.

43 NARA, RG 226, documents concerning Billingsley.

44 NARA, RG 226, documents concerning Todd; Irwin 2010, pp. 16–19.

45 Klep and Schoenmaker, *Oorlog op de flank*, p. 118.

46 NARA, National Archives Microfilm Publications, Roll 8, Target 6, Vol 4, Book 6, Special Operations Branch: Jedburghs, Operations, Team Daniel II, p. 3. Henceforth referred to as 'Report team Daniel II'.

47 Ibid.

48 Margry, *De Bevrijding van Eindhoven*, p. 37; Ellis, *Victory in the West*, II, p. 34.

49 Ellis, *Victory in the West*, II, p. 35.

50 Klep and Schoenmaker, *Oorlog op de flank*, p. 123.

51 Margry, *De Bevrijding van Eindhoven*, p. 45.

52 NARA, RG 226, OSS e101, Folder 8, Jedburghs Clarence, 'Dutch Liaison Mission with Airborne Corps Mission HQ 'Edward', Sub-Mission Clarence with 82nd Airborne Div', n.d., 1. Henceforth referred to as 'Report team Clarence'.

53 Gavin, *On to Berlin*, p. 154.

54 Report of interview with A. D. Bestebreurtje 1966, 8; De Groot 1977, p. 44.

55 De Groot, *Als sterren*, p. 51.

56 According to Beynon, Theo Smiet was a resident of the city of Apeldoorn.

57 Report of interview with A. D. Bestebreurtje 1966, p. 11.

58 Ibid., p. 12.

59 Both Verhaeghe and Bestebreurtje were rewarded with an American Purple Heart due to their injuries. Verhaeghe would be cripple for the remainder of his life as a result from his wounds.

60 Simpson, *The Quiet Operator*, p. 95.

61 TNA, HS 9/627/2, 'Report by 1st Lt H. A. Todd on Claude Mission', 25 May 1945, p. 1. Henceforth referred to as 'Report Todd team Claude'.

62 Ibid.

63 Ellis, *Victory in the West*, II, p. 35; Klep and Schoenmaker, *Oorlog op de flank*, p. 120.

64 Klep and Schoenmaker, *Oorlog op de flank*, p. 121.

65 Report Todd team Claude, p. 1.

66 The exact location of this command post is unknown.

67 See citation of Groenewoud's Military Order of William.

68 Report Todd team Claude, p. 1.

69 Ryan, *Een brug te ver*, p. 248

70 Ibid.

71 Ryan, *Een brug te ver*, p. 350; Foot, *The Special Operations Executive*, p. 135

72 Ryan, *Een brug te ver*, p. 123.

73 Ibid., pp. 126–27.

4. The Bridge Too Far

1 Ryan, *Een brug te ver*, p. 127.
2 Margry, *De Bevrijding van Eindhoven*, p. 47.
3 Telephone conversation with Mr A. Roxs (the Netherlands), 20 February 2008.
4 Ibid.
5 Ibid.
6 Margry, *De Bevrijding van Eindhoven*, p. 52.
7 Ellis, *Victory in the West*, II, p. 36; Klep and Schoenmaker, *Oorlog op de flank*, p. 127.
8 Report team *Edward*, p. 3.
9 Ryan, *Een brug te ver*, p. 249.
10 Report of interview with A. D. Bestebreurtje 1966, p. 15.
11 Gavin, *On to Berlin*, p. 166.
12 Report of interview with A. D. Bestebreurtje 1966, p. 18.
13 De Groot, *Als sterren*, p. 88.
14 Ellis, *Victory in the West*, II, p. 36.
15 TNA, HS 9/627/2, 'Report on Activities of Team Claude with First Airborne Div. landing and subsequent operations at Arnhem 17th September to 26th September 44.', n.d., p. 1. Henceforth referred to as 'Report Knottenbelt team Claude'. Killick was commanding officer of the 89 (Parachute) Field Security Section and would be captured during Operation Market Garden.
16 Ibid.
17 Kershaw, *It Never Snows in September*, p. 131.
18 Report Todd team Claude, p. 2.
19 Tieke, *Im Feuersturm*, p. 328; Kershaw, *It Never Snows in September*, p. 131.
20 Letter from E. (Eric) Robinson to T. A. Boeree, circa 1952, Blok 2171, coll. Boeree, inv.nr. 7 (in Gelders Archief).
21 Report Todd team Claude, p. 2.
22 Tieke, *Im Feuersturm*, p. 328.
23 Report Todd team Claude, p. 2.
24 Klep and Schoenmaker, *Oorlog op de flank*, p. 142.
25 Ibid, p. 138.
26 Ibid, p. 139.
27 Margry, *De Bevrijding van Eindhoven*, p. 110.
28 In various Dutch publications, it is noted that Du Bois was captured by the Germans near Son that day but managed to escape. However, in team Daniel II's report, nothing is mentioned about this. The author has not found any archival documents that confirm Du Bois's capture.
29 Kershaw, *It Never Snows in September*, pp. 145–46.

30 Ellis, *Victory in the West*, II, p. 37; Klep and Schoenmaker, *Oorlog op de flank*, p. 129.

31 Klep and Schoenmaker, *Oorlog op de flank*, p. 134.

32 Ellis, *Victory in the West*, II, p. 37; Klep and Schoenmaker, *Oorlog op de flank*, p. 135.

33 Report team Edward, p. 3.

34 Report of interview with A. D. Bestebreurtje 1966, p. 16.

35 Ibid, p. 15.

36 Ellis, *Victory in the West*, II, p. 38; Klep and Schoenmaker, *Oorlog op de flank*, p. 135.

37 De Groot, *Als sterren*, p. 104.

38 Report team Edward, p. 3.

39 Klep and Schoenmaker, *Oorlog op de flank*, p. 135.

40 Report team Clarence, p. 2.

41 Kruyff, 'Ontstaan en overzicht van de activiteiten van de LKP-groep Arnhem', pp. 10–11.

42 Report Knottenbelt team Claude, p. 1.

43 Douw van der Krap, *Contra de Swastika*, pp. 258–59.

44 Peelen and Van Vliet, *Zwevend naar de dood*, p. 116.

45 Ryan, *Een brug te ver*, p. 350.

46 Tieke, *Im Feuersturm*, p. 330.

47 Report Todd team Claude, p. 2.

48 Ibid.

49 Ibid.

50 Ibid.

51 Ibid.

52 Ibid.

53 R. King, 'Ministory Jedburgh team Claude', annex to *Nieuwsbrief Vrienden van het Airborne Museum*, nr. 61, February 1996, pp. 2–3.

54 Groenewoud's headstone shows that he died on Monday 18 September. In the operational report, however, it is noted he was killed in action on Tuesday 19 September. This book follows Todd's statement.

55 Report Todd team Claude, p. 3.

56 Klep and Schoenmaker, *Oorlog op de flank*, p. 142.

57 Klep and Schoenmaker, *Oorlog op de flank*, p. 143; Ellis, *Victory in the West*, II, p. 38.

58 Klep and Schoenmaker, *Oorlog op de flank*, p. 145.

59 Ibid., p. 144.

60 Report team Dudley, p. 3.

61 Cornelissen, *SIPO en SD in Twente*, p. 324.

62 Hilbrink, *De Illegalen*, p. 188.

63 Didden and Swarts, *Autumn Gale / Herbst Sturm*, pp. 232–36.

64 Ibid., p. 237

65 Margry, *De Bevrijding van Eindhoven*, p. 124.

66 NARA, RG 331, SHAEF G3 Division Airborne Section File Number 24571, 'Operation Market First Allied Airborne Army After Action Report, Report on Operations 'Market' and 'Garden', n.d., p. 12. Henceforth referred to as 'Report FAAA'.

67 The castle at Singraven had indeed been requisitioned by the Germans earlier that month. It is known that General Christiansen, who was commander of all German forces in the Netherlands, was located in Denekamp for some time. It cannot be confirmed whether his command post was actually at Singraven. Correspondence with Mr S. Wynia (the Netherlands), September 2008.

68 Ellis, *Victory in the West*, II, p. 39.

69 Klep and Schoenmaker, *Oorlog op de flank*, p. 136.

70 Reportedly, Jan van Hoof dismantled the German charges during Operation Market Garden. There is, however, no irrefutable evidence for this claim. He was posthumously endowed with the Dutch Knight's Cross of the Military Order of William 4th Class – the Netherlands' highest military award – for his efforts to save the bridge.

71 See citation Bestebreurtje's Military Order of William.

72 Klep and Schoenmaker, *Oorlog op de flank*, p. 198.

73 Horrocks, *Corps Commander*, p. 118. In addition, Horrocks was focused at that time on keeping his 'tenuous supply line' open.

74 Report Todd team Claude, p. 3.

75 Ibid.

76 Report Knottenbelt team Claude, p. 1.

77 Ibid., p. 2.

78 Heaps, *De gans is gevlogen*, pp. 49–50.

79 Report Knottenbelt team Claude, p. 2.

80 See 'Slag om Nijmegen, de Pandoerenclub', available at www.noviomagus.nl/Gastredactie/Meijer/Pandoeren/Pandoeren.htm (consulted 13 March 2016).

81 Report team Edward, p. 4.

82 Ellis, *Victory in the West*, II, p. 41

83 Klep and Schoenmaker, *Oorlog op de flank*, p. 146.

84 Report Todd team Claude, p. 3.

85 Ibid., p. 4.

86 Ibid.

87 Ellis, *Victory in the West*, II, p. 55.

88 Ibid., p. 146.

89 Statements by Knottenbelt in the Dutch EO documentary 'De vergeten Polen in de slag om Arnhem, God Bless Montgomery' (2004).

90 This information was partly correct. The 10th SS-Panzer Division's headquarters had indeed been established in this building. However, the other division's headquarters was located in the village of Beekbergen, north of Arnhem; Tieke, *Im Feuersturm*, p. 304 and p. 313.

91 MacDonald, *The Siegfried Line Campaign*, p. 189.

92 Klep and Schoenmaker, *Oorlog op de flank*, p. 131.

93 Report team Daniel II, pp. 4–5.

94 XXX Corps was part of the Second British Army, which, in turn, was under command of the 21st Army Group.

95 Report team Edward, p. 4.

96 Report Todd team Claude, p. 4.

97 Report Knottenbelt team Claude, p. 2.

98 Ellis, *Victory in the West*, II, 42; Klep and Schoenmaker, *Oorlog op de flank*, p. 147.

99 TNA WO 171/1281, War Diary 5 DCLI, Aug–Sept. 1944.

100 NA 2.13.71, inv.nr. 2982, letter from Major General Van Oorschot to the Minister of War concerning the deployment of Jedburghs in *Market Garden*, 17 November 1944.

101 In a letter from Major General Van Oorschot to the minister of War (NA 2.13.71, Bijl. 57, nr. 2982, 17 November 1944) it is stated that Captains Staal and Sollenberger crossed the Rhine near Driel and reached Arnhem with a DUKW. In the book *The Quiet Operator: Special Forces Signaller Extraordinary* (London 1993) a similar statement is made. In the operational report of team Edward there is, however, no mention of a crossing to Arnhem.

102 Klep and Schoenmaker, *Oorlog op de flank*, p. 147.

103 From a post-war interrogation report of the Dutch POD (a political investigations unit) it appears that Captain Lancker's mistress, who had been caught earlier during a raid by the Germans, led the enemy to Lidwina that day. See C. Hilbrink's, *Vogelvrij Verleden. Oud-illegalen na de oorlog*.

104 Cornelissen, *SIPO en SD in Twente*, p. 117, pp. 119–21.

105 Report team Dudley, p. 4.

106 Cornelissen, *SIPO en SD in Twente*, p. 113.

107 Interview with Lieutenant (ret.) L. Faber; Report team Daniel, p. 5.

108 Report team Daniel II, p. 6.

109 Montgomery, *The memoirs of Field-Marshal the Viscount Montgomery of Alamein*, p. 264.

110 Interview with Lieutenant (ret.) L. Faber.

111 Ellis, *Victory in the West*, II, p. 44.

112 Ibid., p. 55.

113 Dear, *Ten Commando*, p. 187.

114 Report team Clarence, p. 2

115 Pogue, *United States Army in World War II*, p. 287.

116 Montgomery, *Normandy to the Baltic*, p. 149.

117 MacDonald, *The Siegfried Line Campaign*, p. 199.

118 Report FAAA, p. 12.

119 Letter from Lieutenant General J. M. Gavin to General Williams, 17 January 1954 (in US Army Military History Institute, Carlisle Barracks, Carlisle, Pennsylvania).

120 It is remarkable that team Edward sent a telegram to SFHQ in which Du Bois was found 'unsatisfactory' by an unknown member (most likely Major Wilson) of team Daniel II. This comment is astonishing as Du Bois played the leading role within this team. Perhaps a conflict between Major Wilson and Du Bois arose during Market Garden. It is possible Major Wilson, who did not speak Dutch, could not function properly, and was too attached to Du Bois for that reason, leading to frustrations between both officers.

121 Taylor, *Sword and Plowshares*, p. 90.

122 Peelen and Van Vliet, *Zwevend naar de dood*, p. 117.

123 Report Todd team Claude, pp. 4–10. Todd was awarded the American Distinguished Service Cross.

5. The Autumn and Winter of 1944–1945

1 Ashley Hart, *Colossal Cracks*, p. 78.

2 TNA, WO 171/120, '21st Army Group, War Diary, 'Minutes of Chief of Staff's Conference HQ XXX Corps", 2 October 1944,

3 Montgomery, *Normandy to the Baltic*, p. 158.

4 Klep and Schoenmaker, *Oorlog op de flank*, p. 202.

5 Ellis, *Victory in the West*, II, p. 40.

6 Van Ojen, *De Binnenlandse Strijdkrachten*, p. 171.

7 Janssen E. A.., *Stoottroepen 1944–1984*, p. 10.

8 Ibid., pp. 37–38.

9 The author is familiar with only one other Jedburgh team that was given a similar task.

10 NARA, RG 226, OSS e101, Folder 9, Jedburgh Stanley II, 'Dutch Liaison Mission with Airborne Corps Mission HQ 'Edward', Sub-mission Stanley (follow-up of Clarence)', n.d., p. 1. Henceforth referred to as 'Report team Stanley II'.

11 TNA, HS 9/1532/5; Loosemore, 'A postscript, to Arthur Brown's The Jedburghs', Muster roll, p. 32.

12 Report team Stanley II, p. 1.

13 Van Ojen, *De Binnenlandse Strijdkrachten*, p. 235.

14 Ibid.

15 Janssen E. A., *Stoottroepen*, p. 42.

16 Report team Stanley II, p. 1.

17 Captain Vickery refers to the 60th King's Royal Rifle Corps in his operational report. However, this unit was not part of the 8th Armoured Brigade. More likely is the 12th Battalion King's Royal Rifle Corps.

18 See telegram from Stanley II to Northway, 18 October 1944 (in NIOD).

19 Telegram from Van Oorschot to Northaw, 16 October 1944 (These BBO telegrams are part of the BBO archive (440, map 8) of the NIOD.

20 Klep and Schoenmaker, *Oorlog op de flank*, p. 231.

21 Janssen E. A., *Stoottroepen*, p. 38.

22 Report team Stanley II, p. 2.

23 Report team Dudley, p. 4.

24 Olmsted, *Team Dudley*, p. 62.

25 Hilbrink, *De Illegalen*, pp. 239–40.

26 Report team Dudley, p. 4.

27 Hilbrink, *De Illegalen*, p. 293.

28 Ibid.

29 Report team Dudley, p. 4.

30 This terrain is not the heathland at the Hooidijk in Hezingen. The drop zone was actually located several hundred meters south. A supply drop on this terrain was announced via BBC radio via the following code sentence: 'Ga zo door m'n jongen' ('Keep it up my boy'). Information retrieved from several interviews with T. (Teun) Evers, a former Hezingen resistance member, held through October–November 2010. Evers was a member of the reception committee at the Paardenslenkte in October 1944. In May 2015, an information panel and resting bench were unveiled at this former drop zone by the author and Mrs Ynskje van der Meer. See http://en.tracesofwar.com/article/71344/Informatiebord-Wapendroppings-Nederlands-Verzet.htm (consulted 29 December 2015).

31 Hilbrink, *De Illegalen*, p. 294.

32 Ibid.

33 Ibid. Schoonman was executed soon after.

34 Zie kaart *Oberbefehlshaber West: Lage West Okt* [October] 1944, provided to the author by P. Stolte.

35 Bauer, *Het Ardennen Offensief*, 75; Tieke, *Im Feuersturm*, p. 416 and p. 418.

36 Cornelissen, *SIPO en SD in Twente*, pp. 132–33.

37 Captain Staal had received permission in September 1944 to carry out a new Jedburgh mission at short notice. The last briefing of this team, which would be dropped in either the province of Drenthe or Friesland, was planned on

12 October 1944. The mission was cancelled at the last moment. Three weeks later, BBO agents P. (Peter) Tazelaar and Lee Faber (former radio operator of team Daniel II) were parachuted over Friesland to support the resistance.

38 Correspondence with Mr A. Stern (the Netherlands), September 2008.

39 Berends, *Een andere kijk op de slag om Arnhem*, p. 61 and pp. 239–40. Schuylenburg had been warned by the resistance about the upcoming air strike.

40 Hilbrink, *De Illegalen*, p. 295.

41 Ibid., p. 302.

42 Visser, *De bezetter bespied*, p. 368.

43 In the south of Drenthe, just across the Overijssel (provincial) border, the 6th Fallschirmjäger Division was rebuilt. Possibly these troops were also included in the count. The author did not find any information that confirms that a new SS division was established in the Twente region of Overijssel.

44 See telegram from SFHQ to team Dudley, 30 October 1944 (in NIOD).

45 J. Willigers, 'Bankrover met permissie van regering', *de Volkskrant*, 1 December 2011. See www.volkskrant.nl/archief/bankrover-met-permissie-van-regering~a3058907/ (consulted 14 March 2016).

46 TNA, HS 8/250, 'SOE activities, Summary for the Prime Minister, Quarter: October to December 1944, Annex C, Holland', 10 January 1945.

47 Hilbrink, *De Illegalen*, p. 295.

48 Report team Dudley, p. 5.

49 Hilbrink, *De Ondergrondse*, p. 264.

50 Stacey, *The Victory Campaign*, pp. 427–29.

51 Report No. 173, The Watch on the Maas 9 Nov 44–8 Feb 45', 25 March 1947 (In CMHQ, DHH, National Defence and the Canadian Forces).

52 Beynon was transferred to the Far East to and went into action with Chinese guerrillas against the Japanese.

53 Report team Stanley II, p. 4.

54 Ibid.

55 In his operational report, Vickery refers to the Canadian 7th Armoured Brigade. However, at that time Brigadier Bingham commanded the Canadian 2nd Armoured Brigade.

56 Report Stanley II, p. 4.

57 Temmerman, *De Belgische Parachutisten 1942–1945*, 240.

58 Olmsted, Team Dudley, p. 75.

59 This plane crashed into the IJsselmeer, the Netherland's largest lake, near the village of Venhuizen. The six-member crew perished in the crash. The cause of this crash has never been elucidated. A monument is located on the Oostergouw in Venhuizen. See also 'Verliesregister 1939–1945', at http://www.defensie.nl/ binaries/.../verliesregister.../verliesregister-1944.pdf (consulted 13 March 2016).

60 The plans for the pick-up operation would eventually be aborted.

61 See telegram Dudley to SFHQ, 10 November 1944 (in NIOD).

62 Olmsted, 'Team Dudley', p. 91.

64 He would also visit his fiancée several times and have contact with his sister. This information was retrieved from correspondence with Mrs. A. Niessen-Brinkgreve, March 2011.

64 Olmsted, 'Team Dudley', p. 100.

65 On 22October 1944, the first escape operation had taken place under the code name Pegasus I.

66 Olmsted, 'Team Dudley', p. 99.

67 Correspondence with W. Noordman, September 2011.

68 Peelen and Van Vliet, *Zwevend naar de dood*, p. 185. Olmsted was later awarded with the American Distinguished Service Cross.

69 Hilbrink E. A., *De Pruus komt!*, p. 113.

70 Telegram from SFHQ to Maurits (code name Beekman), 20 November 1944 (in NIOD).

71 PAEdR, Jedburgh section, report written by A. van der Poll concerning the activities of Major Brinkgreve, 21 September 1945, p. 2.

72 Hilbrink E. A., *De Pruus komt!*, p. 104.

73 Ellis, *Victory in the West*, II, p. 177.

74 Ibid., p. 179.

75 Klep and Schoenmaker, *Oorlog op de flank*, p. 248.

76 Temmerman, *De Belgische Parachutisten*, p. 243.

77 Cornelissen, *SIPO en SD in Twente*, p. 190.

78 Ibid., p. 191. On December 6 1944 Debefve was given orders to end his mission. It would take until March 1945 before they reached friendly territory.

79 Correspondence with Sergeant (ret.) H. A. Verlander (and his wife Mrs E. Verlander, UK), January 2011.

80 Cornelissen, *SIPO en SD in Twente*, pp. 341–42.

81 Beekman's wife was Jolande Unternährer. It turned out later that she had already been executed early September 1944 in Dachau concentration camp.

82 Blatt, *Rudy*, p. 239.

83 Ibid., p. 238.

84 Ibid., p. 239.

85 Van Ojen, *De Binnenlandse Strijdkrachten*, p. 272.

86 Ibid., p. 485.

87 Ibid., p. 278.

88 Janssen e.a., *Stoottroepen*, p. 56.

89 Stacey, *The Victory Campaign*, p. 450.

90 Ellis, *Victory in the West*, II, p. 241; Montgomery, *Normandy to the Baltic*, p. 185.

91 Ellis, *Victory in the West*, II, pp. 246–47.

92 After his mission in the Netherlands, Vickery was transferred to the Admiral Mountbatten's South East Asia Command. On 1 April 1945, as a member of SOE mission 'Nation Hart', he was killed in British India when the plane that carried him crashed during takeoff.

93 Gavin, *On to Berlin*, pp. 314–15.

94 Ibid.

95 Correspondence with Sergeant (ret.) H. A. Verlander, January 2011.

96 TNA, HS 9/1367/8.

97 Hilbrink, *De Illegalen*, p. 296.

98 Korthals Altes, *Luchtgevaar*, p. 281.

99 Telegram from Squeak (Code name Sjoerdsma) to SFHQ, 25 January 1945 (in NIOD).

100 Blatt, *Rudy*, pp. 244–45.

101 Ellis, *Victory in the West*, II, p. 250.

102 Stacey, *The Victory Campaign*, p. 466.

103 Ibid., p. 491.

104 Ibid., p. 522.

105 Bollen and Vroemen, *Canadezen in actie*, p. 101.

106 Ibid.

107 Telegram from Squeak to SFHQ, 5 March 1945 (in NIOD).

108 This is confirmed by Klep and Schoenmaker. See *Oorlog op de flank*, p. 283.

109 Visser, *De bezetter bespied*, p. 414.

110 Cornelissen, *SIPO en SD in Twente*, p. 221.

111 Ibid., pp. 216–18.

112 Hilbrink, *De Illegalen*, pp. 272–73. Lancker was posthumously awarded with the Bronze Lion. After the war a monument in memory of Lancker was dedicated in the hamlet of Hoge Hexel.

113 Hilbrink, *De Illegalen*, p. 296.

114 PAEdR, report written by A. van der Poll concerning the activities of Major Brinkgreve 21 September 1945, 3. According to Van der Poll, Brinkgreve's courier, who was an eyewitness, the Landwacht and the SS came to the farm to check whether its owners were involved in illegal trade and accidentally stumbled on the Jedburgh officer. On 9 March 1945 Brinkgreve was registered as an unknown person in the local burial records. The author was not able to determine whether the Germans eventually discovered Brinkgreve's identity. However, following this incident the imprisoned Sergeant Austin, was shown a photograph of Brinkgreve. Austin did not acknowledge knowing this person. After the war it became clear that Dutch SS man L. J. J. (Leendert) Dissevelt, the initial adjutant of Dutch national NSB leader A. A. (Anton) Mussert, fired the fatal shot. Dissevelt managed to escape

from captivity and settled in post-war Germany. He was never extradited to the Netherlands. On 5 March 2013, a monument in memory of Henk Brinkgreve was dedicated in Losser.

115 See documentation regarding Austin in the archive of the municipality of Hattem.

116 At this location a monument was dedicated. See http://en.tracesofwar.com/article/56672/Monument-aan-de-Geldersedijk-te-Hattem.htm (consulted 29 December 2015)

6. The Final Missions

1 Stacey, *The Victory Campaign*, p. 539.

2 Ibid.

3 'Report No. 152, The concluding phase: the advance into north-west Germany and the final liberation of the Netherlands, 23 Mar–5 May 1945', 21 March 1946. Historical Section CMHQ.

4 Ibid.

5 Mackenzie, *The Secret History of SOE*, p. 646

6 Cornelissen, *SIPO en SD in Twente*, pp. 273–75; Bollen and Vroemen, *Canadezen in actie*; pp. 172–78; Blatt, *Rudy*, p. 247.

7 War Diary, 1st Canadian Scottish Regiment, 10 April 1945, entry 1700 hours; Stacey, *The Victory Campaign*, p. 551.

8 Appreciation by Brig. J. M. Calvert, 30 Mar 45, First Cdn Army file GOC-in-C 1-07/16. Minutes, 3 Apr 45, of conference on 'Amherst' and 'Keystone' at HQ First Cdn Army, 3 Apr 45, HQ 1st Corps file 1CC/l/Plunder/1.

9 Seymour, *British Special Forces: The Story of Britain's Undercover Soldiers*, p. 262.

10 Stacey, *The Victory Campaign*, pp. 568–70.

11 Stacey, *The Victory Campaign*, p. 575.

12 Klep and Schoenmaker, *Oorlog op de flank*, p. 295.

13 TNA, HS 6/755, 'Joint SAS/SFHQ Plan for Allied Military Operations in the Veluwe', 30 March 1945, p. 1.

14 Ibid.

15 'Joint SAS/SFHQ Plan for Allied Military Operations in the Veluwe', 30 March 1945, p. 2.

16 Ibid.

17 Cooke and Shepherd, *European Resistance in the Second World War*, p. 145.

18 De Roever, *Zij sprongen bij maanlicht*, p. 72.

19 Cieremans, *De ene voet voor de andere*, p. 190.

20 De Roever, *Zij sprongen bij maanlicht*, p. 105.

21 Reisiger and Holvoet did not survive the war.

22 Kruyff, 'Ontstaan en overzicht van de activiteiten van de LKP-groep Arnhem', p. 17.

23 Van Ojen, *De Binnenlandse Strijdkrachten*, p. 738. Dijkman was executed in March 1945.

24 De Roever, *Zij sprongen bij maanlicht*, p. 74.

25 Cieremans, *De ene voet voor de andere*, p. 205.

26 Kruyff, 'Ontstaan en overzicht van de activiteiten van de LKP-groep Arnhem', p. 19.

27 Kirschen, *Zes vrienden*, pp. 159–60.

28 De Roever, *Zij sprongen bij maanlicht*, p. 228.

29 After Operation Market Garden, the wounded Knottenbelt returned to England. Shortly after, he went over to the liberated south of the Netherlands to recruit volunteers for the Dutch commandos. In mid-March 1945 Knottenbelt was again transferred to BBO.

30 TNA, HS 9/329/3; Loosemore, 'A postscript, to Arthur Brown's The Jedburghs', Muster roll, p. 7.

31 TNA, HS 9/1021/4.

32 NA, 2.13.71, nr. 2983, letter from L. A. de Goede to Mrs Alexander of the Department of War, 17 May 1945.

33 TNA, HS 6/755, 'Operation Report Jedburgh team 'Gambling'', 1 May 1945, p. 2. Henceforth referred to as 'Report team Gambling'.

34 Report team Gambling, p. 2.

35 Ibid., p. 3.

36 Ibid., p. 8.

37 Report team Gambling, p. 7.

38 Ibid.

39 Report team Gambling, p. 4.

40 Ibid.

41 Ibid., p. 7.

42 Stacey, *The Victory Campaign*, p. 571.

43 Mulder, 'Het Apeldoorns verzet 1940–1945', pp. 158–59; G. Visser-van Lente, 'Jaarlijkse herdenking van executie twaalf verzetsstrijders bij Klementbrug Heerde', 19 April 1989, *Reformatorisch Dagblad*, see www.digibron.nl/search/share.jsp?uid=000000000012e90dcod439fc30b46e5d2&sourceid=1011 (consulted 13 March 2016).

44 Report team Gambling, p. 9.

45 TNA, WO 218/117; Bollen and Vroemen, *Canadezen in actie*, p. 144.

46 This contact is confirmed in HQ 1 Canadian Infantry Brigade Ops Log, 13 April, 0813 hours.

47 Report team Gambling, p. 5.

48 Klep and Schoenmaker, *Oorlog op de flank*, p. 296.

49 Report team Gambling, p. 9.

50 Ibid., p. 5.

51 Stacey, *The Victory Campaign*, p. 574.

52 Mulder, 'Het Apeldoorns verzet 1940–1945', p. 168.

53 Stacey, *The Victory Campaign*, p. 574.

54 Report team Gambling, 5; War Diary of The Hastings and Prince Edward Regiment, entry 14 April 1945.

55 Bollen and Vroemen, *Canadezen in actie*, p. 147.

56 Ibid.

57 Bollen and Vroemen, *Canadezen in actie*, p. 144.

58 'Major Henry Druce', *The Telegraph*, 7 February 2007, available at www. telegraph.co.uk/news/obituaries/1541780/Major-Henry-Druce.html (consulted 13 February 2016).

59 TNA, WO 218/117; Bollen and Vroemen, *Canadezen in actie*, p. 145.

60 Klep and Schoenmaker, *Oorlog op de flank*, p. 296–97.

61 Mulder, 'Het Apeldoorns verzet 1940–1945', p. 169.

62 Bollen and Vroemen, *Canadezen in actie*, p. 148.

63 Mulder, 'Het Apeldoorns verzet 1940–1945', p. 169; Bollen and Vroemen, *Canadezen in actie*, pp. 148–49. See also the War Diary of the Royal Canadian Regiment, entry 17 April 1945.

64 Mulder, 'Het Apeldoorns verzet 1940–1945', p. 169.

65 Ibid.

66 Report team Gambling, p. 8.

67 Bollen and Vroemen, *Canadezen in actie*, p. 155.

68 Ibid., p. 145.

69 Department of National Defense (Canada), Directorate of History and Heritage, Report No. 32, Historical Section (G. S.) Army Headquarters, 'The Concluding Phase of Operations by the First Cdn Army: Part I', 1949, p. 61.

70 'Operation Amherst, Report by Brigadier J. M. Calvert on an airborne operation in North Holland', n.d., p. 1 (in K11 PAJvD).

71 Flamand and Jansen, *Operatie Amherst*, p. 178.

72 Klep and Schoenmaker, *Oorlog op de flank*, p. 303.

73 Flamand and Jansen, *Operatie Amherst*, p. 33.

74 Ibid., p. 212.

75 Ibid., p. 213.

76 Ibid., p. 28.

77 Klep and Schoenmaker, *Oorlog op de flank*, p. 301.

78 TNA, HS 6/754, Operation Dicing, 'Report on Operation Dicing', 12 June 1945, p. 1. Henceforth referred to as 'Report team Dicing'.

79 Ibid.

80 Ibid.

81 Schoon, *De Knokploeg Noord Drenthe*, p. 53.

82 Van Ojen, *De Binnenlandse Strijdkrachten*, pp. 208–09.

83 Schoon, *De Knokploeg*, p. 67.

84 Ibid., p. 59.

85 Ausems, 'The "Bureau Inlichtingen" (Intelligence Service) of the Netherlands Government in London, November 1942–May 1945: An Overview of its mission, agents and undercover radio traffic'.

86 Van der Veer, *Voor het vaderland weg*, p. 195.

87 Schoon, *De Knokploeg*, p. 220.

88 Van der Wiel, *Assen '40-'45*, p. 98.

89 Ausems, 'The "Bureau Inlichtingen" (Intelligence Service)'.

90 Van der Wiel, *Assen '40-'45*, p. 141.

91 Dutch SvD Ruysch van Dugteren. In preparation of their mission, Ruysch of Dugteren and Harcourt followed parachute training in March 1945. Ruysch of Dugteren, not yet trained in parachuting, made four successful practice jumps, and thereby qualified as a parachutist. Harcourt, too, made a practice jump to check whether he was fit for duty again.

92 THA, HS 9/660/6.

93 TNA, HS 9/1390/1.

94 NA, 2.13.71, letter from SFHQ to Major Klijzing, 9 April 1945, nr. 2983.

95 Report team dicing, p. 7.

96 Statements by A. D. Bestebreurtje in NCRV-documentary 'Operatie Market Garden', 1969. Bestebreurtje was not trained in parachuting with a leg bag.

97 Flamand and Jansen, *Operatie Amherst*, p. 46.

98 Klep and Schoenmaker, *Oorlog op de flank*, p. 303.

99 Flamand and Jansen, *Operatie Amherst*, p. 46.

100 Report team Dicing, p. 7.

101 Ibid., p. 10.

102 Ibid., pp. 7–8.

103 Bollen and Vroemen, *Canadezen in actie*, p. 186.

104 Ibid., p. 187.

105 Flamand and Jansen, *Operatie Amherst*, p. 190.

106 Klep and Schoenmaker, *Oorlog op de flank*, p. 304.

107 Report team Dicing, p. 8.

108 Ibid.

109 Ibid.

110 Bollen and Vroemen, *Canadezen in actie*, p. 191.

111 Klep and Schoenmaker, *Oorlog op de flank*, p. 304.

112 Flamand and Jansen, *Operatie Amherst*, p. 184.

113 Ibid., p. 185.

114 Bollen and Vroemen, *Canadezen in actie*, p. 191.

115 Ibid., p. 189.

116 Report team Dicing, p. 8.

117 Ibid.

118 Bontekoe, *Drentsche kroniek van het bevrijdingsjaar*, p. 211.

119 Bollen and Vroemen, *Canadezen in actie*, p. 196.

120 Flamand and Jansen, *Operatie Amherst*, p. 183.

121 Report team Dicing, p. 9.

122 Ibid.

123 Ibid.

124 Ibid.

125 Bollen and Vroemen, *Canadezen in actie*, p. 193.

126 Report team Dicing, 9; Van der Wiel, *Assen '40-'45*, pp. 151–52.

127 See War Diary 4th Canadian Infantry Brigade.

128 Klep and Schoenmaker, *Oorlog op de flank*, p. 307.

129 Correspondence and telephone conversations with the Schutten family during October 2007.

130 PAEdR, letter from van K. de Graaf to the Minister of War, including a report on Bestebreurtje, 1 November 1945, p. 10.

131 Report team Dicing, p. 4.

132 Report team Gambling, p. 9.

133 Stacey, *The Victory Campaign*, p. 554.

134 Report on Operations – Amherst by 2 and 3 RCP in N.E. Holland, 23 May 1945, p. 2, by Major-General R. N. Gale, Commander I British Airborne Corps.

135 Klep and Schoenmaker, *Oorlog op de flank*, p. 304.

136 'Operation Amherst, Report by Brigadier J. M. Calvert on an airborne operation in North Holland', n.d., p. 10, K11 PAJvD.

137 Ibid., pp. 10–11, K11 PAJvD. The exact number of Germans that were killed during Operation Amherst is unknown. The French estimate is likely on the high side. According to the Dutch researcher and author J. van Doorn, thirty-four French paratroopers were killed in action during Operation Amherst. In the period between 8 April and 14 April 1945, approximately 130 Germans lost their lives while battling the Allies and SAS in Drenthe. The French parachutists have killed about forty Germans during Amherst. Information retrieved via correspondence with J. van Doorn (1 March 2016).

138 'Report on Operations – Amherst by 2 and 3 RCP in N.E. Holland', 23 May 1945, p. 4, by Major-General R. N. Gale.

139 Operation Amherst, Report by Brigadier J. M. Calvert on an airborne operation in North Holland, n.d., pp. 7–8, K11 PAJvD.

Conclusion and Epilogue

1 Loosemore, 'A postscript, to Arthur Brown's The Jedburghs', Section G, Preparing for Burma, pp. 1–3.

2 Lewis, *Jedburgh Team Operations*, p. 65; correspondence with Mr T. J. Sacquety, USASOC, May 2011.

3 The same applies for other special operations units and agents who were active in occupied territory.

4 Mackenzie, *The Secret History of SOE*, p. 603; Lewis, *Jedburgh Team Operations*, p. 3.

5 'Memorandum on organisation and employment of SAS Jeep squadrons operating with infantry or armoured divisions', by Brigadier J. M. Calvert, April 1945, p. 1 (In K30 RG 24 215C1.043 D5, supplied to the author by J. van Doorn, The Netherlands).

6 Irwin, *The Jedburghs*, p. 235.

7 Report team Dicing, p. 10.

8 Irwin, 'A Special Force', pp. 152–53; Lewis, *Jedburgh Team Operations*, p. 62.

9 Report team Gambling, pp. 9–10.

10 See telegram Squeak, 25 January 1945 (in NIOD).

11 Interview with Lieutenant (ret.) M. Cieremans, 3 November 2012.

12 Report of funeral speech by Colonel Hotz, 27 June 1945 (in family archive Brinkgreve)

13 See 'citation' (June 1945) in Brinkgreve's SOE personnel file.

14 Correspondence with Ms M. Staal during September–October 2010.

15 De Man, *Opdracht Sumatra*, pp. 149–50.

16 'Summary of Guide to the Martin Knottenbelt papers', compiled by Cate Putirskis April 2011, in The New York Public Library – Stephen Schwarzman Building Manuscripts and Archives Division; online summary available at www.nypl.org/sites/default/files/archivalcollections/pdf/mss18269.pdf (consulted 20 March 2016). See also www.covgelderland.nl/level3pages.php?f=covgld&pageid=14260 (consulted 13 March 2016).

17 Wilkinson and Astley, *Gubbins and SOE*, p. 232.

18 Foot, *Special Operations Executive*, p. 245.

19 S. Berg, 'Churchill's secret army lived on', *BBC News*, 13 December 2008, available at http://news.bbc.co.uk/today/hi/today/newsid_7780000/7780476.stm (consulted on 13 February 2016)

20 Bank, *From OSS to Green Berets*, p. 221.

21 D. Engelen, 'De Nederlandse stay-behind-organisatie in de koude oorlog 1945–1992. Een institutioneel onderzoek', PIVOT-rapport artikelnummer 166, The Hague 2005, p. 13; Interview with Herman Schoemaker, 30 March 2015. Schoemaker served as an agent in the Dutch stay-behind organisation during a large part of the Cold War.

22 H. G. van den As, 'De Nederlandse Special Forces in ontwikkeling', *Carré* 3, 2007, pp. 1–3; 'Special Forces van het Korps Maniers', See www.defensie.nl/marine/korps_mariniers/special_forces/ (consulted 14 June 2013).

23 Ten Cate and Van der Vorm, *Callsign Nassau*, p. 288.

BIBLIOGRAPHY

Archives

Canada
Department of National Defense, Directorate of History and Heritage, Ottawa, Ontario
Library and Archives Canada, Ottawa, Ontario
The Netherlands
Gelders Archief, Arnhem
Gemeentelijk archief Ede
Gemeentelijk archief Hattem
Nationaal Archief, The Hague
NIOD Instituut voor Oorlogs-, Holocaust- en Genocidestudies, Amsterdam
Semi-Statische Archiefdiensten (Ministerie van Defensie), Kerkrade
United Kingdom
The National Archives, Kew Gardens, London
United States
National Archives and Records Administration, College Park, Maryland
U.S. Army Military History Institute, Carlisle Barracks, Carlisle, Pennsylvania

Personal archives

Canada
The Faber family
The Groenewoud family
The Netherlands
T. A. Boeree (in Gelders archief)
The Bestebreurtje family
The Brinkgreve family
J. van Doorn
The Groenewoud family
G. H. Plekkingra (in Gemeentearchief Ede)

E. de Roever (in Museum der Koninklijke Marechaussee)
South Africa
The Ruysch van Dugteren family
United Kingdom
S. Kippax
United States
The Bestebreurtje family
The Beynon family
Ryan, C. (in Ohio University Library, Archives and Special Collections)
The Sollenberger family
The Todd family

Interviews

M. Cieremans †, Wassenaar, The Netherlands, 3 November 2012
T. Evers †, Reutum, The Netherlands, October - November 2010
L. Faber †, Geldermalsen, The Netherlands, 2 May 2007
J. Hinderink, Laren, The Netherlands, 22 December 2014
A. Roxs, Eindhoven, The Netherlands, 20 February 2008
H. Schoemaker †, Soest, The Netherlands, 30 March 2015
The Schutten family, Hooghalen, The Netherlands, October 2007

Correspondence

A. Bestebreurtje (USA), December 2005
W. W. Beynon † (USA), September 2010–February 2011
M. Brinkgreve † (The Netherlands), Augustus 2008
M. Cieremans † (The Netherlands), September 2012–May 2013
J. van Doorn (The Netherlands), March–April 2016
M. Groenewoud (The Netherlands), September 2008
E. Janssen (The Netherlands), November 2015
M. Kokhuis † (South Africa), December 2014–December 2015
M. Koolhaas (The Netherlands), November 2011 and Augustus 2012
G. Loosemore † (UK), January 2006
A. Niessen-Brinkgreve (The Netherlands), January–May 2011.
W. Noordman (The Netherlands), September 2011.
The Ruysch van Dugteren family (South Africa), May 2012.
T. J. Sacquety (USA), May 2011.

J. K. Singlaub (USA), September 2007.

M. Sollenberger Craig (USA), January 2011.

M. Staal (France), September - October 2010.

A. Stern (The Netherlands), September 2008.

Stichting Apeldoorns Kanaal (The Netherlands), July 2012.

P. Stolte (The Netherlands), July-August 2012

The Todd family (USA), September 2010–February 2011

H. A. Verlander † and Mrs. E. Verlander (UK), January 2011

S. Wynia (The Netherlands), September 2008

Documentaries

A conversation with General Singlaub, by Ben Tedore, KNPB production, n.d. Available at http://vimeo.com/16545128 (consulted 13 March 2016)

De vergeten Polen in de slag om Arnhem, God Bless Montgomery, EO documentary 2004

Operatie Market Garden, NCRV documentary 1969

Unpublished documents

Bestebreurtje, K., 'Arie Dirk Bestebreurtje 1916–1983: een bijzonder mens' (2006)

Brown, A., 'The Jedburghs: A Short History' (1991)

Faber, L., 'This is my story' (2007)

Kruyff, P. C., 'Ontstaan en overzicht van de activiteiten van de LKP-groep Arnhem' (1947)

Loosemore, G., 'A postscript, to Arthur Brown's The Jedburghs: a short history' (2006)

Olmsted, J. M., 'Team Dudley' (1946)

Ryan, C., Report of interviews with A.D. Bestebreurtje (1966)

Articles

As, H. G. van den, 'De Nederlandse Special Forces in ontwikkeling', *Carré* 3 (2007) 1-3

Ausems, A., 'The "Bureau Inlichtingen" (Intelligence Service) of the Netherlands Government in London, November 1942–May 1945: An Overview of its mission, agents and undercover radio traffic', *Military Affairs* 45-3 (1981) 127-32

Berg, S., 'Churchill's secret army lived on', *BBC News*, 13 December 2008

Engelen, D., 'De Nederlandse stay-behind-organisatie in de koude oorlog 1945–1992. Een institutioneel onderzoek', PIVOT-rapport artikelnummer 166 (The Hague 2005)

King, R., 'Ministory Jedburgh team Claude', Annex to *Nieuwsbrief Vrienden van het Airborne Museum*, nr. 61 (February 1996), Vereniging Vrienden van het Airborne Museum.

Putirskis, C., 'Summary of Guide to the Martin Knottenbelt papers', April 2011 (in The New York Public Library – Stephen Schwarzman Building Manuscripts and Archives Division).

Visser-van Lente, G., 'Jaarlijkse herdenking van executie twaalf verzetsstrijders bij Klementbrug Heerde', *Reformatorisch Dagblad*, 19 April 1989

Willegers, J., 'Bankrover met permissie van regering', *de Volkskrant*, 1 December 2011

Books and theses

Bank, A., *From OSS to Green Berets: The Birth of Special Forces* (Novato: 1987)

Bauer, E., *Het Ardennen Offensief* (Rotterdam: 1978)

Bauer, E., *Verraad en Verzet* (Rotterdam: 1978)

Berends, H., *Woeste Hoeve: 8 maart 1945* (Kampen: 1995)

Berends, P., *Een andere kijk op de slag om Arnhem* (Soesterberg: 2002)

Blatt, R., *Rudy, een strijdbare Jood 1940–1945* (Haarlem: 1985)

Bollen, H. A., and P. Vroemen, *Canadezen in Actie: Nederland najaar '44-voorjaar '46* (Warnsveld: 1994)

Bontekoe, G. A., *Drentsche kroniek van het bevrijdingsjaar* (Assen: 1946)

Cammaert, A. P. M., 'Het Verborgen Front, Geschiedenis van de Georganiseerde Illegaliteit in de Provincie Limburg tijdens de Tweede Wereldoorlog' (Ph.D. dissertation Rijksuniversiteit Groningen, Groningen 1994)

Cate, A. ten, and M. van der Vorm, *Callsign Nassau: Dutch Army Special Forces in Action in the 'New World Disorder'* (Leiden: 2016)

Cieremans, M., *De ene voet voor de andere: verhaal van een Engelandvaarder die geheim agent werd* (Baarn: 1994)

Colby, W. E., *Honorable men: my life in the CIA* (New York: 1978)

Cornelissen, C. B., *SIPO en SD in Twente 1940-1945* (Albergen: 2010)

Dear, I., *Ten Commando, 1942–1945* (New York: 1987)

Didden, J., and M. Swarts, *Autumn Gale / Herbst Sturm* (Drunen 2013)

Douw van der Krap, C. L. J. F., *Contra de Swastika: De strijd van een onverzettelijke Nederlandse marineofficier in bezet Europa, 1940–1945* (Bussum: 1981)

Ellis, L. F., *Victory in the West, Volume II, The Defeat of Germany* (London: 1968)

Enquête commissie regeringsbeleid 1940–1945, 'Verslag houdende de uitkomsten van het onderzoek, deel 4A en B, De Nederlandse geheime diensten te London, de verbinding met het bezette gebied' (Den Haag: 1949)

Flamand, R., and J. H. Jansen, *Operatie Amherst: Franse para's vochten in Drenthe, April 1945* (Amsterdam: 2002)

Foot, M. R. D., *SOE in the Low Countries* (London: 2001)

Foot, M. R. D., *The Special Operations Executive: An outline of the Special Operations Executive 1940–46* (London: 1984)

Gavin, J. M., *On to Berlin: Battles of an Airborne Commander, 1943–1946* (New York: 1978)

Groot, N. A. de, *Als sterren van de hemel* (Bussum: 1977)

Gutjahr, R. G., 'The Role of Jedburgh teams in Operation Market Garden' (Masterscriptie U.S. Army Command and General Staff College Leavenworth, Leavenworth: 1990)

Hart, S. A., *Colossal Cracks: Montgomery's 21st Army Group in Northwest Europe, 1944–45* (Mechanicsburg: 2007)

Heaps, L., *De gans is gevlogen* (Bussum: 1976)

Hilbrink, C., *De Illegalen, Illegaliteit in Twente & het aangrenzende Salland 1940–1945* (Den Haag: 1989)

Hilbrink, C., *De Ondergrondse: Illegaliteit in Overijssel 1940–1945* (Den Haag: 1998)

Hilbrink, C., M. Kienhuis and K. Vos, *De Pruus komt! Overijssel in de Tweede Wereldoorlog* (Zwolle: 1990)

Hilbrink, C., *Vogelvrij Verleden. Oud-illegalen na de oorlog* (Amsterdam: 2001)

Horne, A., and D. Montgomery, *Monty: the Lonely Leader, 1944–1945* (New York: 1994)

Horrocks, B., *Corps Commander* (London: 1977)

Huston, J. A., *Out of the blue: U.S. Airborne Operations in World War II* (West Lafayette: 1998)

Irwin, W. W., 'A Special Force: Origin and Development of the Jedburgh Project in Support of Operation Overlord' (Leavenworth: Master thesis U.S. Army Command and General Staff College Leavenworth, 1991)

Irwin, W. W, *Abundance of Valor, Resistance, Survival, and Liberation: 1944–1945* (New York: 2010)

Irwin, W. W., *The Jedburghs: The Secret History of the Allied Special Forces, France 1944* (San Clemente 2005)

Janssen, J. A. M. M., P. M. H. Groen and C. M. Schulten, *Stoottroepen 1944–1984* (Utrecht: 1984)

Johns, P., *Within two cloaks: missions with SIS and SOE* (London: 1979)

Kemp, P., *No colours or crest* (London: 1958)

Kershaw, R. J., *It Never Snows in September: The German View of Market Garden and The Battle of Arnhem* (New York: 1990)

Kirschen, G. S., *Zes vrienden komen heden avond* (London: 1946)

Klep, C., and B. Schoenmaker, *De bevrijding van Nederland 1944–1945. Oorlog op de flank* (Den Haag: 1995)

Korthals Altes, A., *Luchtgevaar: luchtaanvallen op Nederland 1940–1945* (Amsterdam: 1984)

Lewis, S. J., 'Jedburgh Team Operations in Support of the 12th Army Group, August 1944' (Fort Leavenworth: 1991)

LoFaro, G., *The sword of St. Michael: the 82nd Airborne Division in World War II* (Cambridge: 2011)

MacDonald, C. B., *The Siegfried Line Campaign* (Washington: 1990)

Mackenzie, W., *The Secret History of SOE: Special Operations Executive 1940–1945* (London: 2000)

Man, J. Th. A. de, *Opdracht Sumatra: Het Korps Insulinde 1942–1946* (Houten: 1987)

Margry, K., *De Bevrijding van Eindhoven* (Eindhoven: 1992)

Montgomery, B. L., *Normandy to the Baltic* (London: 1947)

Montgomery, B. L., *The memoirs of Field-Marshal the Viscount Montgomery of Alamein* (Cleveland: 1958)

Mulder, H., 'Het Apeldoorns verzet 1940–1945' (Utrecht: Master thesis Universiteit Utrecht, 1971)

Nie, J. A. van, '*Bericht voor groote Jan*' (Den Haag: 1946)

Ojen, G. J. van, *De Binnenlandse Strijdkrachten* (Den Haag: 1972)

Payne Best, S., *The Venlo Incident: A True Story of Double-Dealing, Captivity, and a Murderous Nazi Plot* (London: 2009)

Peelen, Th. en A. L. J. van Vliet, *Zwevend naar de dood* (Bussum: 1977)

Pogue, F. C., *United States Army in World War ii European Theater of Operations, The Supreme Command* (Washington: 1954).

Riessen e.a., H. van, *Het grote gebod: gedenkboek van het verzet in LO en LKP* (Kampen: 1979)

Roever, E. de, *Zij sprongen bij maanlicht: de geschiedenis van het Bureau Bijzondere Opdrachten en de agenten London 1944–1945* (Baarn: 1986)

Roever, E. de, *London roept Amsterdam: de missie van geheim agenten Tobs Biallosterski en Henk Veeneklaas: Amsterdam, Noord-Holland, 1944–1945* (Amsterdam: 1992)

Ryan, C., *Een brug te ver* (Bussum:1974)

Schoon, S., *De Knokploeg Noord Drenthe* (Assen: 1970)

Seymour, W., *British Special Forces: The Story of Britain's Undercover Soldiers* (Barnsley: 2006)

Simpson, J., *The Quiet Operator: Special Forces Signaller Extraordinary* (London: 1993)

Stacey, C. P., *The Victory Campaign, The Operations in North-West Europe 1944–1945* (Ottawa: 1966)

Strawson, J., *A History of the S.A.S. Regiment* (London: 1984)

Taylor, M. D., *Swords and Plowshares* (New York: 1972)

Temmerman, J., *De Belgische Parachutisten 1942–1945: 'Kunstenmakers zonder enig belang'* (Gent: 1994)

Tieke, W., *Im Feuersturm letzter Kriegsjahre: II. SS-Panzerkorps mit 9. SS-Panzerdivision 'Hohenstaufen' und 10. SS-Panzerdivision 'Frundsberg'* (Osnabrück: 1978)

Veer, W. van de, *Voor het vaderland weg: het verhaal van een Engelandvaarder* (Haarlem: 1996)

Visser, F., *De bezetter bespied: De Nederlandse Geheime Inlichtingendienst in de Tweede Wereldoorlog* (Zutphen: 1983)

Wiel, H. van der, *Assen '40-'45: Oorlog en Bevrijding* (Assen: 1995)

Wilkinson, P., and J. Bright Astley, *Gubbins and SOE* (London: 1997)

INDEX

Geographical locations